Insights to Performance Excellence in Education 1999

Also available from ASQ Quality Press

Malcolm Baldrige National Quality Award Materials
1999 Education Criteria for Performance Excellence

Principles of Quality Costs: Principles, Implementation, and Use, Third Edition
ASQ Quality Costs Committee, Jack Campanella, editor

Business Process Improvement Toolbox
Bjørn Andersen

Global Cases in Benchmarking: Best Practices from Organizations Around the World
Robert C. Camp, editor

The Reward and Recognition Process in Total Quality Management
Stephen B. Knouse

Understanding and Applying Value-Added Assessment: Eliminating Business Process Waste
William E. Trischler

Quality Quotes
Hélio Gomes

The Change Agents' Handbook: A Survival Guide for Quality Improvement Champions
David W. Hutton

Benchmarking: The Search for Industry Best Practices That Lead to Superior Performance
Robert C. Camp

Business Process Benchmarking: Finding and Implementing Best Practices
Robert C. Camp

To request a complimentary catalog of ASQ Quality Press publications, call 800-248-1946.

Insights to Performance Excellence in Education 1999

An Inside Look at the 1999 Baldrige Award Criteria for Education

Mark L. Blazey

Karen S. Davison

John P. Evans

ASQ Quality Press

Milwaukee, Wisconsin

Insights to Performance Excellence in Education 1999: An Inside Look at the 1999 Baldrige Award Criteria for Education
Mark L. Blazey, Karen S. Davison, and John P. Evans

10 9 8 7 6 5 4 3 2 1

ISBN 0-87389-458-8

Acquisitions Editor: Ken Zielske
Project Editor: Annemieke Koudstaal
Production Coordinator: Shawn Dohogne

ASQ Mission: The American Society for Quality advances individual and organizational performance excellence worldwide by providing opportunities for learning, quality improvement, and knowledge exchange.

Attention: Bookstores, Wholesalers, Schools and Corporations:
ASQ Quality Press books, videotapes, audiotapes, and software are available at quantity discounts with bulk purchases for business, educational, or instructional use. For information, please contact ASQ Quality Press at 800-248-1946, or write to ASQ Quality Press, P. O. Box 3005, Milwaukee, WI 53201-3005.

To place orders or to request a free copy of the ASQ Quality Press Publications Catalog, including ASQ membership information, call 800-248-1946. Visit our web site at http://www.asq.org.

Printed in the United States of America

∞ Printed on acid-free paper

American Society for Quality

ASQ

Quality Press
611 East Wisconsin Avenue
Milwaukee, Wisconsin 53202
Call toll free 800-248-1946
http://www.asq.org
http://standardsgroup.asq.org

Contents

Preface

This book examines systems and practices that enable organizations of all types to achieve optimum levels of performance excellence. This book grew out of many discussions centered on the Malcolm Baldrige criteria and how education at all levels could benefit from applying this management system in educational organizations. We have spent a substantial portion of our professional lives focused on two major endeavors: the first is education, and our brief biographies attest to our broad coverage of the field from early childhood to postgraduate institutions and from gifted and talented to business education; the second is performance management systems.

We wish to offer our readers some insights from experiences derived from our work with high-performing organizations as well as those not performing to high levels. We recognize that every organization is unique. Each organization has its own people, culture, work, and customers that create unique challenges for leadership and management. The work of education must be managed more effectively at all levels—from the classroom teacher to top administrators—to enable our children to remain competitive in a global economy.

For many years, public schools in the United States enjoyed an enviable position at the K–12 and higher education levels. They have faced very little competition. At the K–12 level, charter schools and vouchers are beginning to challenge the current system. At the higher education level, competition for students has become global and intensified accordingly. The most serious competition, however, may be the kind that our students face in the next century. This will be for continued leadership in the global marketplace.

Our goal for this book is that leaders at all levels of education will understand how to improve their organizations and regain a competitive edge. To do this they must understand not only the parts of a high-performance management system, but also how these parts connect and align. We believe that readers need to understand fully what each area of the performance management system means for educational organizations and find the synergies among the seven major parts of the management system: leadership, strategic planning, student and stakeholder focus, information and analysis, faculty and staff focus, educational and support process management, and school performance results.

Educational leaders have reported that this book has been valuable as a step-by-step approach to help identify and put in place continuous improvement systems. As this progresses, improvement efforts in one area will lead to improvements in other areas. This book will help identify areas that need immediate improvement as well as areas that are less urgent but, nevertheless, vitally linked to overall improvement.

Acknowledgements

Curt Reimann, Harry Hertz, and the dedicated staff of the Malcolm Baldrige National Quality Award office have provided long-standing support and guidance in promoting quality excellence. The book would not be possible in a timely fashion without the design and layout expertise, dedication, and commitment of Enterprise Design and Publishing, the assistance of Heather Lupinski in typing and collecting information on state award practices, and Russell Buyse for editing and contributing to the content and document accuracy.

The chapter on site visits is used with permission of Quantum Performance Group, Inc. Material for the core values, criteria, selected glossary terms, and background information in this book are drawn from the *Malcolm Baldrige National Quality Award 1999 Education Criteria for Performance Excellence*. Portions of the Organizational Assessment Survey are used with permission from the National Council for Performance Excellence.

The following people have been inspirational and pivotal to our educational development and insights: Carol Davison, a dedicated and creative teacher and role model/mother of an author; the late Trudy Watson, who was a mentor; professor Maurice Johnson, who introduced the concept of Intentionality in Education; Sandra Kessler, for early pioneering in Cooperative Learning; and John Michalko, an inspirational teacher and friend to his students. Great educational leaders helped shape our concepts of leadership at all levels, including Gary Jones, Stephen Uebbing, Richard Rose, Daniel Hayes, John O'Rourke, Susan Snyder, and James Latham and Paul Darnall. The research of authors Peggy Seigle and Sandra Byrne was important to our work. Special acknowledgment goes to Marshall "Mike" Smith, Marc Tucker, Janice Weinman, and the dedicated people at the Institute for Educational Leadership, including Mike Usdan, Betty Hale, and Joan Wills, for continual national leadership in education.

Two dedicated and very special students, Mark Harold Blazey and Elizabeth Rose Blazey, have helped our work with critical review and feedback based on their experience in the public schools.

For developing new paradigms to promote performance excellence in all their students—Tim Sergeant, Matt Mahoney, Kelly Harris, Dave Metting, and Kathy Albright.

The School System of Pinnelas County, Florida has won the Florida Sterling Award and continues to be a pioneer and role model school system that holds great promise for our public education system. We especially recognize the efforts of James Shipley and Marie Shipley, J. Howard Hinesley, Ken Rigsby, Jerry Goolsby, Marilyn Caldwell and Chris Collins, Brenda Clark, Shirley Lorenzo, Cathy Athenson, and John Leanes.

Mark L. Blazey, Karen S. Davison, and John P. Evans

Introduction

The *Malcolm Baldrige National Quality Award Education Criteria for Performance Excellence* and related scoring guidelines are powerful new assessment instruments that will help leaders of educational organizations identify strengths and key areas for improvement. Their primary task will then be to use the information to achieve higher levels of performance.

This will not be an easy task for education organizations or their leaders. There are complex and ever-changing relationships involving the community, parents, educational administrators, students, research facilities, teachers, customers, partners, and suppliers. These complex relationships make building an effective educational management system to drive performance improvement an ongoing challenge.

Over the past decade, organizations of all types have used the Baldrige criteria to drive improvement to ever-higher levels. The criteria evaluate every *key* facet of activity and closely monitor organizational performance. Leaders of these organizations set high expectations, value employees and their input, communicate clear directions, and align the work of everyone to achieve organizational goals and optimize performance. As a result of the efforts of these organizations, Americans have enjoyed higher productivity and living standards.

There are now similar but specialized criteria for education. To provide value, streamline operations and meet stakeholder demands, the criteria and scoring guidelines presented in this book offer a new roadmap for educators. As Dr. Stephen Uebbing, superintendent of the Canandaigua City School District and New York State's current Superintendent of the Year said of the

Performance Excellence Criteria, "The old system has taken us about as far as it's going to go. In order for us to make the jump to the next level of improvement in student achievement, we have to move away from the existing paradigms and look for a new vehicle. The quality principles, we believe, are the vehicle that will take us to the next level."

Because of the complexity of modern organizations, the continually increasing demands of customers, and the challenge from competitors, the criteria used to examine organizational management systems and processes are often complex and difficult to understand. This introduction outlines the framework, key concepts, and "lessons learned" by educational organizations that are beginning to get better at what they do.

The introduction includes the following information:

- A practical rationale for using the Baldrige criteria to improve educational organizational performance.
- Education Award criteria goals, and core values that drive organizational change to high levels of performance and underlie the Baldrige Education criteria.
- Key characteristics and key themes of the 1999 Education Criteria.
- Practical insights and lessons learned—ideas on strategies to put high-performance systems in place and promote organizational learning. This section emphasizes themes driven by the criteria and the core values. It also includes suggestions about how to start down the path to systematic organizational improvement; how to go about "getting better at what you do."

A note about the language and terms we chose to use for this book. First of all, a detailed glossary is included in the back of the book that will clarify unfamiliar terms and terms used in specific ways. The terms used in the criteria attempt to make concepts from business more user-friendly for education. For example, "faculty and staff" instead of human resources, "schools" instead of organizations, and "students and stakeholders" instead of customers. An attempt was made to not use or minimize terms that are not frequently used in education. "School" and "organization" or "enterprise" are used interchangeably. "Teacher" is used generically and includes the classroom teacher, professor, instructor, and lecturer. All these terms refer to K–12, higher education and research institutions, for-profit schools, and technical schools.

Special Note:

Each criteria item is accompanied by a linkage diagram that depicts the relationships of item requirements to each other. The major or primary linkages are designated using a solid arrow (———▶). The secondary linkages are designated using a dashed arrow (– – – –▶). Also, for each criteria item we have included examples of effective practices that some organizations have developed and followed. We have also included samples of effective practices for teachers, instructors, professors, or lecturers. These samples present some ideas about how to meet requirements. Examiners should not take these sample effective practices and convert them into requirements for organizations they are examining. *Sample practices for teachers were included for many but not all of the items; the authors welcome examples of additional sample effective practices for the year 2000 book.*

Insights to Education Performance Excellence

This section provides information for leaders who are transforming their schools to achieve substantially higher levels of performance excellence. This section presents

- A "business case" or rationale for using the Baldrige education criteria to improve school performance.
- The core values, themes, and concepts that drive organizational change to high levels of performance and underlie the Baldrige criteria.
- Practical insights and lessons learned— ideas on transition strategies to put high-performance systems in place and promote organizational learning. It emphasizes themes driven by the 1999 criteria and core values. It also includes suggestions about how to start down the path to systematic organizational improvement, as well as lessons learned from those who chose paths that led nowhere or proved futile despite their best intentions.

A Practical Rational for Using the Baldrige Performance Excellence Education Criteria

All leaders know that change is tough. Because they know they will be asked and perhaps tempted to turn back many times, they appreciate improvement examples and encouraging results from organizations that are ahead of them on the journey and still progressing. Because disciplined processes to improve performance in education are relatively new and generally immature, compared with those in the business sector, a relatively

small number of role model examples of best practices exist. However, the authors will draw examples and practices from schools that have instituted or are in the process of instituting fundamental and systematic changes in the way they meet the demands of the future for more highly educated and skilled people.

World Cup Education

Many soccer fans had a "wake-up call" this past summer when the United States soccer team placed last in the 1998 World Cup Soccer Games. Prior to the games, newspapers and soccer enthusiasts reported that our team was "good." Maybe they were—compared with local clubs and leagues. But compared with the rest of the world, we obviously didn't stack up very well.

When adults from a local school community discuss or evaluate their K–12 schools they often rate them as "good." Maybe they are—compared with others in the region or the state or with schooling they received as children. Or perhaps they are rating their schools on the strength of the sports program. But on academic performance, compared to the rest of the world, United States kids aren't scoring very well. In fact, for almost a decade U.S. students' test scores have been about where our soccer team placed—last.

In 1990, the National Center for Education Statistics described the condition of elementary and secondary education as poor relative to students in other countries, American students performed poorly on assessments of mathematics and science. On both assessments, they were in the lowest group of countries, and in mathematics they ranked last. Results from science assessments were similar. In an international assessment, U.S. students placed in the lowest group of nations and second to last overall. Since "A Nation at Risk" was published in 1983 by the Department of Education, the trend for educational achievement has been flat or downward. A 1998 report wrote, "Not much has changed in terms of educational achievement—we are still a nation at risk educationally." (Standards Count: Papers prepared for the tenth anniversary of the national assessment governing board, November 19, 1998, Washington D.C.)

Lower skills at the elementary and secondary levels have a direct effect on higher education and eventually the workforce. Secondary school graduates entering college with lower skill levels means more time must be spent on remedial instruction. These students are not prepared to read, compute, and write at the college level. Remedial instruction to correct deficiencies adds costs and diverts resources from college-level instruction. Policy discussions are currently underway to prohibit some public institutions of higher education from using taxpayer money to fund this academic rework. If we are to achieve the goal of the U.S. governors that U.S. students will be first in the world in science and mathematics achievement by the year 2000, we have much work to do. Clearly, sustaining the status quo or relying on minor adjustments to the current system will not enable us to achieve that goal.

In student graduation rates, the United States has also fallen to the bottom of the industrialized world. Ranked against such nations as Japan and Belgium, our graduation rate has not kept up. We have not regressed, but our competitors have improved. We have not kept pace with the rate of improvement in this critical area around the world.

In higher education, we are all aware that tuition rates in U.S. institutions of higher education have increased more rapidly than the cost of living. This indicates that our colleges and universities are either making larger profits (or surplus rev-

enue) or not improving performance effectiveness as quickly as the rest of the organizations that contribute to our economy and cost of living. Accordingly, these schools are under increasing pressure to be accountable for and improve the management of their resources and provide more educational value. Additionally, global competition and information technology have created a number of challenges for higher education. For example, business schools in the United States were once considered the crown jewel in education, enjoying undisputed leadership in the world. They experienced growing enrollments and attracted students from the United States and many other countries as well. Now, just as business activity has become truly global in scope, education of and for those who will lead business organizations in the future has become global in both content and competition. Thus competition in the business education market has become global and has intensified accordingly.

Information technology has also created a new kind of competitive environment. The information technology revolution provides new and exciting ways to deliver learning experiences at all levels of education. With this new capacity comes increasing pressure to upgrade teaching methods that exploit the new technology's capabilities and match student enthusiasm for the technology. New ways of delivering instruction such as long-distance delivery now compete with traditional "stand-up" lectures, which have been a mainstay of higher education institutions. New pathways for information technology have created thousands of virtual classrooms—even in the lower grades of schools. The increasing interdependency that is occurring creates a special educational challenge to deal with entirely new competition.

Businesses have had to compete globally for some time. Education at all levels must now face the same tests. The "Asian flu" that affected stock markets in early 1999 demonstrated dramatically the interconnectiveness and linkages of our world. Brought together by webs and pathways that span the globe, the whole world is at the fingertips of our students. They will be competing for jobs and market share in that world. Unfortunately, given their performance on standardized tests, it seems they will be easy to beat.

The practical rationale for using the Baldrige Education Criteria is basically about these ideas: the United States cannot maintain its leadership without superior skills and competencies. It is the job of schools, colleges, and universities to do this, and they are not changing fast enough to meet the challenge.

U.S. students will compete in the world economy, not just their region and state. To be realistic, their performance must be judged globally, not locally. Accordingly, U.S. schools at all levels must set their standards higher, and improve teaching, learning, and the management of education in order to continue our global leadership.

Competition for the existing structure of schools in the form of vouchers, charter schools, home schools, and long-distance learning is here. The current educational establishment must deal with the reality of changing to meet and exceed the demands of its students and stakeholders and actually *achieve* the high levels of performance required.

The *Malcolm Baldrige Education Criteria for Performance Excellence* outline effective practices and core values that have helped U.S. businesses, government agencies, and a few schools improve their performance. Schools of all types will find that these criteria, if applied systematically, will improve their performance and the academic achievement of their students. Both are needed to help us meet the challenges of the new millennium.

Education Criteria
Goals and Values

Education Criteria Purposes

The *Malcolm Baldrige Education Criteria for Performance Excellence* are the basis for assessment and feedback to education organizations. In addition, the criteria have four other purposes.

- To help improve educational performance practices by making available an integrated, results-oriented set of key performance requirements.
- To facilitate communication and sharing of best practices information within and among educational organizations of all types based upon a common understanding of key performance requirements.
- To foster the development of partnerships involving schools, businesses, human service agencies, and other organizations via related criteria.
- To serve as a working tool for understanding and improving school performance, planning, training, and institutional assessment.

Education Criteria Goals

The criteria are designed to help schools enhance their educational services through focus on interconnected, results-oriented goals. These goals include providing ever-improving educational value to students, contributing to their overall development and well-being, and also the improvement of overall educational organization effectiveness, and use of resources and capabilities.

Core Values and Concepts

The Baldrige Education Criteria are built on a set of common values that characterize all types of high-performing organizations and are present in the best schools in the nation. This section presents the eleven core values that underlie the criteria. These values bind an organization together and are the foundation upon which success is built. These core values are critical for successful educational organizations of any size and in any sector—from rural schools to city universities to private academies. By integrating these values into the everyday life of education as schools engage students in their own learning, educators can convert their institutions into improving organizations.

For many years, schools seemed to operate on the empty vessel idea—fill the brain up by pouring in the knowledge. Students today need much more from their teachers and professors and schooling than just knowledge. They need to be fully engaged in seeking and interpreting the knowledge and facts. All of the following core values are linked with this underlying need to engage students in the learning process.

These core values and concepts are:

Learning-Centered Education

Learning-centered education places the focus of education on learning and the real needs of students. Such needs are derived from the requirements of the marketplace and the responsibilities of citizenship. Changes in technology and in the national and world economies are creating increasing demands on employees to become knowledge workers and problem solvers, keeping pace with the rapid changes in the marketplace. Most analysts conclude that schools of all types need to focus more on students' active learning and on the development of problem-solving skills.

Schools exist primarily to develop the fullest potential of all students, affording them opportunities to pursue a variety of avenues to success. A learning-centered school needs to fully understand and translate marketplace and citizenship requirements into appropriate curricula. Education offerings need to be built around learning effectiveness. Teaching effectiveness needs to stress promotion of learning and achievement.

Key characteristics of learning-centered education include the following:
- Setting high developmental expectations and standards for all students.
- Understanding that students may learn in different ways and at different rates. Also, student learning rates and styles may differ over time, and may vary depending upon subject matter. Learning may be influenced by support, guidance, and climate factors, including factors that contribute to or impede learning. Thus, the learning-centered school needs to maintain a constant search for alternative ways to enhance learning. The school also needs to develop actionable information on individual students that bears upon their learning.
- Providing a primary emphasis on active learning. This may require the use of a wide range of techniques, materials, and experiences to engage student interest. Techniques, materials, and experiences may be drawn from external sources such as businesses, community services, or social service organizations.

- Using formative assessment to measure learning early in the learning process and to tailor learning experiences to individual needs and learning styles.
- Using summative assessment to measure progress against key, relevant external standards and norms regarding what students should know and be able to do.
- Assisting students and families to use self-assessment to chart progress and to clarify goals and gaps.
- Focusing on key transitions such as school-to-school and school-to-work.

The first value is Learning-Centered Education. Without fully engaging students in learning, performance excellence cannot be achieved. Focusing on learning means
- Setting standards and expectations of excellence, not mediocrity, for students.
- Recognizing that students differ in learning rates and styles and using information about learning preferences to enhance learning.
- Emphasizing that learners should be active in selecting their learning vehicles and engaged in the process as much as their maturity and the subject matter allow.
- Using assessment formatively (during the learning process) and summatively (after the learning process) to improve the learning at different stages in the process.
- Providing rapid and immediate feedback to students on their performance so improvement cycles become shorter.

Leadership

A school's senior leaders play a crucial role in the development of a student-focused, learning-oriented climate. This requires the setting of clear and visible directions and high expectations. Senior leaders need to take part in the development of strategies, systems, and methods for achieving excellence. Such strategies, systems, and methods should include a foundation of continuous improvement and learning in the way the school operates. This requires the commitment and development of all faculty and staff. Senior leaders need to ensure that school policies reinforce the learning and improvement climate and encourage initiative, self-directed responsibility, and leadership throughout the school—including students.

In addition to their important role within the school, senior leaders have other avenues to strengthen education. Reinforcing the learning environment in the school might require building community support and aligning community and business leaders and community services with this aim.

Every school system, educational strategy, and method for achieving performance excellence must be guided by effective Leadership.

- Effective leaders convey a strong sense of urgency to counter the natural resistance to change that can prevent the organization from taking the steps that these core values for success demand.
- Such leaders serve as enthusiastic role models, reinforcing and communicating the core values by their words and actions. Words alone are not enough.
- Schools must have leadership at all levels with common and clearly understood goals. Relationships must be built on trust, kept alive by open and honest communication. This includes leaders from Boards and the top level of administration; school, college, building and department level leaders; and significantly, classroom leaders—instructors and teachers.
- Leaders must take steps to ensure that all systems in the organization—including compensation, reward, and recognition—align to support these values and goals.

Continuous Improvement and Organizational Learning

Achieving ever-higher levels of school performance requires a well-executed and systematic approach to continuous improvement. A well-executed continuous improvement process has several important characteristics: (1) it has clear goals regarding what to improve; (2) it is fact-based, incorporating measures and/or indicators; (3) it is systematic, including cycles of planning, execution, evaluation, and subsequent improvement; and (4) it focuses primarily on key processes as the route to better results.

The approach to improvement needs to be "embedded" in the way the school operates. Embedded means (1) improvement is a regular part of the daily work of all faculty, staff, and students; (2) improvement processes seek to eliminate problems at their source; and (3) improvement is driven by opportunities to do better, as well as by problems that need to be corrected. Opportunities for improvement come from many sources, including student, faculty and staff ideas; successful practices of other schools and organizations; and educational and learning research findings.

The approach to continuous improvement should seek to engage students as full participants in and contributors to improvement processes. A major opportunity exists to build active student learning around goal setting, assessment (including self-assessment), and improvement. In addition to creating an improvement-oriented climate, this approach could help to identify the best approaches to learning on an individual basis, and to build upon demonstrated improvement to strengthen student confidence and commitment to learning.

The most potent value is Continuous Improvement and Organizational Learning. High-performing schools are learning organizations that create a culture of evaluating and improving everything they do. They not only provide programs, offerings, or services; they also consciously create information that will be used to guide improvement efforts. They strive to get better and get faster at getting better. In order to do this, educational organizations need to

- Create a culture of continuous improvement essential to maintaining and sustaining true competitive advantage. They need to embed this culture into the everyday life of the school. They need to make continuous improvement an automatic reflex, like eyeblinking.
- Reward improvement of processes *and* performance as part of the culture change.

With systematic continuous improvement, time becomes a powerful ally. As time passes, the organization grows stronger and smarter. Without continuous improvement, time becomes an enemy. Competitors gain, causing us to fall further behind.

Valuing Faculty and Staff

A school's success in improving performance depends critically upon the knowledge, capabilities, skills, and motivation of its faculty and staff. Faculty and staff success depends upon having meaningful opportunities to develop and practice new knowledge and skills. Schools need to invest in the development of faculty and staff through ongoing education, training, and opportunities for continuing growth.

For faculty, development means building not only discipline knowledge, but also knowledge of student learning styles and of assessment methods. Faculty participation may include contributing to school policies and working in teams to develop and execute programs and curricula.

Increasingly, participation should become more student-focused and more multidisciplinary. School leaders need to work to eliminate disincentives for groups and individuals to sustain these important, learning-focused professional development activities.

For staff, development might include classroom and on-the-job training, job rotation, and pay for demonstrated skills. Increasingly, training, education, development, and work systems need to be adapted to a more diverse workforce and to more flexible, high-performance work practices.

Major challenges in the area of valuing employees include integration of human resource practices—selection, performance, recognition, training, and career advancement; and alignment of human resource management with strategic change processes.

Valuing Faculty and Staff means providing the resources and support for each employee to develop and learn continually. The organization as a whole learns if knowledge and learnings are shared. This value must be at the heart of the culture of any educational institution. Educational organizations need to reflect on the relationship between the Board and its top administrators and then between the top administrators and faculty and staff. The relationships at the top, if based on trust and common goals, will cascade down into the organizational structure. Trust will then be the basis for the relationship between teachers and students in most classrooms. If top administrators are valued by the Board, college deans and principals valued by central administrators, and teachers valued by site administrators, then students are more likely to be valued by teachers. If an organization values its members and provides support for development, initiative, and self-directed responsibility, it is able to create a workforce that is motivated to become continually better and fully use their capabilities.

Partnership Development

Schools should seek to build internal and external partnerships to accomplish their overall goals more effectively.

Internal partnerships might include those that promote cooperation among faculty and staff groups such as unions, departments, and work units. Agreements might be created involving faculty and staff development, cross-training, or new work organizations, such as high-performance work teams. Internal partnerships might also involve creating network relationships among school units to improve flexibility and responsiveness.

External partnerships might include those with other schools, businesses, business associations, and community and social service organizations—all stakeholders and potential contributors.

Partnerships should seek to develop longer-term objectives, thereby creating a basis for mutual investments. Partners should address objectives of the partnership, key requirements for success, means of regular communication, approaches to evaluating progress, and means for adapting to changing conditions.

> Achieving long-range goals is increasingly difficult without internal and external partnerships. Internal partnerships with faculty and staff, labor unions, and other units is essential to achieving the collaboration necessary to achieve high-performance outcomes. These partnerships must also exist between different levels of the school, such as middle to high school or high school to college. External alliances and strategic partnerships are key to enhancing the overall capabilities of the education enterprise.

Design Quality and Prevention

Education improvement needs to place very strong emphasis on effective design of educational programs, curricula, and learning environments. The overall design should include measurable learning objectives, taking into account the individual needs of students. Accordingly, design must also include effective means for gauging student progress. A central requirement of effective design is the inclusion of an assessment strategy. Such a strategy needs to emphasize the acquisition of formative information—information that provides early indication of whether or not learning is taking place—to minimize problems that might arise if learning barriers are not promptly identified and addressed.

> To improve educational outcomes and programs, schools need a strong focus on improving Design Quality and Prevention of problems. The cost to schools of preventing problems by effectively designing educational products and services is significantly less than the cost of taking corrective action later. It is critical to design programs taking into account student learning needs and the need to engage students in their learning. Assessment strategies need to be designed as part of the program so it is apparent immediately whether learning is taking place at the desired rate and to the desired extent. Early indicators of success and potential problems need to be part of the design strategy. Combined with the value of continuous improvement, once learning problems are identified, students must be given opportunities to study, relearn, and demonstrate the new learning. This may involve ongoing assessment and reassessment.

Management by Fact

An effective education improvement system based upon cause-effect thinking needs to be built upon measurement, data, information, and analysis. Measurements must derive from and support the school's mission and strategy and address all key requirements. A strong focus on student learning requires a comprehensive and integrated fact-based system—one that includes input data, environmental data, and performance data. Analysis refers to extracting larger meaning from data to support evaluation and decision making throughout the school. Such analysis might entail using data to reveal information—such as trends, projections, and cause and effect—that might not be evident without analysis. The effective use of measurement and analysis to support student learning and school performance improvement requires a strong focus on information system design. This might entail organizing data systems to provide key information to support design of improvement strategies. Examples include organization of data by cohorts, longitudinal information, and comparative information.

> Management by Fact is the cornerstone value for effective planning, decision making, faculty and staff involvement, engaging students, and leadership. Educators make decisions every day that directly affect student performance and learning. However, without data, the basis for decision making is intuition—gut feel. Most drivers decide when to fill their fuel tanks based on data from the fuel gauge and get very uncomfortable if the gauge is broken. Yet people routinely make decisions of enormous consequence about learning methods, strategies, goals, and students with little or no data. This is a recipe for disaster, not one designed to ensure high performance. All participants in the organization, from top leaders and teachers to students, must have access to data to promote informed, effective decision making.

Long-Range View of the Future

Pursuit of education improvement requires a strong future orientation and a willingness to make long-term commitments to students and to all stakeholders—communities, employers,

faculty, and staff. Planning needs to anticipate many types of changes, including changes in education requirements, instructional approaches, resource availability, technology, and demographics. A major longer-term investment associated with school improvement is the investment in creating and sustaining a mission-oriented assessment system focused on learning. This entails faculty education and training in assessment methods. It also entails school leadership becoming familiar with research findings and practical applications of assessment methods and learning style information.

> Every educational organization must be guided by its own set of measurable goals and Long-Range View of the Future. These measurable goals, which emerge from the strategic planning process, serve to align the work of everyone in the organization. Without this view, the entire organization will find it difficult to achieve common goals with a common mission and purpose. Measurable goals that have been aligned for consistency clarify issues about objectives, priorities, and accomplishments. They serve as a basis for consistent communication and allow everyone to know where they are going and determine when things are off track. Without consistent, measurable goals, everyone may still work hard, but they are likely to go in different directions—suboptimizing the success of the organization.

Public Responsibility and Citizenship

A school's leadership should stress the importance of the school serving as a role model in its operation as an institution. This includes protection of public health, safety, and the environment, ethical practices, and nondiscrimination in all that it does. Planning related to public health, safety, and the environment should anticipate adverse impacts that might arise in facilities management, laboratory operations, classrooms, and transportation. Ethical business practices need to take into account proper use of public and private funds. Nondiscrimination should take into account factors such as student admissions, hiring practices, and treatment of all students and stakeholders. Inclusion of public responsibility areas within a school's performance system means meeting all local, state, and federal laws and regulatory requirements. It also means treating these and related requirements as opportunities for continuous improvement "beyond mere compliance." This requires that appropriate measures of progress be created and used in managing performance.

School citizenship refers to leadership and support—within the reasonable limits of its resources—of publicly important purposes. Such purposes might include environmental sensitivity, community service, and sharing of quality-related information. An example of school citizenship might include influencing other organizations, private and public, to partner for these purposes.

> Public Responsibility and Citizenship is a strategic initiative. Schools, colleges, and universities serve at the center of their communities and role model ethical and data-driven decision making at all levels. These organizations are highly visible and under constant scrutiny. Schools are constantly being judged by their students, parents, and other stakeholders. Educational organizations must determine and anticipate any adverse effects to the public of their products, services, and operations. Failure to do so can undermine public trust. These are not altruistic principles but minimum requirements for effective schools to demonstrate as they mold the minds of future generations.

Fast Response

An increasingly important measure of organizational effectiveness is faster and more flexible response to the needs of customers—the students and other stakeholders of the school. Many organizations are learning that explicit focus on and measurement of response times help to drive the simplification of work systems and work processes. There are other important benefits derived from this focus: response time improvements often drive improvements in organization, quality, and productivity. The world's best organizations are learning to make simultaneous improvements in quality, productivity, and response time while strengthening their customer focus.

> Fast Response is a value that is key to academic performance improvement. Faster feedback on performance at all levels will mean faster corrections and improvement in learning. Students are also motivated by immediate feedback to continue to do better. One of the biggest impacts on student performance appears to be the quality and speed of instructor feedback. Variables such as methods of instruction, instructor training, and even reduced class size have produced uneven performance results. The variable that is having a dramatic impact on student learning is reduction in the cycle time involved in teaching, assessing learning, and correcting mistakes. The quicker students get feedback, and the more meaningful and specific the feedback, the larger the performance gains.

Results Orientation

A school's performance system should focus on results—reflecting and balancing the needs and interests of students and all other stakeholders. To meet the sometimes conflicting and changing aims that balance implies, school strategy needs to address all student and stakeholder requirements explicitly to ensure that actions and plans meet differing needs and avoid adverse impact on students and/or other stakeholders. The development and use of a balanced composite of performance indicators offers an effective means to communicate requirements, monitor actual performance, and marshal broadly based support for improving results.

> A Results Orientation helps educational organizations communicate requirements, monitor actual performance, make adjustments in priorities, and reallocate resources. Results should include a balance of lagging indicators, such as student achievement, graduation rates, and financial measures, as well as leading measures such as attendance, learning rates, rework required, and time on task. Without a balanced results focus, organizations can become fixated on processes and lose sight of the important factors for success.

There are always better ways to do things. The challenge for educators and schools is to find them. Schools, colleges, and universities that base efforts on the core values that underlie the Baldrige Education Criteria will build organizations that foster trust, effective learning, high performance, and steady improvement.

Key Characteristics of the Education Criteria

1. **The criteria are directed toward improved overall school performance results.** The criteria focus principally on key areas of school performance, listed below. School performance results are a composite of the following:
   - Student performance
   - Student success/satisfaction
   - Stakeholder satisfaction
   - School performance relative to comparable schools
   - Effective and efficient use of resources

   Improvements in these results areas comprise overall school performance.

   The use of a composite set of indicators helps to ensure that strategies are balanced—that they do not inappropriately trade off among important stakeholders or objectives. The composite set of indicators also helps to ensure that school strategies bridge short- and long-term goals.

   > The criteria are intended to improve overall school performance. School performance can be broken into five components: student performance, student success and satisfaction, stakeholder satisfaction, school performance compared to comparable schools, and effective/efficient use of resources. The criteria are designed to help organizations enhance their competitiveness through focus on results-oriented goals.

2. **The criteria are nonprescriptive and adaptable.** The criteria are a set of 18 basic, interrelated, results-oriented requirements. However, the criteria do not prescribe
   - Specific tools, techniques, technologies, systems, or starting points.
   - Whether an educational organization should or should not have work units for quality, planning, or other functions.
   - How the organization units within the organization should be organized.
   - Whether different organizational units should be managed in the same way.

   Processes to achieve performance excellence are very likely to change as needs and strategies evolve. Hence, the criteria themselves are regularly evaluated as part of annual performance reviews to ensure that they continue to distinguish high-performing schools from all others.

   The criteria are nonprescriptive because
   - The focus is on results, not on procedures, tools, or organizations. Schools are encouraged to develop and demonstrate creative, adaptive, and flexible approaches for meeting basic requirements. Nonprescriptive requirements are intended to foster incremental and major (breakthrough) improvement as well as basic change.
   - Selection of tools, techniques, systems, and organizations usually depends on many factors such as size, school type, the organization's stage of development, and faculty and staff capabilities and responsibilities.

• Focusing on common requirements within a school, rather than on common procedures, fosters better understanding, communication, sharing, and alignment, while supporting creativity and diversity in approaches.

> The criteria are not prescriptive. They do not specify particular tools, techniques, methods, or technologies. Also, they do not specify specific functions of a school or require that different units of a school be managed in the same way. They focus on the systems that drive high-performance results. Schools are encouraged to develop solutions and creative approaches to meet their unique requirements in a disciplined, systematic manner.

3. **The criteria support a systems approach to organization-wide goal alignment.** The systems approach to goal alignment is embedded in the integrated structure of the criteria and the results-oriented, cause-effect linkages among the criteria parts.

Alignment in the criteria is built around connecting and reinforcing measures, derived from the school's strategy. The measures in the criteria tie directly to student and stakeholder value and to overall performance that relate to key internal and external requirements of the school. Measures serve both as a communications tool and a basis for deploying consistent overall performance requirements. Such alignment ensures consistency of purpose while at the same time supporting speed, innovation, and decentralized decision making.

A systems approach to goal alignment, particularly when strategy and goals change over time, requires dynamic linkages among criteria categories and items that together foster systems learning. In the criteria, action-oriented learning takes place through feed-back between processes and results facilitated by learning or continuous improvement cycles. The learning cycles have four clearly defined and well-established stages.

1. Plan. Formulate plans, including design of processes, selection of measures, and deployment of requirements.
2. Do. Execute plans.
3. Check. Assess progress, taking into account internal and external results.
4. Act. Revise plans based on assessment findings, learning, new inputs, and new requirements.

> The criteria support a systems approach that will align the goals and the work of the entire organization. The systems approach, including interconnections among criteria items and results orientation, is essential to achieving optimum performance. It is the role of measures, derived from the organization's strategy, to connect and communicate performance requirements for the entire educational system. It is important to note that the organization must realign its goals as its strategy and goals change over time. It must continue to use feedback between processes and results to foster systems learning.

4. **The criteria permit goal-based diagnosis.** The criteria *and* the scoring guidelines make up the diagnostic assessment system. The criteria, as discussed previously, are a set of results-oriented items. The scoring guidelines define the assessment dimensions—approach, deployment, and results—and the key factors used to assess against each dimension. An assessment provides a profile of strengths and areas for improvement to help schools identify areas that, if addressed, will move the school ahead. As a result, this diagnostic assessment is a useful management tool that goes beyond traditional performance reviews.

The criteria, together with the scoring guidelines, are intended to be diagnostic in nature. They will be useful in profiling strengths and weaknesses against the three assessment dimensions of approach, deployment, and results. This type of assessment is useful for management and educational decisions and provides substantially more information than that of usual performance and accreditation reviews. Furthermore, the criteria and scoring guidelines provide insight into the elements of performance excellence— a view that traditional accreditation and "blue ribbon" reviews fail to achieve.

Key Education Themes of the 1999 Criteria

Concept of Excellence

The concept of excellence relates to demonstrated performance outcomes rather than inputs of the education system. Such performance considers year-to-year improvement in key measures and/or indicators of performance, as well as demonstrated leadership in performance and performance improvement relative to comparable schools and/or appropriate benchmarks.

This concept of excellence places the major focus on teaching and learning strategies; poses similar types of challenges for all schools regardless of resources and/or incoming student preparation and abilities; is likely to stimulate learning-related research and offer a means to disseminate the results of such research; and offers the potential to create an expanding body of knowledge of successful teaching and learning practices in the widest range of schools.

The focus on value-added contributions by the school does not suggest manufacturing-oriented, mechanistic, or additive models of student development. Nor does the use of a value-added concept imply that a school's management system should include documented "procedures" or attempt to define "conformity" or "compliance." Rather, the performance concept in the Education Criteria means that the school should view itself as a key developmental influence (though not the only influence), and that the school should seek to understand and optimize its influencing factors, guided by an effective assessment strategy.

In today's global competitive environment, excellence must be based on achievements, not inputs. Demonstrated performance, rather than intention, is vital. For decades, schools have taken pride and some solace in measures of success based on inputs—well-trained teachers, good facilities, and good curriculum and instructional techniques. However, when inputs do not produce desired outputs, then excellence has been denied. This means year-to-year improvement in key measures and/or indicators of performance outcomes, as well as demonstrated leadership in performance and performance improvement, must be assessed relative to comparable schools or benchmarks. This theme is important to all levels and types of education for these reasons: it places the major focus on outcome measures of excellence to adjust teaching and learning strategies; it poses similar challenges to all schools regardless of resources or student pool; it may stimulate teaching/learning research and dissemination of the results of such research; and it may create an expanding body of knowledge to share the best of teaching and learning practices.

Accreditation processes should be mentioned briefly here because they are so pervasive throughout education. The role of these processes as mechanisms for quality assurance to the public, frequently done via peer review as a form of self-governance, has been of considerable historical importance. However, the typical accreditation process starts primarily from a set of input-based standards and produces an evaluation of organizational compliance with those standards. The perspective of these processes is primarily oriented toward providing or renewing a "license to do business." These reviews evaluate conformity to the minimum standards necessary for the organization to exist. Any nonconformities found during the evaluation usually imply a requirement on the part of the organization either to implement an immediate correction or at least to provide a plan for achieving compliance. Important as this function is, it does not inherently produce a striving for excellence in performance, or even for continuous improvement.

The very title of the criteria that serve as the basis for this book suggests a different orientation. The underlying mindset is that every process can be improved. It is the continuing experience of the authors of this book that the leaders of high-performing organizations are justifiably proud of the progress their organizations have made, yet keenly interested in ways to take performance still higher. Compliance with a common denominator is not enough for these organizations and their people and stakeholders. They are hungry for mechanisms that will continually raise the bar by supporting, facilitating, and driving high performance.

- Assessment as embedded, ongoing, with prompt feedback; assessment is curriculum-based and criterion-referenced, addressing key learning goals and overall performance requirements.
- Clear guidelines regarding how assessment results will be used and how they will not be used.
- An ongoing evaluation of the assessment system itself to improve the connection between assessment and student success. Success factors should be developed based on external requirements derived from the marketplace, other schools, and so on, on an ongoing basis.

> Assessment is central to the achievement of excellence. A sound assessment strategy will include the following: alignment between the school's mission and goals and what is being assessed; a focus on improvement, not status quo of student performance, faculty capabilities, and school program performance; prompt feedback and ongoing assessment; a curriculum-based and criteria-referenced strategy; clear guidelines of how assessment results will and will not be used; and an ongoing evaluation and improvement cycle for the assessment system.

Assessment Strategy

Central and crucial to the success of the excellence concept in the Education Criteria is a well-conceived and well-executed assessment strategy. The characteristics of such a strategy should include the following:
- Clear ties between what is assessed and the school's mission objectives. This means not only what students know, but also what they are able to do.
- A strong focus on improvement—of student performance, faculty capabilities, and school program performance.

Mission Specificity

Although schools share common aims, individual school missions, roles, and programs vary greatly. Use of a single set of criteria to cover all requirements of all schools means that these requirements need to be interpreted in terms of specific organizational missions. That is, specific requirements and critical success factors differ from school to school. For this reason, effective use of the criteria depends upon operationalizing mission requirements consistently across the seven categories of the criteria framework. In particular, the Strategic Planning category needs to address all key mission requirements, setting the stage for the interpretation of the other requirements. For example, results reported in the School Performance Results category need to be clearly consistent with the school's mission objectives.

The Education Criteria are most explicit in the area of student learning, as this requirement is common to all education organizations, regardless of their larger missions. Despite this commonality, the focus of student learning and development depends upon organizational mission. For example, results reported by trade schools, engineering schools, and music schools would be expected to differ. Nevertheless, all three types of schools would be expected to show year-to-year improvements in their mission-specific results to demonstrate the effectiveness of their performance improvement efforts.

> The criteria take into account that specific requirements and critical success factors differ from organization to organization. For this reason, organizations need to use mission requirements to drive operations across the seven categories of the criteria. The strategic planning process must address all key mission requirements. School Performance Results (Category 7) must report on the degree of attainment of strategic and operational initiatives including the school's mission objectives. The Education Criteria are most detailed in the area of student learning because this is a critical mission requirement of all educational organizations.

Customers

The Baldrige Award criteria for Performance Excellence use the generic term "customers" to reflect the users of products or services. Although marketplace success depends heavily upon user preference, setting organization requirements needs to consider other stakeholders as well. Successful operation of an organization may depend upon satisfying environmental, legal, and other requirements. Thus, meaningful criteria need to incorporate all relevant requirements that organizations must meet to be successful.

Schools also must respond to a variety of requirements, all of which need to be incorporated into the Education Criteria. The adaptation of the Baldrige Award criteria to education poses alternative approaches for defining key requirements. The approach selected seeks to distinguish between students and other stakeholders for purposes of clarity and emphasis. Stakeholders include parents, employers, other schools, and communities, to name a few. To further clarify the requirements related to students, the requirements for current students are separated from those of future students. Requirements for current students are more concrete, specific, and immediate; determining requirements for future students is part of the school's planning, and needs to take into account changing student populations and changing requirements future students must be able to meet. A major challenge schools face is "bridging" between current student needs and the needs of future students. This requires an effective learning and change strategy.

> The Education Criteria recognize many types of groups and persons who have a stake in their school; they make demands and have requirements of schools. The criteria distinguish between students and stakeholders in an effort to help distinguish the requirements of these two classes of customers. Stakeholders include parents, employers, other schools, and communities. Students are further delineated into current students and future students. Requirements from current students are more specific and immediate, whereas requirements of future students take into account more long-range factors. Successful schools must address both groups of customers to consistently achieve high levels of performance.

Primary Focus on Teaching and Learning

Although the Education Criteria are intended to address all organizational requirements, including research and service, primary emphasis is placed on teaching and learning. This is done for three main reasons:

- Every education organization has teaching and learning as a goal even when other very important goals such as university research exist simultaneously. Thus, sharing of teaching and learning strategies and methods would have the greatest impact on education system improvement.

- Those who encourage the creation of an award category for education cite improvement in teaching and learning as their primary or only rationale for such an award.

- Only a small percentage of schools engage in research. Peer review systems exist to evaluate research. Funding organizations and businesses provide avenues to channel the directions of much research. Numerous excellent forums and media already exist for sharing research results. Much of the research performed in schools involves students as part of the students' overall education. Thus, the educational value of research is incorporated in the Education Criteria as part of teaching and learning. Other important aspects of research, such as faculty development and student/faculty recruitment, are also addressed in the criteria.

> The criteria are intended to address all organizational requirements, including those mainly focused on research and service. However, the primary emphasis is on teaching and learning, because the criteria are intended to have the greatest possible impact on educational system improvement, and the percentage of schools that engage in research is small compared to teaching and learning institutions.

> Schools that have research, service, and/or other scholarship as part of their core missions must ensure these activities achieve optimum performance. In other words, if research, for example, is critical to organization success (as at a research university), the effective design and execution of research must be a part of the core operations, evaluated and continually improved. This activity would not be required of organizations for which research is *not* critical to organization success.

Systems Concept

The systems concept is reflected in the integrated structure of the criteria. The structure consists of the seven categories, with category items listed beneath the category titles. The integrated structure of the criteria consists of the numerous direct linkages between the categories and Items as depicted in Figure 1 on page 42. Such linkages are intended to ensure alignment and integration of the overall requirements. The criteria stress cause-effect thinking and a process orientation. The intent is to accumulate a body of knowledge to help the school learn and improve from that learning. One of the main elements in the systems approach is the set of measures and/or indicators used. Such measures and indicators link key processes to key mission results.

> The criteria structure itself is interconnected and integrated, reflecting the systems concept. The systems concept is woven throughout the criteria, connecting mission, goals, objectives, and measures that link the organization together. The integrated structure of the criteria consists of the linkages between the categories and items presented in Figure 1 on page 42 of this book, and in the thin linkage diagrams throughout this book.

Practical Insights, Connections, and Linkages

Connect the dots, a popular children's activity, helps kids understand that, when properly connected, apparently random dots create a meaningful picture. In many ways, the seven categories, 18 items, and 26 areas to address in the Baldrige Education Criteria are like the dots that must be connected to reveal a meaningful picture. This is part of the systems approach mentioned as a key theme that underlies the criteria. With no paths to make the web, or join the dots, staff development and use are not related to strategic planning; information and analysis are isolated from educational process management; and academic performance improvement efforts are disjointed, fragmented, and do not yield robust results. This book describes the linkages and interrelationships among the items of the criteria. The exciting part about having them identified is you can look for these linkages in your own school and, if they don't exist, start building them.

Transition Strategies

Putting high-performance school management systems in place is a major commitment that will not happen quickly. At the beginning, you will need a transition strategy to get you started on the road to the steeper slopes—from management by opinion, power, or intuition to more data-driven management. The next part of this section describes one approach that has worked for many organizations in various sectors: driving performance improvement through an existing top management structure.

Performance Improvement Council

The performance improvement council should be the administrative cabinet or its equivalent—the primary policy-making body for the organization. The name change is significant and brings with it a new role and renewed focus on shared goals and mission with a focus on continuous improvement. It should spawn other groups at different levels in the school system to take on roles as performance improvement councils.

The major role of the performance improvement councils is to be a conscience for the strategic plan and mission of the school. Council members must communicate, share practices and policies, and involve faculty, staff, and stakeholders. All faculty and staff and, when appropriate, students and stakeholders, must know the mission and goals, and how their work contributes to achieving the goals. Members of the performance improvement council become leaders for major improvement efforts and sponsors for several process or continuous improvement teams throughout the organization. The council structure, networked and cascaded fully, can effectively align the work and optimize performance at all levels and across all functions of the school.

Council Membership

Selecting new members for the performance improvement council should be done carefully. Each member should be essential for the success of the operation, and together they must be sufficient for success. Partnerships with the school community including unions, parents, faculty, staff, and students should be forged using these councils. The most important member is the senior leader of the school, college, or other entity seeking to optimize performance. This person must participate actively, demonstrating the kind of leadership that all should emulate. Improvement can be led from the top, but it cannot be "dictated and delegated." Of particular importance is a commitment to consensus building as the modus operandi for the council. This tool, a core of performance improvement programs, is often overlooked by leadership. Other council members selected should have leadership responsibility for broad areas of the organization such as faculty and staff resources, operations planning, curriculum, and data systems.

The Use of Champions

Members of the performance improvement council should each lead a major category across the system. They need to be the "champion" of this category. For example, the Category 3 champion would focus across disciplines, departments, and other units on students and stakeholders. He or she, for example, may gather information from key student groups and share concerns and perspectives from students on their needs and expectations. If major complaints are identified, they would be shared with other category champions and corrective actions agreed upon. In this way, major initiatives include perspectives and requirements from all categories.

Performance Improvement Council Learning and Planning

The performance improvement council should eventually become extremely knowledgeable about high-performance management systems. Council members should be among the first in the organization to learn about continuous improvement tools and processes.

To be effective, every member of the council (and every member in the organization) must understand the Baldrige criteria because the criteria describe the components of the entire management system. Participation in carefully designed training focused on the criteria and the importance of performance improvement for educational enterprises has proven to be the best way to understand the complexities of the system needed to achieve performance excellence. Any additional training should be carried out in the context of planning—that is, learn tools and use them to plan the performance improvement implementation, practices, and policies.

The following are suggested actions for the performance improvement council:

- Develop one integrated, strategic performance improvement plan.
- Create the communication plan and infrastructure to transmit performance improvement policies throughout the school.
- Define the roles of faculty and staff, including new recognition and reward structures to support needed behavioral changes.
- Develop a master training and development plan. Involve team representatives in planning so they can learn skills close to when they are needed. Define what training is provided to whom, and when and how success will be measured.
- Launch improvement projects that will produce both short- and long-term successes. Improvement projects should be clearly defined by the performance improvement council and driven by the strategic plan. Typical improvement projects include important faculty and staff processes such as career development, performance measurement, and diversity, as well as improving operational products and services in the line areas.
- Develop a plan to communicate the progress and successes of the organization. Through this approach, the need for performance improvement processes is consistently communicated to all employees. Barriers to optimum performance are weakened and eliminated.

Core Competencies

A uniform set of skills or core competencies and constancy of purpose are critical to success. Schools or colleges or other educational institutions should be trained together as a unit. Content must lead participants to understand why change is critical and how this Baldrige-based change strategy will work for their school.

Ongoing training will also be necessary in the context of performance improvement team work, and councils should provide all faculty, staff, and most importantly students with the knowledge and skills on which to build a learning organization that continually gets better. Such training typically includes team building, leadership skills for the classroom and organization, consensus building, communications, and effective meeting management. These are necessary for effective teams to become involved in solving critical problems in a disciplined and systematic way.

An important competency involves using a common process to define student and stakeholder requirements, determine the ability of the school to meet those requirements, measure success, and determine the extent to which stakeholders— internal and external—are satisfied. Stakeholders may include parents of students, businesses, the next level of education (such as grade three as the stakeholder for grade two, high school English teachers as stakeholders for middle school English teachers or college undergraduate studies as a stakeholder for high schools). Students also have roles as stakeholders when they purchase food from the cafeteria or ride the bus. When a customer-related problem arises, staff and faculty close to the problem must be able to define the problem correctly, isolate the root causes, generate and select the best solution to eliminate the root causes, and implement the best solution.

It is also important to be able to understand data and make decisions based on facts, not merely intuition or feelings. Students, faculty, and staff need to share a common culture of fact-based decision making, particularly when making decisions about programs and student learning. Guessing that an instructional approach is or isn't working should not be part of the culture. Therefore, familiarity with statistical and decision-making tools to analyze student and staff work and performance data is important. With these tools, processes can be analyzed and vastly improved. Reducing unnecessary steps in processes, increasing process consistency, reducing variability, and reducing cycle time are powerful ways to improve quality and reduce cost simultaneously.

Knowledge of techniques for acquiring comparison and benchmarking data, curricular and instructional process improvement, leadership strategies and roles, strategic planning, and student and stakeholder satisfaction will help faculty and staff expand their optimization and high-performance thrust across the entire organization.

Lessons Learned

Marc Tucker, president of the National Center on Education, was a member of the commission that reported on education and the economy in the book *America's Choice: High Skills or Low Wages* (The Report of the Commission on the Skills of the American Workforce, June 1990). Although today Americans seem content and even euphoric about the economy, the report isn't talking about 1999 or 2000. This report looks far into the future of our students. Today's students, the same ones who are scoring last academically against the rest of the developed world, are going to be in charge of our corporations, schools, and government in the coming years. Those who are calling for vouchers or charter schools are giving our current schools a clear message—we want leading, not lagging, skills and capabilities. Those ideas that used to be radical are now in the editorials of major mainstream newspapers under such banners as "School Boards Association, instead of rejecting charter schools, should welcome them." Education, a constitutionally established responsibility of the states, is going to be a national election determinant in the 2000 presidential election. Demands for performance excellence to move into our schools is widespread.

Performance improvement has permeated major sectors of the American economy from manufacturing and service industries to professional services, health care, public utilities, and government. Education has pioneered some efforts as well. All of these segments have contributed valuable lessons to the performance improvement movement and have played an important part in our recovery from the economic slump caused by poor service and products of the 1970s. Relying on the Baldrige model, we will share some of the insights and lessons learned from leaders of high-performing organizations.

Educational Institutions Are Unique, but Do Not Let That Be an Excuse to Do Nothing

As a school or college moves forward with performance improvement, the first reaction of faculty and staff may be that they are not businesses—they deal with human learning. The business of education indeed centers around student learning. However, as with any other business, achieving excellence is essential to ensure success. To achieve excellence, schools need the best management practices at the organization and classroom levels. Good leaders, both teachers and administrators, in the right place make a significant difference in performance.

Products of education are unique to the business of education—skills, competencies, techniques, and research results. But the requirements of students and stakeholders are similar to those of any business—on-time delivery, reliability, professional treatment, responsiveness, and good value for the money. To satisfy students and other stakeholders and optimize student learning, the best management practices must be put in place.

Research and scholarship in particular raise an important issue for the interpretation and application of the Baldrige criteria for educational organizations. On one hand, research is an increasingly important element of an educational institution as the level of education proceeds to higher education and to graduate level instruction. The Baldrige criteria do not specifically mention research as a process requirement, although its role is discussed with respect to the concept of excellence under Key Themes. The fact that research is not mentioned specifically in the criteria as a process requirement, however, does not mean one can draw the conclusion that is not applicable to the criteria. In fact, if research is critical to mission success, then research becomes a key business factor. As such, the organization must address research design and execution as any other core process. Accordingly, a university scholar or administrator in the research infrastructure cannot accurately conclude that the criteria do not apply to research activities. All relevant aspects of producing and supporting research must be effectively managed and improved to optimize performance results. In addition, results from research and applied scholarship are important in the continuing refinement of curricula. As key business factors, research and scholarship should be guided and improved by the careful interpretation and application of the concepts and principles that are the foundation of the Baldrige Education Criteria.

Resistance to Change Is Likely to Come First and Strongest from the Best People

A middle school wrote of a difficult experience when a small committee enthusiastically planned its first all-school quality training. Two days before the session was to be held, a letter signed by about twenty teachers was delivered to the school administrator. It basically said that the training was ill timed and not needed. It was signed by the best teachers in the school. Administrators did not know how to handle this letter but they did the right thing. They discussed openly the need for the training with the group and built more debriefing time into the training session. They also stuck to the plan of performance improvement they had promised to the community.

There are many excellent faculty and staff on board who have pushed the envelope of excellence as far as they can with traditional methods. They represent the best of the traditional school structure and methodology. They typically have difficulty understanding why they need to change when they have always been in the forefront of achievement. It is critical that dialog with these excellent contributors continue so they do not create a barrier to moving forward. The best and brightest need to understand the limits of the paradigms that made them successful, in order to change to become even more successful.

Category 1: Leadership

Great Educational Leaders Lead by Example and Message

One characteristic of a high-performance educational organization is outstanding academic results. How does a school achieve such results? How does it become world class? While no scientific studies have been able to document a single road that leads to such success, we have found unanimous agreement on the critical and funda-

mental role of leadership. There is not one example of an organization or unit within an organization that achieves profound improvement without the personal and active involvement of its top leadership. Top leaders in these organizations create a powerful vision that focuses and energizes the workforce. Everyone is pulling together toward the same goals. Frequently, an inspired vision is the catalyst that overcomes the organizational status quo.

As you transition your school, sending the right signals can be pivotal in getting your message across. Some powerful examples that have worked include

- Canceling your own administrative cabinet meetings when the agenda does not include substantive issues of policy that are critical to the mission and key goals.
- Defining your role as the conscience of the mission and strategic plan of the school.
- Redrawing reporting relationships so that administration is seen as the support for the instruction rather than the "big boss." One school district renamed their administrative cabinet the District Support Council.
- Promoting those who demonstrate advanced performance management leadership skills. One school system only promoted those who had successfully completed its very rigorous "Quality Academy," consisting of Baldrige-based criteria training and studies of various quality principles.
- Delivering in person presentations of key goals and mission to schools, colleges, or other units of the organization by the president, superintendent, or Board members.

Great educational leaders are great communicators. They identify clear objectives and a game plan so the school succeeds in its mission of producing student learning. They assign accountability, ensure that employees have the tools and skills required, and create a work climate where transfer of learning occurs. They reward teamwork and data-driven improvement. While practicing what they preach they serve as role models for continuous improvement, consensus building, and fact-based decision making, and push authority and accountability to the lowest possible levels.

One lesson from great leaders is to minimize the use of the word *quality*. Too often, when skilled, hard working, dedicated employees are told by leaders, "We are going to start a quality effort," they conclude that their leaders believe they have not been working hard enough or producing quality work. The employees hear an unintended message—"We have to do this because we are not good." They frequently retort with "We already do quality work!" Unfortunately, the use of the word *quality* can create an unintended barrier of mistrust and negativism that leaders must overcome before even starting on the road to performance excellence.

As an alternative, we advise leaders to create a work climate that enables employees to develop and use their full potential, to improve continually the way they work—to seek higher performance levels and reduce activities that do not add value or optimize performance. Most employees readily agree that there is always room for improvement. This leads to our second lesson learned.

Leaders will have to overcome two organizational tendencies—to reject any quality model or theory "not invented here," and to think that there are many equally valid models. Most traditional awards and certifications are either not Baldrige-based or based on a very low level of Baldrige achievement. This includes processes such as various accreditation reviews and blue ribbon school awards. The Baldrige model—including the many national, state, and organization assessment systems based on it—is accepted worldwide as *the* standard for defining performance excellence in organizations. Its criteria focus on validated, leading-edge practices for managing an organization. A decade of extraordinary performance results shown by Baldrige Award winners and numerous state-level, Baldrige Award–based

winners (including schools) have helped convince those willing to learn and listen.

To be effective, leaders must understand the Baldrige model and communicate to the workforce and leadership system their intention to use that model for assessment and improvement. Without clear leadership there will be many "hikers" walking around but no marked trails for them to follow. Once leaders understand the system and realize that it is their responsibility to share the knowledge and mark the trails clearly, alignment and performance optimization are attainable. This brings us to our third leadership lesson learned.

A significant portion of senior leaders' time—as much as 60% to 80%—should be spent in visible Baldrige-related leadership activities such as goal setting, planning, reviewing academic performance and improvement, recognizing and rewarding high performance, and spending time understanding and communicating with faculty, staff, stakeholders, and students, not micromanaging subordinates' work. The senior leaders' perspective in goal setting, planning, and reviewing performance must look at the inside from the outside. Looking at the organization through the critical eyes of external stakeholders is a vital perspective.

The primary role of the effective senior leader is not to manage internal operations, but rather to be visionary and focus the organization on satisfying students and stakeholders through an effective leadership system. Leaders must role model the tools of consensus building and decision making as the organization focuses on its vision, mission, and strategic direction to keep stakeholders loyal.

Falling back on command-and-control behavior will be self-defeating. The leadership system will suffer from crossed wires and mixed messages. Commandments such as "I want this project completed by the end of the second semester" fall into the self-defeating, major-mistake category.

Using the consensus approach to focus the organization on its mission and vision will take time, of course. However, this is similar to taking more time during the course and curriculum design phase to ensure that learning problems are prevented later. The additional time is necessary for organizational learning, support, and buy-in, particularly around two areas—the competitive environment, and the requirements of stakeholders. The resulting vision will have more depth. The leadership system will be stronger. Finally, the deployment of the vision and focus will take a shorter time because of the buy-in and support created during the process.

Teachers Are Leaders of the Classroom Learning System

School systems are made up of many interconnected systems. The leader of the most fundamental system is in the classroom—the leader, instructor, professor, teacher, or lecturer. It is this leadership that will determine whether the students are engaged, or just "filled with stuff"; whether parents and stakeholders are involved in the process or seen as only "payors," "field trip chaperones," and "cookie makers." For this reason, under sample effective practices, we have included a section for teachers on their role in each of the seven categories. It is not an exhaustive list but it provides examples of what teachers should be considering under each category.

L Is for Listen

Successful leaders know the power in listening to their people—those they rely on to achieve their goals. One vital link to the pulse of the school is faculty, staff, and student feedback. To find out whether what you have said has been heard, ask for feedback and then listen carefully. To know whether what you have outlined as a plan makes sense or has gaping faults, ask for feedback and then listen. Your system cannot improve without leadership that listens to and acts on feedback from faculty, staff, students, and stakeholders.

Improvement on goals and action plans depends on this process of listening and refining.

Lead and Drive Change

Educational leaders can count on relentless, rapid change being part of the academic world. The rate of change confronting business today is far faster than that driven by the industrial revolution. Skills driven by the industrial revolution carried our parents through a forty-year work cycle. Today, our children are told to expect five career (not job) changes during their work life. Human knowledge now doubles every five to seven years, instead of the forty years it took in the 1930s.

There are several lessons in this for leaders today. Change may not occur on the schedule they set for it. It is difficult to predict. Also, change is often resisted not only by those entrenched in the status quo, but by those most successful—they have difficulty seeing the need to change.

Leaders who hold the values of high performance will need to drive change to make the necessary improvements. Embracing the concepts of organizational learning (not just individual) will facilitate change in the school. Leaders will need to promote organizational learning as a tool to manage change and drive it through the school.

Category 2: Strategic Planning

Deploy through People, Not Paper

Strategic planning is performance improvement planning, deployment, and implementation. The organization's strategic plan is also its business, human resources, and performance improvement plan. Easily enough said, but trying to get agreement on exactly what strategic planning is will result in a variety of ideas. Therefore, the planning process should begin by ensuring that all contributors agree on terminology. Otherwise the strategic plan may in fact be a curriculum plan, a budget plan, or a master building plan, depending on who is leading the effort.

Leaders should concentrate on the few critical improvement goals necessary for organizational success, such as improving academic performance and reducing rework and learning cycle time. The well-developed strategic plan
- Documents the impact of achieving these few goals.
- Details actions and resources needed to support the goals.
- Discusses the competitive environment that drives the goals.

One highly successful organization simplified this document to a single electronic page, to which senior leaders referred each month by computer during academic progress and performance review meetings.

The most critical lesson learned when it comes to strategic plans is that there can be no rest until every person in the organization knows the strategic plan and can describe how he or she contributes to achieving the plan's goals and objectives. Remember the hiking analogy: don't let hikers onto the trails until they all know where they are going, what they have to do to get there, and how to measure progress so that they know they are going in the right direction and maintaining satisfactory progress. The same basic principles apply to running a high-performance educational organization.

Imagine this test in your school: a visitor meets with the school superintendent or dean to gain an understanding of the personal vision and plan for the school. Suppose the visitor then interviews teachers, research faculty, support staff, students, and many others at all levels, asking them to explain the school's vision and plan and their role in achieving the plan. In high-performance organizations, a consistent story emerges from people at all levels. Additionally, the visitor gets a sense that the vision and plan are real and attainable.

The visitor could be any stakeholder: a parent, a prospective student, a trustee, legislator, or any taxpayer or donor. The visitor could also be an examiner for the Baldrige Award, because the test suggested here is an actual process used by these examiners. It can also be used effectively by any organization to assess itself.

In any case, ensure two things:
- That the strategic plan does not merely rest in a prominent position on the bookshelves of top administrators.
- That it is used to drive and guide actions and is understood by all. That means all decisions must consider the impact on achieving strategic goals and objectives.

If these actions are not taken, work will not be aligned. People may work hard, but are likely to pull in many directions. This scenario leads to nonproductive pet projects and programs competing for time and other resources. It is critical to get all faculty and staff pulling in the same direction. At the same time, alignment does not require or even suggest conformity and standardization across units as diverse as different departments in a college of arts and sciences, or different grade levels in a school. There is, however, a need to create clear understandings about priorities and the actions needed to achieve them. If a faculty member is hired by a department in which research is a primary part of the mission and that individual expects to be rewarded primarily for teaching and student advising, both the school and the individual have made mistakes that will be costly in human terms and in organization productivity.

Category 3: Student and Stakeholder Focus

Students Bring Multiple Perspectives to a School, Including Those of Stakeholder, Customer, and Worker

Customers are those who use products and receive services. A strong source of resistance to performance management has come from teachers who do not fully understand the role of students in the new system. They are rightly concerned that students, if seen as customers, might have requirements that would be contrary to sound education or, more generally, might wish to apply a "consumerist" view to education. For example, students may make the unreasonable requirement that they should all receive grades of A. Or, students might favor entertainment over challenge. Clearly, this is not consistent with management of high-performance schools. The focus of this discussion needs to address one prominent issue: How can we best engage students in their learning to optimize it?

Student feedback on the attributes of the learning process and environment can be very valuable in identifying opportunities for improvement, without undermining the responsibility of the instructor to select content and establish the level of challenge. Harry Roberts, now retired from the Graduate School of Business at the University of Chicago, said: "Students know when they're confused by a presentation. Yet, because students can feel intimidated about asking questions, an instructor may not be aware of the problem without a mechanism for obtaining feedback."

All students have certain requirements of their instructors and teachers. Some educators may see these as "customer requirements," while others see them as part of "workforce requirements." These include expectations of fairness and consistency, clear directions for assignments, classes that begin and end on time, respectful treatment, and a safe, secure environment. In other kinds of businesses these kinds of expectations generally are included in basic workforce or employee requirements, without which the organization cannot be successful. In a school these issues are central to creating a constructive learning environment, without which a school cannot be successful.

At all levels of education, kindergarten through postgraduate, students need to be engaged in planning and evaluating their learning. Tools and techniques for assessment such as using rubrics and student portfolios have helped instructors engage students in planning and evaluating their learning. Students need to have a much higher degree of involvement in planning their curriculum, assessments, and class projects as they move on in their education.

Students as customers or stakeholders in schools are more easily defined at higher levels when employment, admission to college or graduate school, and certain levels of competency are clear customer requirements. At lower levels, it is easy to see students as customers with specific expectations as they buy their food from the cafeteria, ride the bus, receive homework instructions, and attend dances or fun nights at school.

As students progress from kindergarten through graduate school and beyond, they take on different roles and have differing requirements. There is an invisible continuum of increasing responsibility for their own education and learning as they mature. To optimize learning requires more involvement of the student in their own learning and more student engagement as they mature. Not engaging students in their learning will suboptimize programs and waste time and resources.

For example, a school district chose the character development of its students as one of its key goals. This was a goal of the Board and the community. Many businesses and individuals in the community contributed funds and support for this program. As the planning team developed the curriculum, a parent suggested that students needed to be involved in planning, and faculty needed to be trained with students. This did not happen and students saw the program as "something done to them." Further, they noted many discrepancies between the promises of their teachers and what was delivered. Although they were being asked to take personal responsibility for keeping promises and turning in homework on time, teachers were not grading and returning papers when they said they would. Their coaches were telling students that if they work hard and attend practices they will play during games. Yet in reality only a few players were playing, and this had more to do with natural skill than hard work. This tended to make the message of the program "Do as I say, not as I do." This was a sure recipe for the program's failure, particularly among teenagers.

Engaging students in the educational planning and decisions that affect them will have the largest payback in terms of performance and a positive school climate. There are numerous examples of how institutions that are supposedly focused on student learning ignore students when planning their learning experiences.

A middle school decided to improve its efficiency by banning students from carrying book bags from class to class. Faculty thought that this would ensure students wouldn't be fidgeting with their book bags during class to get out pencils, papers, and notes. Students were never involved in this decision and did not appreciate the unwelcome and burdensome rule. The net result of this policy was that more students arrived at class late and unprepared. They had to go to their lockers, which were located all over the building, before every class. Students routinely arrived at class without their homework because it was in their lockers. This policy adversely affected student learning and grades suffered because students were marked down for not bringing homework to class—homework that was complete but left in the locker.

A college decided to send out student transcripts in batches of 20 for their own convenience instead of when students needed them. Some students missed deadlines for financial aid for transfer credits while waiting for the 20th transcript to be requested, even though their requests were made weeks ahead of time.

Schools cannot afford to ignore students at any level when they make policies and decisions that affect their learning and attitudes toward the school.

Another lesson has to do with external customers and stakeholders such as parents, businesses, and taxpayers. Organizations that make it easy for customers to complain are in a good position to hear about problems early so that they can fix them and plan ahead to prevent them. If organizations handle customer complaints effectively at the first point of contact, customer loyalty and satisfaction will increase and the organization will learn about its processes more quickly.

The next lesson has to do with educating the organization's leadership in the fundamentals of customer satisfaction research models before beginning to collect customer satisfaction data. Failure to do this may affect the usefulness of the data as a strategic tool. At the very least, it will make the development of data collection instruments a long, misunderstood effort, creating rework and unnecessary cost.

Do not lose sight of the fact that the best customer feedback method, whether it is a survey, focus group, or one-on-one interview, is only a tool.
- Make sure the data gathered are actionable.
- Aggregate the data from all sources to permit complete analyses.
- Use the data to improve planning and operating processes.

Finally, be aware that students and other stakeholders are not interested in the school's problems, just as you are not interested in the problems of your grocer or mechanic. Your interest is in receiving the product or service as required. Similarly, students and other stakeholders merely want products or services delivered as promised.

Category 4: Information and Analysis

Focus on the Power of Measures

First of all, most people accept the proposition that measures are not just numbers and facts and who ever has the largest pile of information wins. Educational organizations are very committed to collecting information. Unfortunately, the facts and information they collect do not always relate to their key goals and priorities. So the first lesson is to design what you collect to answer the questions that you want answered (and must answer due to local, state, and national requirements), and then make sure the information is available to all who need it to make decisions.

For example, schools around the country have been running an expensive ($6 billion) and popular program to help students avoid drugs. It is funded by the Safe and Drug-Free Schools and Communities Act. Elementary and secondary schools partner with local police departments to learn about the perils of drug use and hand out T-shirts and trinkets to students when they "graduate." If the program's goals were good will or effective partnerships in the community, the program would be an overwhelming success. The goal of the program, however, is to reduce the number of students taking drugs. Evidence suggests that students who participate and graduate from this program are not any more likely to avoid drugs than other students.

What Gets Evaluated Gets Done, What Gets Rewarded Gets Done First

Key goals need to be measurable in clear and understandable ways. The following are lessons learned that can help educational organizations make their measures truly powerful. Because not everything is subject to counting or quantification, we include under the heading of "measurement" many valuable concepts that require careful judgment in the context of approaches to assessment and evaluation.

Data-Driven Management and Avoiding Contephobia

The high-performance school collects, manages, and analyzes data and information to drive excellence and improve its overall performance. Said another way: in the best schools and classrooms, information is used to drive actions. Using data and information as strategic weapons, effective leaders use comparisons aggressively. First they compare actual performance within the organization to goals or plans. In addition, they compare their school constantly to competitors, similar educational service providers, and world-class schools. They uncover performance excellence and performance problems.

While people tend to think of data and measurement as objective and hard, there is often a softer by-product of measurement. That by-product is the basic human emotion of fear. This perspective on data and measurement leads to the next lesson learned about information and analysis. Human fear must be recognized and managed in order to practice data-driven management.

This fear can be found in two forms: First there are those who have a simple fear of numbers—those who hated mathematics in school and may simply practice avoidance behavior when faced with anything quantitative. These individuals are uncomfortable in discussions of numerical data. When asked to measure or when presented with data, they can become fearful, angry, and resistant. Their reactions can undermine improvement efforts.

A second form of fear may be present in one who understands numbers and realizes that numbers can impose higher levels of accountability. The fear of accountability, *contephobia* (from 14th-century Latin *to count*, modified by the French *to account*), is based on the fear of real performance failure that numbers might reveal or, more often, an overall fear of the unknown that will drive important decisions. Power structures can and do shift when decisions are data-driven. The power of the loudest voice or last person leaving the boss's office erodes in the face of reliable information and data.

Fearful individuals can undermine effective data-driven management systems. In managing this fear, leaders must believe and communicate through their behavior that the purpose of data is to promote better decision making, not punishment. It is important for leaders at all levels to demonstrate that system and process improvements are the objective, not mechanisms for punishment or sanction.

A mature, high-performance organization will collect data on competitors and similar providers and compare itself against world-class leaders. Some individuals may not be capable of seeing the benefit of using this process. Benchmarking data are a means of identifying, learning from, and adopting best practices or methods from similar processes, regardless of industry or product similarity. Adopting the best practices of other organizations has driven quantum leap improvements and provided great opportunities for breakthrough improvements.

Schools that are new to the experience of making systematic improvement aimed at excellent performance may choose to postpone benchmarking processes against known superior performers within the education arena or against other world-class performers. Eventually, however, only by using valid and reliable data from outside the organization can leaders confirm that performance is good or excellent. Benchmarking serves that purpose.

This lesson relates to not being a DRIP. This refers to a tendency to collect so much data (which contributes to contephobia) that the orga-

nization becomes "Data Rich and Information Poor." This reflects inadequate planning of the measurement system. Avoid wasting resources and stretch the resources available for managing improvement by asking this question: "Will these data help make improvements for our students, faculty, and staff, or in other top result areas such as reducing drug use or increasing science test scores?" If the answer is no, do not waste time collecting, analyzing, and trying to use the data (unless required by law or regulation).

Category 5: Faculty and Staff Focus

In high-performing schools, faculty and staff are the most valuable asset of the organization—investment and development are critical to optimize performance. Faculty and staff should be perceived as internal stakeholders and a vital part of the chain. They provide a valuable service—helping to produce students and graduates with enhanced knowledge, skills, thinking abilities, and competencies, who become motivated workers and responsible citizens.

The Big Challenge Is Trust

The high-performing school values its faculty and staff and demonstrates this by enabling people to develop and realize their full potential while providing them incentives to do so. The school that is focused on faculty and staff excellence maintains a climate that builds trust. Trust is essential for faculty and staff participation, engagement, personal and professional growth, and high performance. Without it, the relationship in the classroom also suffers. Student-faculty relationships, in turn, will not be based on trust, and students will not be meaningfully engaged in their learning.

A new principal of a troubled middle school with many safety and drug issues tried to forge new relationships built on trust with his faculty and staff. He sent them signals. For example, teachers and faculty were treated like "adults" and allowed to leave the building for emergencies and appointments without his permission. He did not make decisions and take the role of parent of the school, but let faculty and staff work with him on a new mission, to make new rules and a governance structure based on data and consistency. This helped produce much higher levels of trust with students and subsequently higher performance.

A community college empowered a committee of faculty and staff to make decisions about funding projects based on institutional priorities. The president and trustees were impressed that the committee did not allocate all the funds because they did not think many projects were actually based on institutional priorities. Imagine the message this sent about next year's projects—focus them on our common goals and institutional priorities. Stronger alignment and focus resulted.

Schools need to take a critical look at their current reward and recognition systems. Leaders must be willing to revise—overhaul, if necessary—recognition, compensation, promotion, and feedback systems to support whatever constitutes high performance for that institution. Promotion, compensation, recognition, and reward must be tied to the achievement of educational results, including student and stakeholder satisfaction, innovation, academic performance improvement, and, where applicable, effective research. The promotion/compensation tool is a powerful tool in aligning, or misaligning, the work of the school. Most organizations have the authority to provide effective rewards and recognition, but few leaders have either the courage or energy to make the necessary changes.

A second human resource lesson learned relates to training and development. Training is not a panacea or a goal in itself. The organization's direction and goals must support training, and training must support organization priorities. Empowered and skilled people are the competitive edge of a high-performing organization. Training must be aligned with overall strategy. If

not, money and resources are probably better spent on a memorable holiday party.

Timing is critical. Overall awareness training for entire faculties and groups that work together with common goals can be very effective in educational organizations. However, broad-based workforce skill training should not come until needed. Many schools rush out and train their entire faculty and staff on tools and techniques only to find they have to retrain months or years later. Key participants should be involved in planning skill training so that important skills are developed just in time for them to use in their assignments. Many schools have had great success with "just-in-time" training that is delivered shortly before the recipients are expected to need or be asked to apply it.

For example, there are dozens of decision-making and group process tools that will be useful for classroom use. Learning them all at once will not result in their use. Rather, it makes more sense for teachers to look at their goals and decide how to engage students more in the learning process. This may be in selecting a project. They may then learn how to use "rubrics" or "fishbone diagrams." This will require the use of several tools and an "internal expert" to teach them how to use the tools they will need to engage students more fully in their studies.

Continuous skill development requires that administrators support, reinforce, and strengthen skills on the job. Leadership development at all levels of the organization must be built into faculty and staff development. New technology has increased training flexibility so that all knowledge does not have to be transferred solely in a classroom setting. Consider many options when planning how best to update skills. After initial awareness training occurs, high-performing schools emphasize organizational learning where faculty and staff take charge of their own learning, using training courses as only one avenue for skill upgrading. Transferring learning to other parts of the school or projects is a valuable organizational learning strategy and reinforcement technique. Training must be offered when an application exists to use and reinforce the skill. Otherwise, most of what is learned will be forgotten. The effectiveness of training must be assessed based on the impact on the job, not merely the likability of the instructor or the clarity of course materials.

Faculty and staff surveys are often used to measure and improve satisfaction. Surveys are especially useful to identify key issues that should be discussed in open forums. Such forums are truly useful if they clarify perceptions, provide more in-depth understanding of faculty and staff concerns, and open the communication channels with leaders. Schools have success in improving faculty and staff satisfaction by conducting routine satisfaction surveys, meeting with them to plan improvements, and tying improvements in satisfaction ratings to promotion and recognition.

Two final faculty and staff excellence lessons have to do with engaging and involving faculty in decisions about their work. This is particularly critical because when faculty or staff are engaged and involved, they understand better the importance of involving and engaging their students. Involving faculty, staff, and students in decision making without the right skills or a sense of direction produces chaos, not high-performance. The two lessons are these:

- First, leaders who empower faculty and staff before ensuring that a sense of direction has been fully understood will find that they are managing chaos.
- Second, not everyone wants to be empowered. There may be teachers/faculty and staff members who truly seek to avoid responsibility for making improvements, claiming "that's the administration's job." These individuals do not last long in a high-performing school. They begin to stick out like lone birds in the winter. Most responsible administrators and faculty who want the school to thrive and excel do not

want such people to drag down the organization.

The bigger reason why individuals fail to "take empowerment and run with it" is the administration's mixed messages. In short, administrators must convince faculty and staff that they really believe faculty, staff, and students are in the best position to improve their own work processes. Consistent leadership is required to help faculty and staff overcome legitimate, long-standing fear of traditional administrative practices used so often in the past to control and punish.

Remember, aligning compensation and reward systems to reinforce performance plans and core values is one of the most critical ways to enhance organizational performance; however, getting faculty and staff to believe their leaders really trust them to improve their own processes is difficult but vital. Training and development should be done not just to accumulate training hours, but to ensure that knowledge and skills needed for improvement are acquired. Finally, just as feedback from students is important to instructors, feedback from faculty and staff is important for administrators.

Category 6: Educational and Support Process Management

Involve Faculty and Staff Closest to the Work

Process management involves the continuous improvement of processes required to meet educational and operational requirements. Every high-performance school identifies key processes and manages them to ensure that student and stakeholder requirements are met consistently and performance is continuously improved.

The first lesson learned has to do with the visibility of processes. Many processes are highly visible, such as serving a meal or purchasing equipment. However, many educational processes are hard to observe, such as course design or student responses. It cannot be assumed that everyone will see the organization as a collection of processes. The simple exercise of drawing a process flow diagram with people involved in an invisible process can be a struggle, but also a valuable revelation. With no vantage point from which to see work as a process, many people never think of themselves as engaged in a process. Some even deny it. The fact that all work—visible and invisible—is part of a process must be understood throughout the organization before faculty and staff can begin to manage and improve key processes.

Schools often succeed at making their internal processes better, faster, and (perhaps) cheaper for them. However, this may or may not actually improve student performance. When analyzing internal processes, someone must stubbornly play the role of advocate for the student and stakeholder perspective. Ensure that the improved processes will help meet key organizational goals, such as improving student learning or providing the key researcher an opportunity to be more creative and productive. Process improvement should reduce unnecessary costs or work steps, and/or boost performance results. Avoid wasting resources on process improvements that do not benefit stakeholders, students, staff, or faculty as tracked by the key performance indicators of your school.

A fourth lesson involves design processes, an important but often neglected part of process management. The best schools have learned that improvements made early in the process, beginning with design, save more time and money than those made farther "downstream." To identify how design processes can be improved, it is necessary to include ongoing evaluation and improvement cycles. Reducing the time for designing new curriculum not only reduces costs, but can return the teacher to student-centered activities more quickly.

Category 7: School Performance Results

Encourage Activities that Lead to Desired Performance Results

Results fall into four broad categories:
* School performance results
* Student and stakeholder satisfaction results
* Faculty and staff results
* School-specific results

Student performance results are based upon mission-related factors and assessment methods. Student performance should reflect holistic and mission-related results; current levels and trends should be reported; and data should be segmented by student group. This is an important item for all educational organizations because it looks at student achievement over time, related to comparable schools and/or student populations.

Student and stakeholder satisfaction is a critical and ongoing result that every successful school must achieve. Educational systems must ensure that the data from student and stakeholder satisfaction and dissatisfaction are used at all levels to plan and make improvements. Remember that when students and stakeholders are asked their opinion, an expectation is created in their minds that the information will be used to make improvements that benefit them—even in kindergarten.

Some organizations have found it beneficial to have their students and other stakeholders analyze some of their academic performance results with the idea of learning from them as well as building and strengthening relationships. This may or may not be appropriate for your organization, but many successful schools have shared results with key groups at a level appropriate for their specific school.

Faculty and staff results provide an early alert to problems that may threaten success. Absenteeism, turnover, accidents, low morale, grievances, and poor skills or ineffective training suboptimize school effectiveness. By monitoring performance in these areas, educational leaders can adjust quickly and prevent little problems from overwhelming the organization.

School-specific product and service results provide useful information on key measures of the program, offering, or service itself. This information allows a school to predict whether students and other stakeholders are likely to be satisfied—usually without asking them. For example, the likelihood that student satisfaction would be high with a given teacher would increase if the teacher knew and behaved consistently with factors students want in their teachers. These factors might include the following:

- Being knowledgeable about content
- Using relevant examples
- Returning assignments promptly
- Showing relationships between unknown content and known content
- Being fair
- Being genuinely interested in learning and teaching

One important lesson in this area is to select measures that correlate with, and predict, student and other stakeholder preference, satisfaction, and loyalty.

School-specific operational and service results pertain to measures of internal effectiveness that may not be of immediate interest to students and stakeholders. Examples include cycle time (how long it takes to administer a test and return the grades), waste (how many tests or test items have to be rewritten or thrown out because of faulty wording or mistakes), and test-reporting accuracy (which may upset the affected students and faculty). Ultimately, improving internal work process efficiency can result in reduced cost, rework, waste, scrap, and other factors that affect performance, whether academic results–driven or budget-driven. As a result, students and stakeholders benefit indirectly. To remain competitive, or to meet increased performance demands with fewer resources, schools will be required to improve processes that enhance operational and support service results.

Effective performance management is as much a key to survival for educational organizations as for any other organization. This is true for both private sector (for-profit) and public sector (not-for-profit) schools. It is important to avoid over-reliance on financial results. Financial results are the most lagging indicators of all school performance measures. Leaders who focus primarily on financials often overlook or cannot respond quickly to changing needs. Focusing on finances to run educational enterprises—to the exclusion of more leading indicators such as operational performance and student and stakeholder satisfaction—is like driving your car by looking only in the rearview mirror. You can not avoid potholes and turns in the road, and eventually you crash.

Supplier quality performance can significantly affect organizational operating effectiveness and student and stakeholder satisfaction. This is particularly true for food suppliers; nutrition has a direct effect on learning. To the extent a school depends on suppliers, it must ensure that supplier performance improves—otherwise it must absorb (or pass on) supplier waste, errors, inefficiency, and rework. Suppliers of information technology and support for processes related to information technology have become vitally important for educational organizations. A school that tolerates poor supplier performance places its own success at risk.

Do Not Tolerate System Craziness

The following illustration of supplier waste was caused by system craziness. It affected student and stakeholder satisfaction as well as wasted resources. A parent asked her student why he was not eating the lunches the school provided. He replied that he would not eat peanut butter and cheese sandwiches. The parent went to school and asked the cafeteria manager why she was serving peanut butter and cheese sandwiches. The manager acknowledged that these were not eaten but in fact thrown out by the majority of students. She said that federal guidelines for nutrition required a certain number of grams of protein and that if they put enough peanut butter to satisfy the requirement, it would literally be so thick as to choke the student. So they added a slice of cheese to make up the protein requirement. Of course, students have to actually eat the sandwich to get any protein at all, but this apparently was not figured into the menu design. This is a perfect example of compliance, but not performance excellence.

Stakeholders' requirements are of two types: (1) surrogate requirements based on student needs that should be reflected in the school's educational services; and (2) personal needs of stakeholders themselves. For example, parents might request services related to their children's educational program (type 1), and the parents might also request special meeting times with the school to accommodate their work schedules (type 2). Many of the needs of employers and other stakeholders are actually needs that must be addressed in the school's educational services to students. The Education Criteria place primary emphasis upon such needs because the school's success depends heavily upon translating these needs into effective educational services and experiences.

Education Criteria for Performance Excellence Systems Framework

The Performance Excellence Education Criteria framework contains three basic elements.
- Strategy and action plans—the context for aligning work and achieving performance excellence
- System—consisting of the driver triad, work core, and outcomes
- Information and analysis—the brain center of high-performing organizations

Figure 1 depicts the entire system. Figures 2, 3, and 4 break out the major components of the system.

Strategy and Action Plans

Strategy and action plans are the set of student- and stakeholder-focused school-level require- ments, derived from short- and long-term strategic planning, that must be done well for the school's strategy to succeed. Strategy and action plans set the context for action in high-performing organizations and provide the vehicle through which leaders drive the school to achieve success. Strategy and action plans guide overall resource decisions and drive the alignment of measures for all work units to ensure student and stakeholder satisfaction and overall success.

Strategy and action plans are represented in the framework as an umbrella that covers the organization's entire work system and guides discussions of the organization and its people.

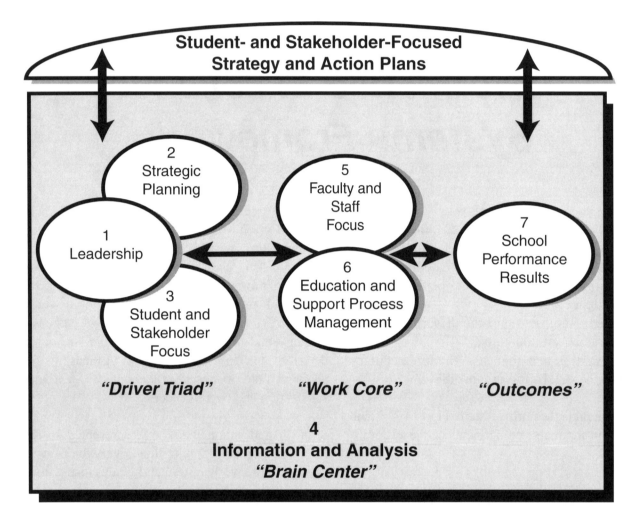

Figure 1. Education criteria for performance excellence—systems framework.

System

The *system* is comprised of the six categories in the center of the figure that define the organization, its operations, and its results. These categories form three groups, the driver triad, the work core, and outcomes.

Outcomes are a composite of student performance, student and stakeholder satisfaction, faculty and staff results, and school-specific results, including measures such as productivity and operational effectiveness, innovations, research, and improvements in school safety.

The links from the driver triad to the work core and outcomes are critical to school success. Leadership must keep its eyes on the results and must learn from them to drive improvement.

The Driver Triad

As Figure 2 indicates, the *driver triad* consists of three categories: leadership, strategic planning, and student and stakeholder focus.

The processes that make up these categories require leaders to set direction and expectations for the organization to meet student and stakeholder requirements (Category 1). Student and stakeholder focus (Category 3) processes produce the information that leaders use to determine what current and potential students and stakeholders want. Strategic planning (Category 2) and goal setting provide the vehicle for determining the short- and long-term strategies for success, as well as communicating and aligning the work of the organization. Leaders use this information to set direction and goals, monitor progress, make resource decisions, and take corrective action when progress does not proceed according to plan.

Figure 2. Driver triad.

The Work Core and Outcomes

The *work core* describes the processes through which the core work of the school takes place. As Figure 3 indicates, the work core consists of Faculty and Staff Focus (Category 5) and Educational and Support Process Management (Category 6), which produce the outcomes reported in School Performance Results (Category 7).

These categories recognize that the people of an educational organization are responsible for doing the work. To achieve performance excel-lence, these people must possess the right skills and must be allowed to work in an environment that promotes initiative and self-direction. The work processes provide the structure for continu-ous learning and improvement to optimize performance.

School Performance Results reflect the organiza-tion's outcomes critical for success. These include student performance results, student and stakeholder satisfaction, faculty and staff perfor-mance, and school-specific results such as supplier performance and internal operating effectiveness.

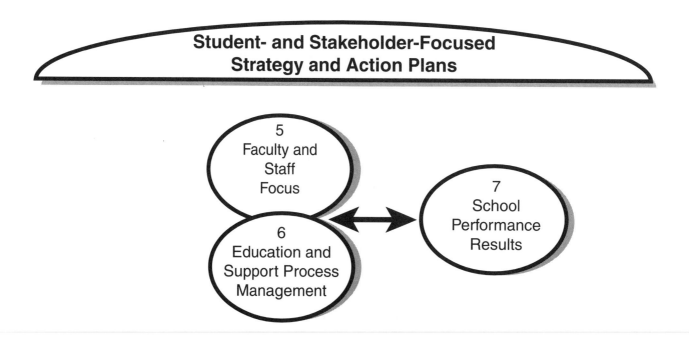

Work Core   **Outcomes**

Figure 3. Work core and outcomes.

Information and Analysis

Figure 4 indicates that information and analysis (Category 4) are the foundation for the entire management system. Information and analysis are the "brain center" of the management system. They are the platform on which the entire system operates. Information and analysis processes are critical to the effective management of the organization and to a fact-based system for improving organizational performance and competitiveness.

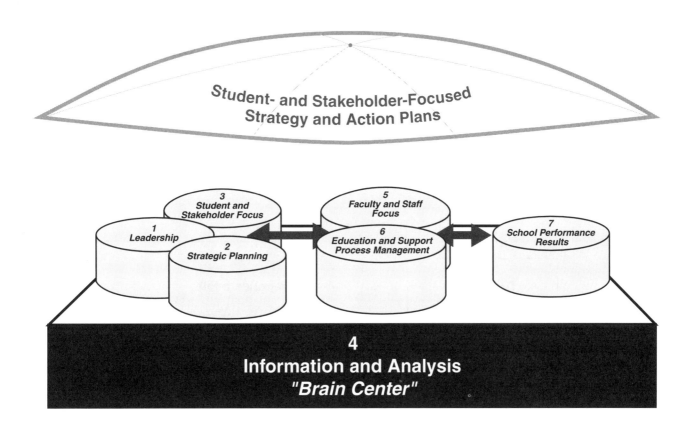

Figure 4. The systems framework.

Award Criteria Organization

The seven criteria categories are subdivided into Items and Areas to Address. Figure 5 demonstrates the organization of Category 1.

Items

There are 18 items, each focusing on a major requirement. Item titles and point values are listed on page 47.

Areas to Address

Items consist of one or more areas to address. Information for assessment is prepared in response to the specific requirements of these areas. There are 26 areas to address.

Subparts

There are 53 subparts. Areas consist of one or more subparts, where numbers are shown in parentheses. A response should be made to each subpart.

Notes

Notes provide a better explanation of the item requirements and identify some of the more obvious linkages. *Notes do not add requirements.* Do not interpret the explanations in the notes as if they were criteria requirements.

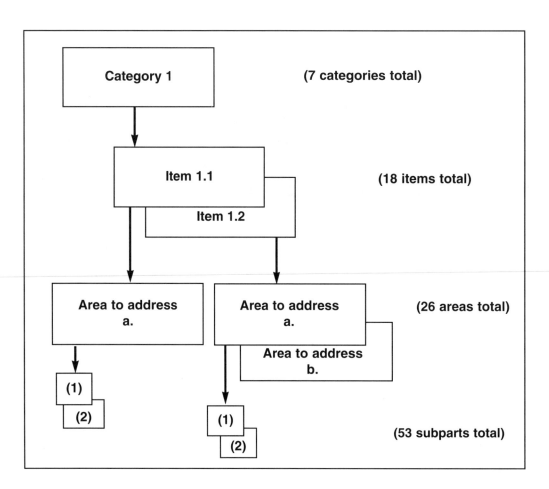

Figure 5. Sample flow chart.

Baldrige Education Criteria Categories and Point Values

Examination Categories/Items	Maximum Points
1 Leadership (110 points)	
1.1 Leadership System	80
1.2 Public Responsibility and Citizenship	30
2 Strategic Planning (80 points)	
2.1 Strategy Development Process	40
2.2 School Strategy	40
3 Student and Stakeholder Focus (80 points)	
3.1 Knowledge of Student Needs and Expectations	40
3.2 Student and Stakeholder Satisfaction and Relationship Enhancement	40
4 Information and Analysis (80 points)	
4.1 Selection and Use of Information and Data	25
4.2 Selection and Use of Comparative Information and Data	15
4.3 Analysis and Review of School Performance	40
5 Faculty and Staff Focus (100 points)	
5.1 Work Systems	40
5.2 Faculty and Staff Education, Training, and Development	30
5.3 Faculty and Staff Well-Being and Satisfaction	30
6 Education and Support Process Management (100 points)	
6.1 Education Design and Delivery	60
6.2 Education Support Processes	40
7 School Performance Results (450 points)	
7.1 Student Performance Results	150
7.2 Student and Stakeholder Satisfaction Results	100
7.3 Faculty and Staff Results	100
7.4 School-Specific Results	100
Total Points	**1000**

1 Leadership—110 Points

The Leadership category examines the school's leadership system and senior leaders' personal leadership. It examines how senior leaders and the leadership system address values, a focus on student learning, and performance excellence. Also examined is how the school addresses its societal responsibilities and provides support to key communities.

Leadership is the focal point within the criteria for addressing how the school's senior leaders guide the school in setting directions, seeking future opportunities, and building and sustaining a learning environment. Primary attention is given to how the senior leaders create a leadership system based upon clear values and high performance expectations that address the needs of all stakeholders. The category also includes the school's responsibilities to the public and how the school practices good citizenship.

1.1 Leadership System (80 Points)
Approach/Deployment Scoring

Describe the school's leadership system and how senior leaders guide the school in setting directions and in developing and sustaining effective leadership throughout the organization.

In your response, address the following area:

a. Leadership System

Describe the school's leadership system, how senior leaders provide effective leadership, and how this leadership is exercised throughout the school, taking into account the needs and expectations of all key stakeholders. Include:

(1) a description of the school's leadership system and how it operates. Include how it addresses values, performance expectations, a focus on students and other stakeholders, student learning, and goals.

(2) how senior leaders
  • set and communicate school directions, taking into account all key stakeholders.
  • communicate and reinforce values, performance expectations, a focus on students and other stakeholders, student learning, and commitment to improvement throughout the faculty and staff.
  • maintain a climate conducive to learning, including safety and equity.
  • participate in and use the results of performance reviews.
  • evaluate and improve the leadership system, including how they use their review of the school's performance and faculty and staff feedback in the evaluation.

Note:

N1.   The term *school*, as used in the criteria, refers to the assessment participation unit. The participation unit might actually be a school, a school district, a postsecondary institution, or a major academic unit within a college or university.

N2.   The term *senior leaders*, as used in the criteria, refers to those with main responsibility to manage the school. The leadership system would also include the school's governance entities such as school boards, as appropriate.

N3.   School performance reviews are addressed in Item 4.3. Responses to 1.1a(2) should therefore focus on the senior leaders' role in and uses of the review of overall performance, not on the details of the review.

This item addresses how the school's senior leaders set directions and sustain a leadership system conducive to high performance, individual development, initiative, organizational learning, and innovation. The item asks how leadership takes into account the needs and expectations of all key stakeholders. Key stakeholders might include families, employers, and other schools. In many cases, the leadership system would include not only those who have day-to-day responsibility to manage the school, but also the governance entities such as school boards or trustees.

The item calls for information on the major aspects of leadership—creating values and expectations; setting directions; projecting a strong focus on students and learning; encouraging innovation; developing and maintaining an effective leadership system; and effectively communicating values, directions, expectations, and a strong focus on students and learning. Setting directions includes creating future opportunities for the school and its stakeholders. An effective leadership system promotes continuous learning, not only to improve overall performance, but also to involve all faculty/staff in the ongoing challenge to enhance student/stakeholder value. To be successful, leadership must ensure that the school captures and shares learnings. Leadership's communications are critical to school success. Effective communication includes ongoing demonstration that stated values, directions, and expectations are indeed the basis for the school's key decisions and actions.

This item asks how leaders maintain a climate conducive to learning. Important parts of this climate are safety and equity. Equity refers to opportunities and benefits fairly distributed among different population groups. Communications also need to include performance objectives and related measures that help provide focus as well as integration and alignment among school units and activities.

This item also includes the senior leaders' role in reviewing the leadership system, using faculty/staff feedback, and reviewing overall school performance. This aspect of leadership is crucial, not only because reviews help provide focus on student learning, but also because reviews are an effective means for early detection of problems and timely redirection of resources, which usually require leadership support and involvement. A major aim is to create schools that are flexible and responsive, changing easily to adapt to new needs and opportunities. Through their roles in developing strategy and reviewing school performance, senior leaders develop leadership and create schools capable of adapting to changing opportunities and requirements.

At the smallest organizational level in schools—the classroom—teachers are the leaders and students make up the "workforce," (although they are obviously not employees). Within schools, teachers, as classroom leaders, can be considered part of the leadership system.

1.1 Leadership System

How senior leaders guide the school in setting direction and developing and sustaining an effective leadership system throughout the school.

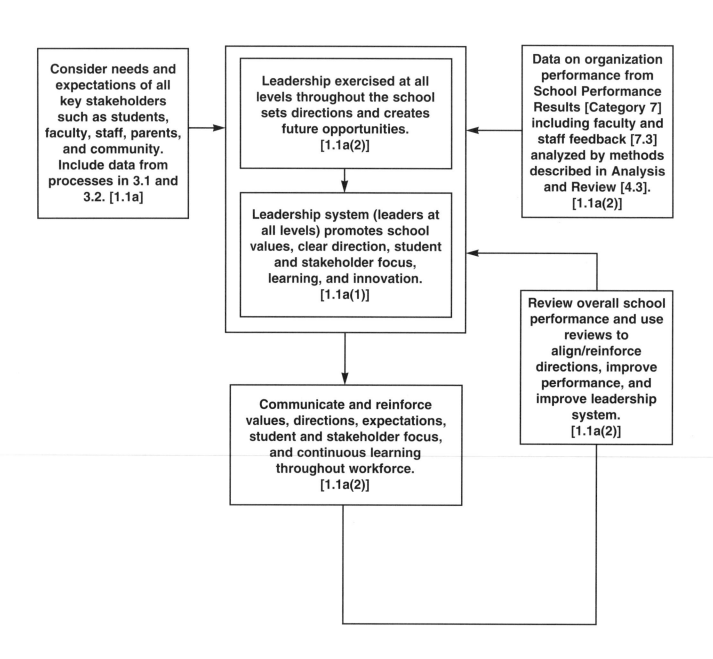

1.1 Leadership System Item Linkages

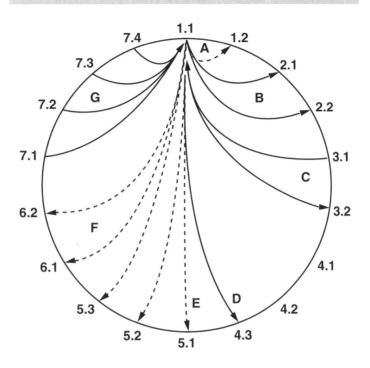

Nature of Relationship

A Leaders at all levels [1.1] must role model and support public responsibility and practice good citizenship [1.2].

B Leaders [1.1] participate in the strategic planning process [2.1] and ensure that plans are deployed at all levels throughout the organization and used to align work [2.2a]. Leaders [1.1] also approve the goals and measurements set forth in the plan [2.2b]. They are responsible for using comparative data to set stretch goals.

C Leaders [1.1] use information from students and stakeholders [3.1 and 3.2] to set direction and create opportunity for the school. Leaders [1.1] also have a responsibility for personally building relationships with key stakeholders [3.2a] (creating a bidirectional relationship).

D Leaders [1.1] use analyses of data [4.3] to monitor school performance and understand relationships among school program

performance and student and stakeholder performance. These analyses are also used for decision making at all levels to set priorities for action and allocate resources for maximum advantage.

E Leaders [1.1] at all levels work to improve the school's work and job design [5.1a] and ensure that the compensation and recognition system [5.1b] encourages faculty and staff at all levels to achieve the school's performance objectives, including student and stakeholder satisfaction and performance excellence. Leaders [1.1] are also responsible for supporting appropriate skill development of all faculty and staff through training and development systems and the use of learning on the job [5.2] as well as creating effective systems to enhance faculty and staff satisfaction, well-being, and motivation [5.3]. Leaders are also responsible for evaluating and refining all of these processes.

F Leaders [1.1] at all levels are responsible for creating an environment that supports high performance, including monitoring processes for education design and delivery [6.1], and education support processes [6.2]. Leaders must ensure that educational programs and offerings are aligned and consistently evaluated and refined.

G Leaders [1.1a(2)] at all levels use performance results data [Category 7] for many activities including strategic planning [2.1] and for setting goals and priorities, allocating resources [2.2], reinforcing or rewarding faculty and staff performance [5.1b], and for improving the leadership system [1.1a(2)].

1.1 Leadership System
Sample Effective Practices for Senior Leaders

- The CEO of a major university and his direct reports take new faculty on a bus tour of the state in the summer preceding their first year of appointment. This allows senior leaders to communicate core values to new faculty. At the same time, it communicates the university's interest in state customers and stakeholders.
- All senior leaders are personally involved in performance improvement.
- Senior leaders spend a significant portion of their time on performance improvement activities.
- Senior leaders carry out many visible activities, such as goal setting, planning, and recognition and reward of performance and education process improvement.
- Senior leaders regularly communicate values to leaders and administrators and ensure that they demonstrate those values in their work.
- Senior leaders participate on performance improvement teams and use tools and practices to enhance performance.
- Senior leaders spend time with students and stakeholders, seeking input about strengths and opportunities for improvement.
- Senior leaders mentor faculty and staff and ensure that promotion criteria reflect organizational values.

- Senior leaders study and learn about the improvement practices of other organizations.
- Senior leaders clearly and consistently articulate values such as student and stakeholder focus, student and stakeholder satisfaction, role model leadership, continuous improvement, faculty and staff involvement, and performance optimization throughout the organization.
- Senior leaders base their decisions on reliable data and facts pertaining to students and stakeholders, teaching and learning processes, and faculty and staff performance and satisfaction.
- Senior leaders ensure that organizational values are used to provide direction to all students, faculty, and staff in the organization to help achieve the mission, vision, and performance goals.
- Senior leaders hold regular meetings to review performance data and use two-way communication for problems, successes, and effective approaches to improve work.
- Senior leaders use effective and innovative approaches to reach out to all faculty and staff to spread the organization's values and align its work to support organizational goals.
- Senior leaders effectively surface problems and encourage faculty and staff creativity.
- Senior leaders conduct monthly reviews of organizational performance. This requires

that school leaders and department chairs conduct biweekly reviews and that faculty and staff and teams provide daily performance updates. Corrective actions are developed to improve performance that deviates from planned performance.

- Roles and responsibilities of leaders are clearly defined, understood by them, and used to judge their performance.
- Leaders and administrators "walk the walk," serving as role models in leading systematic performance improvement.
- Job definitions with performance indices are clearly delineated for each level of the organization, objectively measured, and presented in a logical and organized structure.
- Many different communication strategies are used to reinforce high-performance values.
- Leader behavior (not merely words) clearly communicates what is expected of the organization and its faculty and staff.
- Systems and procedures are deployed that encourage cooperation and a cross-functional approach to administration, team activities, and problem solving.
- Leaders monitor faculty and staff acceptance and adoption of vision and values using annual surveys, focus groups, and e-mail questions.
- Reviews against measurable performance standards are held frequently.
- Actions are taken to assist units that are not meeting goals or performing to plan.
- A systematic process is in place for evaluating and improving the integration or alignment of performance excellence values throughout the organization.
- Senior leaders systematically and routinely check the effectiveness of their leadership activities (for example, seeking annual feedback from faculty, staff, students, and peers in an upward evaluation, and taking steps to improve.
- Leaders at all levels determine how well they carried out their activities (what went right or wrong and what could be done better).
- There is evidence of changes made to improve leader effectiveness.
- Priorities for organizational improvement are driven by student performance, faculty, and staff results, stakeholder and student satisfaction, and other results key to the school's mission.

1.1 Leadership System
Sample Effective Practices for Teachers;
Leaders of the Classroom Learning System

- Teachers involve students in creating mission, vision statements, and values for classes and these are posted prominently. This involves and engages students in their studies and contributes to a feeling that the school is their school.
- Teachers role model fact-based decision making using data and performance tools.
- The management of classrooms is based on the Baldrige values.
- Continuous improvement is encouraged by seeking routine feedback from students about teaching strengths and opportunities for improvement. On a daily basis, students develop a list of strengths and opportunities for improvement to be acted upon and drive classroom (or team) process improvements. These are frequently called +/delta comments.
- There are clear behavioral metrics (rubrics) and nearly immediate feedback to enable all students to monitor their own academic, social, and personal performance.

1.2 Public Responsibility and Citizenship (30 Points)
Approach/Deployment Scoring

Describe how the school addresses its responsibilities to the public and how the school practices good citizenship.

In your response, address the following areas:

a. Societal Responsibilities

How the school addresses the current and potential impacts on society of its operations. Include:

(1) key practices, measures, and targets for regulatory, legal, and ethical requirements, and for risks associated with school operations; and

(2) how the school anticipates public concerns with its operations, assesses potential impacts on society, and addresses these concerns in a proactive manner.

b. Support of Key Communities

How the school, its senior leaders, and its faculty and staff support and strengthen their key communities.

Notes:

N1. Public responsibilities in areas critical to the school also should be addressed in Strategy Development Process (Item 2.1) and in Educational and Support Process Management (Category 6). Key results, such as results of regulatory/legal compliance, should be reported as School-Specific Results in Item 7.4.

N2. Areas of community support appropriate for inclusion in 1.2b might include efforts by the school to strengthen local community services, education, the environment, and practices of professional, trade, and business associations.

N3. Health and safety of students and stakeholders are included in Item 1.2. However, health and safety of faculty and staff are not included in Item 1.2; they are addressed in Item 5.3.

- Teachers provide students with endless examples of continuous improvement in classroom management and teaching. They use tests as tools to provide feedback, to sharpen instruction, and to enhance learning—not to limit progress, rank performance, or punish.
- Progress toward goals is tied to the overall school's goals. These are displayed and communicated to students, and parents through various means such as parent visitation days, assemblies, newsletters, posters etc.

This item addresses how the school integrates its values and expectations regarding its public responsibilities and community involvement into its performance management practices.

Area 1.2a calls for information on the school's practices relative to risks and legal responsibilities—those associated with school operations, management of funds, regulatory requirements, and related concerns. Schools face numerous responsibilities in day-to-day operations. This includes student safety, equity in hiring, and ethical practices in fund management and athletic programs. Relevant information relates to how the school makes risk factors and legal and ethical requirements an integral part of performance improvement, and how the school maintains sensitivity to issues of societal concern, whether or not these issues are currently embodied in law.

Area 1.2b calls for information on how the school practices good citizenship in its key communities as a contributing member and as a positive influence upon other schools. Opportunities for involvement and leadership include efforts by the school, its senior leaders, and its faculty/staff to strengthen community services, the environment, athletic associations, and professional associations. Some of the activities appropriate for inclusion might involve partnering with other organizations, sometimes through use of school facilities. Levels of involvement and leadership are dependent upon school size and resources.

This item is not about altruism, doing good for its own sake, but rather about positioning the organization to serve as a respected and valued community resource. As such, it should be able to sustain essential support and funding.

1.2 Public Responsibility and Citizenship

How the school addresses its responsibilities to the public and how the school practices good citizenship.

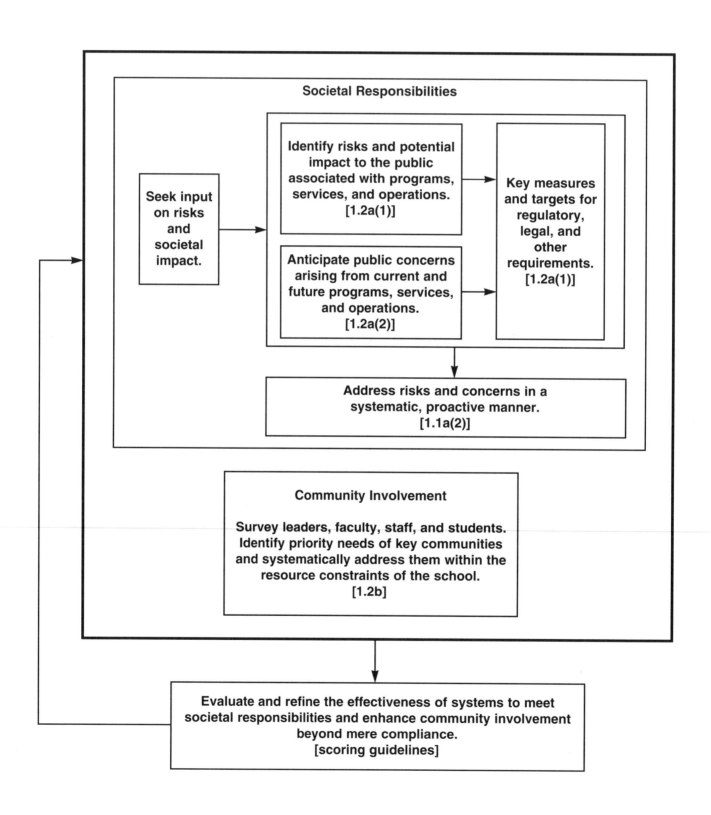

1.2   Public Responsibility and Citizenship Item Linkages

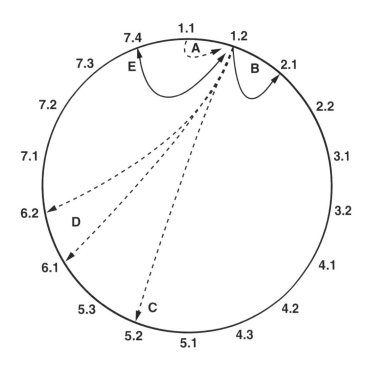

Nature of Relationship

A   Leaders [1.1] have a responsibility for setting policies and ensuring that practices and products of the school and its faculty, staff, and students do not adversely impact society or violate ethical standards, regulations, or law [1.2a]. Leaders are also responsible for ensuring that the school and its faculty, staff, and students strengthen key communities in areas such as local community services, education, the environment, business and professional associations, and health and welfare [1.2b].

B   Public health and safety concerns, environmental protection, and waste management issues [1.2] are important factors to consider in strategy development [2.1].

C   Training [5.2] is provided to ensure all faculty and staff understand ethical educational practices as well as the importance of strengthening key communities [1.2].

D   Managers at all levels have responsibility for ensuring that work practices of the school [6.1 and 6.2] are consistent with the school's standards of ethics and public responsibility [1.2].

E   Key results, such as results of regulatory compliance, environmental improvements, and support to key communities, are reported in School-Specific Results [7.4]. In addition, these results are monitored to determine if process changes are needed. (Compliance results in areas of employee safety are reported in 7.3, based on processes described in Item 5.3, Faculty and Staff Well-Being and Satisfaction, and are not a part of the requirements in 1.2.)

1.2 Public Responsibility and Citizenship
Sample Effective Practices

A. Societal Responsibilities

- The school's principal business activities include systems to analyze, anticipate, and minimize public hazards or risk.
- Indicators for risk areas are identified and monitored.
- Continuous improvement strategies are used consistently, and progress is reviewed regularly.
- The school considers the impact its operations, programs, and services might have on society and considers those impacts in planning.
- The effectiveness of systems to meet or exceed regulatory or legal requirements is systematically evaluated and improved.

B. Support of Key Communities

- Faculty and staff at various levels in the organization are encouraged to be involved in professional organizations, committees, task forces, or other community activities.
- Organizational resources are allocated to support involvement in community activities outside the organization.
- Faculty and staff participate in local, state, or national performance award programs and receive recognition from the organization.
- Faculty and staff participate in a variety of professional educational and leadership improvement associations.
- The effectiveness of processes to support and strengthen key communities is systematically evaluated and improved.

1.2 Public Responsibility and Citizenship
Sample Effective Practices for Teachers:
Leaders of the Classroom Learning System

- Students are encouraged to be involved in community activities, committees, and task forces.
- Students can earn extra credit as recognition for involvement in community and civic improvement/volunteerism relevant to their course content.

- Teachers partner with parents and community groups to improve the classroom, the school, and the community.

2 Strategic Planning—
80 Points

The Strategic Planning category examines how the school sets strategic directions, and how it develops key action plans to support the directions. Also examined are how plans are deployed and how performance is tracked.

Strategic planning addresses all aspects of school-level planning and the deployment of plans. This includes primarily the development and deployment of key educational and other mission-related requirements, taking into account the needs of students and other key stakeholders.

The criteria emphasize that performance improvement should be part of the daily work of all school units. The special roles of the Strategic Planning category are (1) to provide a results-oriented focus, accommodating to change; and (2) to align daily work with school directions.

The Strategic Planning category examines how schools
- Understand key student and stakeholder and societal requirements as input to setting directions. This is to help ensure that ongoing process improvements are aligned with the school's strategic directions.

- Optimize the use of resources, ensure faculty and staff capability, and ensure bridging between short- and longer-term requirements.
- Ensure that plan deployment will be effective—that there are mechanisms to communicate requirements and achieve overall alignment.

The Strategic Planning category requirements are intended to encourage strategic thinking and acting, and to bring about key alignments in support of goals. These requirements do not imply formalized plans, planning systems, departments, or specific planning cycles. Nor does the category imply that all improvements could or should be planned in advance. Rather, the requirements in the category imply that the school maintains a future-oriented basis for decisions and priorities.

2.1   Strategy Development Process (40 points)
Approach/Deployment Scoring

Describe how the school sets strategic directions to better address key student and stakeholder needs and school performance requirements.

In your response, address the following area:

a. Strategy Development Process

Provide a brief description or diagram of the strategy development process. Include how the school takes the following factors into account:

(1) student and stakeholder needs and expectations;

(2) key external factors, requirements, and opportunities; and

(3) key internal factors, including faculty and staff capabilities and needs, and the school's capability to assess student learning.

Notes:

N1.   The strategy development process refers to the school's approach, formal or informal, to a future-oriented basis for making or guiding decisions, priorities, resource allocations, and schoolwide management. This process might use models, forecasts, scenarios, analyses, and/or key stakeholder requirements and plans.

N2.   Strategy should be interpreted broadly. It might include any or all of the following: addition or termination of programs; modifications in instructional design; use of technology; changes in testing and/or assessment; adoption of standards; services to new or changing student populations; research priorities; and partnerships with other schools. Responses to Item 2.1 should address the factors from the point of view of the school, taking into account opportunities and constraints the school faces.

N3.   Item 2.1 addresses overall school directions and strategy, including changes in services and programs. However, the item does not address education design; this is addressed in Item 6.1.

This item addresses how the school develops its view of the future, sets directions, and translates these directions into a clear basis for communicating, deploying, and aligning critical requirements. Alignment refers to effective integration of faculty development, curriculum, instruction, and assessment.

The item calls for information on all the key influences, challenges, and requirements that might affect the school's future directions and decisions—taking as long a view as possible. The main purpose of the item is to provide a thorough and realistic context for the development of educational services and for the overall management of the school. The item addresses student and stakeholder needs and expectations and external factors affecting the school. This includes changing requirements brought about by other schools, employers, educational mandates, instructional technology, changing demographics, and changing student career interests. Also addressed are important internal factors, such as faculty and staff capabilities and needs. Especially important here is the need to assess student learning relative to key outcomes the school seeks to achieve.

2.1 Strategy Development Process

How the school sets strategic directions to better address key student and stakeholder needs and school performance requirements.

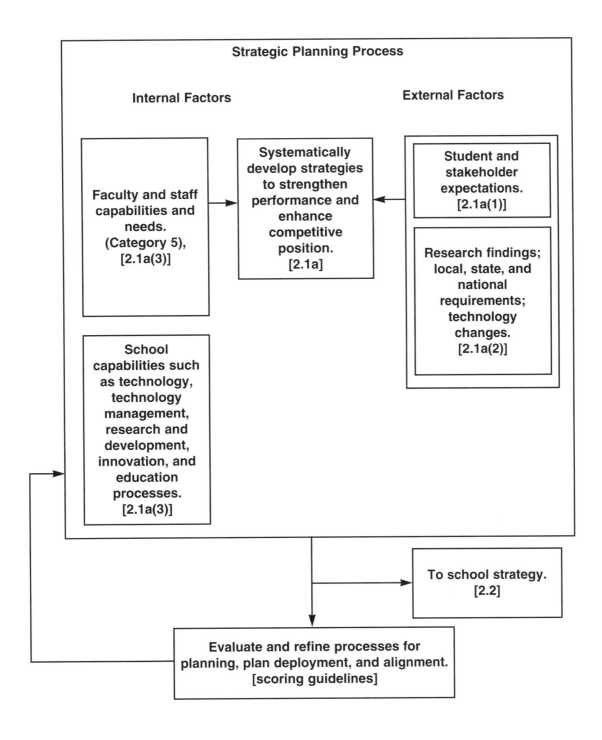

2.1 Strategy Development Process Item Linkages

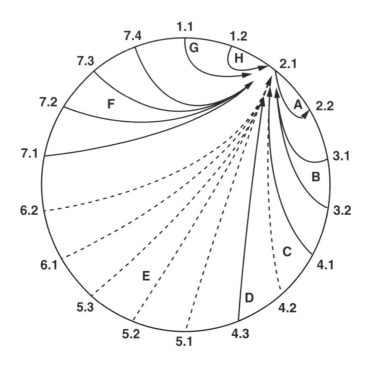

Nature of Relationship

A   The planning process [2.1] produces a plan [2.2] and set of actionable items.

B   The strategy development process [2.1] includes information on current and future student and stakeholder requirements [3.1] as well as intelligence obtained from customer-contact people (complaints and comments) [3.2a]

C   Key school [4.1] and comparison data [4.2] are used for planning [2.1].

D   Analytical data [4.3] including data on work process improvement strategies, realigning work processes, improving operational performance, and reducing waste are used in the planning process [2.1].

E   Information on faculty and staff capabilities [Category 5] and work process capabilities [Category 6] is considered in the strategic planning process as part of the determina-tion of internal strengths and weaknesses. To avoid cluttering diagrams 5.1–6.3, these arrows will not be repeated there.

F   Student performance results and student and stakeholder satisfaction results [7.1 and 7.2] and faculty and staff and school-specific results [7.3 and 7.4] are used in the planning process [2.1] to set priorities and goals (which are reported in 2.2).

G   The planning process [2.1] includes senior leader participation and guidance as well as participation by leaders at all levels [1.1].

H   Public health, environmental, waste man-agement, and related concerns [1.2a] are considered, as appropriate, in the strategy development process [2.1].

NOTE: The many inputs to strategy development will not all be repeated on other linkage diagrams to avoid clutter.

2.1 *Strategy Development Process*
Sample Effective Practices

- Goals, strategies, and issues are addressed and reported in measurable terms. Goals consider future requirements needed to achieve organizational leadership after considering the performance levels other organizations are likely to achieve.
- The planning and goal-setting process encourages input (but not necessarily decision making) from a variety of people at all levels throughout the organization.
- Data on stakeholder and student requirements, key communities, benchmarks, faculty and staff, and organizational capabilities are used to develop strategic plans.

- Plans are evaluated each cycle for accuracy and completeness—more often if needed to keep pace with changing requirements.
- Areas for improvement in the planning process are identified systematically and carried out each planning cycle.
- Refinements in the process of planning, deploying plans, and receiving input from work units have been made. Improvements in plan cycle time, plan resources, and planning accuracy are documented.

2.1 *Strategy Development Process*
Sample Effective Practices for Teachers;
Leaders of the Classroom Learning System

- Teachers survey parents and students prior to the course to gain a better understanding of requirements and expectations.
- The course and curriculum planning process encourages input (but not necessarily decision making) from students and stakeholders.

- Students are involved in educational planning appropriate for their age and educational level (intensely in higher education, as much as possible in elementary school) to identify and meet their needs.

2.2 School Strategy (40 points)
Approach/Deployment Scoring

Summarize the school's strategy and action plans, how they are deployed, and how performance is tracked. Include key performance requirements and measures, and an outline of related faculty and staff resource plans. Estimate how the school's performance projects into the future relative to current performance, comparisons, and/or key benchmarks.

In your response, address the following areas:

a. Strategy and Action Plans

Provide a summary of the action plans and related faculty and staff resource plans derived from the school's overall strategy. Briefly explain how critical action plan requirements, including faculty and staff resource plans, performance measures and/or indicators, and resources are aligned and deployed. Describe how performance relative to plans is tracked. Note any important differences between short- and longer-term plans and the reasons for the differences.

b. Performance Projection

Provide a two-to-five-year projection of key performance measures and/or indicators of performance based on the likely changes resulting from the school's action plans. Include appropriate comparisons with the school's past performance, comparable schools, and/or key benchmarks. Briefly explain the comparisons, including any estimates or assumptions made in projecting comparative performance and/or benchmark data.

Notes:

N1. The development and implementation of school strategy and action plans are closely linked to other items in the criteria and to the overall performance management framework given on page 38 of the *1999 Education Criteria for Performance Excellence* booklet. Specific linkages include
- Item 1.1 and how senior leaders set and communicate school directions
- Category 3 for gathering student and stakeholder knowledge as input to strategy and action plans, and for implementing action plans for building and enhancing relationships
- Category 4 for information and analysis to support development of school strategy and track progress relative to strategies and action plans
- Items 5.1 and 5.2 for work system and faculty and staff development needs resulting from school action plans and related faculty and staff resource plans
- Category 6 for process requirements resulting from school action plans

This item addresses the school's strategy and action plans and how they are deployed. The item also calls for a projection of the school's performance. The main intent of the item is effective operationalizing of action plans, incorporating measures that permit clear communication and tracking of progress and performance.

Area 2.2a calls for information on the school's action plans and how these plans are deployed. This includes spelling out critical action plan requirements such as faculty and staff development plans and needs, use of learning technologies, key measures and indicators, and how resources are deployed, aligned, and tracked. Of critical importance in this area is how alignment and consistency are achieved—for example, in key learning strategies and key measurements. The alignment and consistency are intended also to provide a basis for setting priorities for ongoing improvement activities.

Without effective alignment, routine work and acts of improvement can be random and serve to suboptimize organizational performance. In Figure 2.2-1, the arrows represent the well-intended work carried out by employees of organizations who lack a clear set of expectations and direction. Each person, each leader, and each department works diligently to achieve goals they believe are important. Each is pulling hard—but not necessarily in ways that ensure performance excellence. This encourages the creation of "fiefdoms" within organizations.

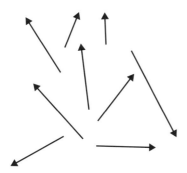

Figure 2.2-1. Nonaligned work.

With a clear, well-communicated strategic plan, it is easier to know when daily work is out of alignment. The large arrow in Figure 2.2-2 represents the strategic plan pointing the direction the organization must take to be successful and achieve its mission and vision. The strategic plan and accompanying measures make it possible to know when work is not aligned and help faculty and staff, including leaders, to know when adjustments are required.

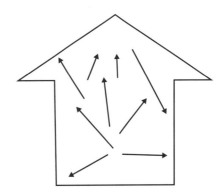

Figure 2.2-2. Strategic direction.

A well deployed and understood strategic plan helps everyone in the organization distinguish between random acts of improvement and aligned improvement. Random acts of improvement give a false sense of accomplishment and rarely benefit the organization. For example, a decision to improve a teaching process that is not aligned with the strategic plan (as the small bold arrow in Figure 2.2-3 represents) usually results in a wasteful expenditure of time, money, and faculty and staff resources—improvement without benefiting students or stakeholders or enhancing operating effectiveness.

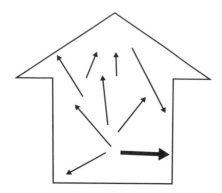

Figure 2.2-3. Random improvement.

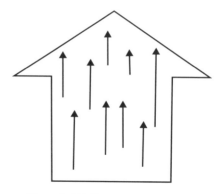

Figure 2.2-5. Systematic alignment.

On the other hand, by working systematically to strengthen processes that are aligned with the strategic plan, the organization moves closer to achieving success, as Figure 2.2-4 indicates. Ultimately, all processes and procedures of an organization should be aligned to maximize the achievement of strategic plans, as Figure 2.2-5 demonstrates.

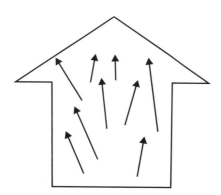

Figure 2.2-4. Moving toward alignment.

Critical action plan requirements include faculty/staff resource plans to support the overall strategy. Examples of faculty/staff resource plan elements that might be part of a comprehensive plan are

- Education and training of faculty in outcomes assessment practices and student learning styles
- Introduction of quality improvement initiatives
- Initiatives with the business community to support faculty development
- Redesign of staff work organizations and/or jobs to increase staff responsibility and decision making

Area 2.2b calls for a two-to-five-year projection of key measures and/or indicators of the school's performance. It also calls for comparison of projected performance relative to past performance and relative to comparable schools and benchmarks. This projection/comparison is intended to encourage schools to improve their ability to understand and track dynamic performance factors and to take into account rates of improvement and change relative to others as a diagnostic management tool.

2.2 School Strategy

Summary of strategy, action plans, and performance projections, how they are deployed, and how performance is tracked.

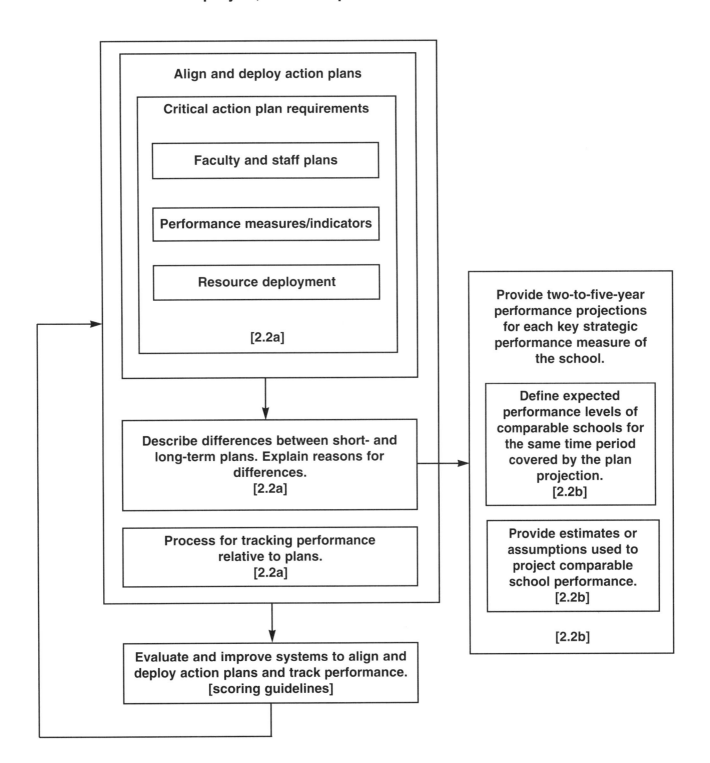

2.2 School Strategy Item Linkages

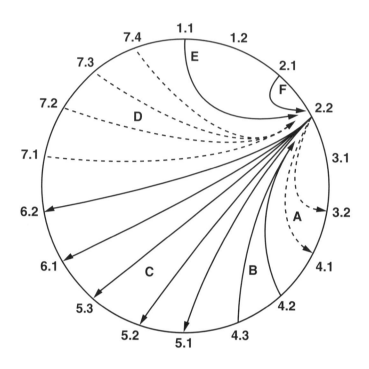

Nature of Relationship

A   The goals and strategy [2.2] will influence the data and measures that need to be collected to monitor alignment [4.1], student and stakeholder relations management, and satisfaction determination [3.2].

B   Benchmarking comparison data [4.2] and analytical processes [4.3] are used to set school measures and objectives [2.2].

C   Measures, objectives, and plans, deployed to the faculty and staff [2.2], are used to drive and align actions to achieve improved performance [Category 6] and develop faculty and staff [Category 5].

D   Results data [Category 7] are used to help set goals [2.2]. (To avoid clutter, these relationships will not be repeated on the Category 7 linkage diagrams.)

E   The leadership team [1.1] sets the school's goals and objectives [2.2].

F   The planning process [2.1] produces the school's action plan [2.2].

2.2 School Strategy
Sample Effective Practices

A. *Strategy and Action Plans*

- Student and stakeholder surveys focus on critical faculty and staff development needs for meeting requirements.
- Plans are in place to optimize operational performance and improve student and stakeholder focus using tools such as streamlining and reducing cycle time.
- Strategies to retain or establish leadership positions exist for major products and services for key student and stakeholder groups.
- Strategies to achieve key organizational results are defined.
- Performance levels are defined in measurable terms for key features of educational products and services.
- Planned actions are challenging, realistic, achievable, and understood by faculty and staff and, in some instances, students, throughout the school. Each understands his or her role in achieving strategic and operational goals and objectives.
- Resources are available and committed to achieve the plans (no unfunded mandates).
- Plans are realistic and used to guide performance improvements.
- Incremental (short-term) strategies to achieve long-term plans are defined in measurable terms.
- Strategic plans, short- and long-term goals, and performance measures are understood and used to drive actions throughout the organization.
- Each individual in the organization (including students as possible), understands how his or her work contributes to achieving organizational goals and plans.
- Plans are followed to ensure that resources are deployed and redeployed as needed to support goals.

- Capital projects are funded according to business improvement plans.
- Faculty and staff plans support strategic plans and goals. Plans show how the workforce will be developed to enable the organization to achieve its strategic goals.
- Key issues of training and development, hiring, retention, faculty and staff participation, involvement, empowerment, and recognition and reward are addressed as a part of the faculty and staff plan.
- Innovative strategies may involve one or more of the following:
  - Redesign of work to increase faculty/staff responsibility.
  - Improved labor-management relations (that is, prior to contract negotiations, both sides are trained in effective negotiation skills so that people focus on the merits of issues, not on positions. The goal is to improve relations and shorten negotiation time by 50 percent).
  - Forming partnerships to develop faculty and staff and ensure a supply of well-prepared future employees.
  - Broadening faculty/staff responsibilities; creating self-directed or high-performance work teams.
- Key performance measures (for example, faculty/staff satisfaction or work climate surveys) have been identified to gather data to manage progress. (Note: Improvement results associated with these measures should be reported in Item 7.3.)
- The effectiveness of faculty and staff planning and alignment with strategic plans is evaluated systematically.
- Data are used to evaluate and improve performance and participation for all types of faculty and staff (for example, absenteeism, turnover, grievances, accidents, recognition and reward, and training participation).

- Routine, two-way communication about performance of faculty/staff occurs.

B. Performance Projection

- Projections of two-to-five-year changes in performance levels are developed and used to track progress.
- Data from competitors and/or key benchmarks form a valid basis for comparison.

- The organization has strategies and goals in place to exceed the planned levels of performance for these competitors and benchmarks.
- Plans include expected future levels of competitor or comparison performance and are used to set and validate the organization's own plans.

2.2 School Strategy
Sample Effective Practices for Teachers:
Leaders of the Classroom Learning System

- Routine two-way communication about performance of students occurs.
- Data are used to evaluate and improve performance and participation for all types of students (for example, tardiness, suspensions, absenteeism, and participation in class).

- Key performance measures have been identified for classes.
- Students are involved and engaged, and given the broadest possible amount of responsibility.

3 Student and Stakeholder Focus—80 Points

The Student and Stakeholder Focus category examines how the school determines requirements, expectations, and preferences of its students and stakeholders. Also examined is how the school builds relationships with students and stakeholders and determines their satisfaction.

Student and Stakeholder Focus is the criteria category that examines how the school seeks to understand the needs of current and future students and of its stakeholders on an ongoing basis. The category stresses the importance of school relationships and of the use of an array of listening and learning strategies. Although many of the needs of stakeholders must be translated into educational services for students, the stakeholders themselves have needs that schools must also accommodate. A key challenge to schools frequently may be to balance differing needs and expectations between students and stakeholders, and among different groups of stakeholders.

3.1 Knowledge of Student Needs and Expectations
(40 points) Approach/Deployment Scoring

Describe how the school determines longer-term requirements, expectations, and preferences of students and future students. Describe also how the school uses this information to understand and anticipate needs and to create an overall climate conducive to learning for all students.

In your response, address the following area:

a. **Knowledge of Student Needs and Expectations**
   Provide a brief description of how the school learns from its former, current, and future students to understand and anticipate needs and to develop and maintain a climate conducive to optimal learning. Include
   (1) how the school maintains awareness of key general and special needs and expectations of current students. Describe how needs and expectations are determined, aggregated, and analyzed, and how this information is deployed to all appropriate school units;
   (2) how the school monitors student utilization of offerings, facilities, and services to determine their influence upon active learning and satisfaction. Include how information on student segments and/or individual students is developed for purposes of engaging all students in active learning; and
   (3) how the school determines and anticipates changing needs and expectations of future students. Summarize the following: (a) demographic data and trends that may bear upon enrollments and needs; (b) changing requirements and expectations its graduates will face; (c) changing needs and expectations resulting from national, state, or local requirements; (d) educational alternatives available to its pool of future students; and (e) how the school analyzes the information to develop actionable data and information as input to planning.

Notes:
N1. Student needs (3.1a) might take into account information from students and key stakeholders such as families, employers, and other schools. Needs include educational and other requirements such as safety.

N2. Student segments [3.1a(2)] refers to groups of students with similar needs. The basis for the groupings might reflect their career interests, learning styles, living status (residential vs. commuter), family income, or other factors.

N3. Changing requirements of graduates [3.1a(3)] should reflect requirements set by stakeholders—other schools and employers, taking into account paths followed by the school's graduates. This might include qualification standards, licensure requirements, workplace skills, admission requirements, and so on.

N4. Use of trend data [3.1a(3)] refers to information the school collects that shows year-to-year changes. Such changes might reflect specific and/or local factors important to the school. In some cases, such local factors could be different from national trends.

This item seeks information on how the school maintains awareness of key general and special needs and expectations of current students. Such needs and expectations cover all aspects of education content and delivery, as well as the learning environment, including safety. An important part of this information comes from the school's observations of student utilization of offerings, facilities, and services to determine their influence on active learning.

This item also examines how the school determines and anticipates changing needs and expectations for future students. This determination should take into account the following: demographic data and trends; changing requirements of graduates in the workplace or other schools; changing local, state, national, and global requirements; and educational alternatives for its prospective students. Also examined is how the school analyzes the overall information to develop actionable data for planning.

This item also addresses how the school improves its listening and learning strategies, with a focus on keeping current with changing school needs.

A wide variety of listening and learning strategies should be used, depending on the type and size of the school and other factors.

3.1 Knowledge of Student Needs and Expectations

How the school determines longer-term requirements, expectations, and preferences of students and future students. Describe also how the schools use this information to understand and anticipate needs and to create an overall climate conducive to learning for all students.

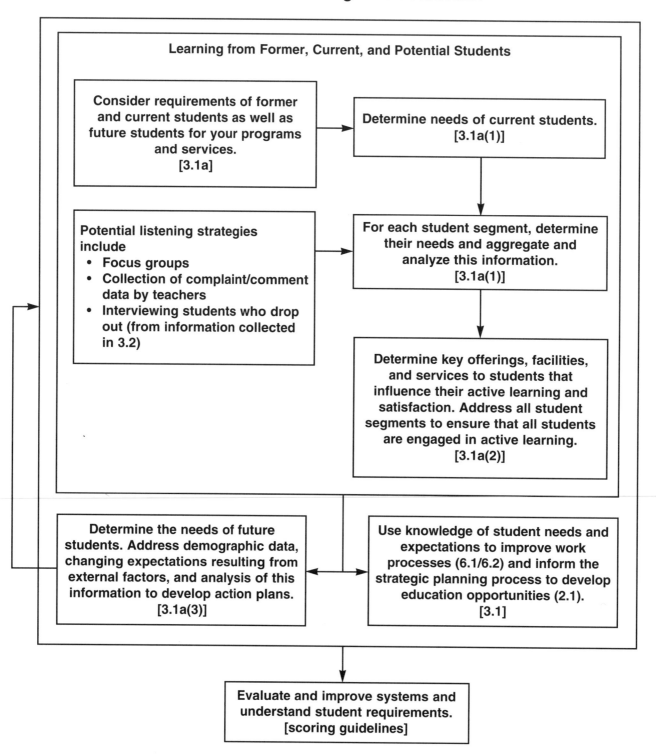

3.1 *Knowledge of Student Needs and Expectations Item Linkages*

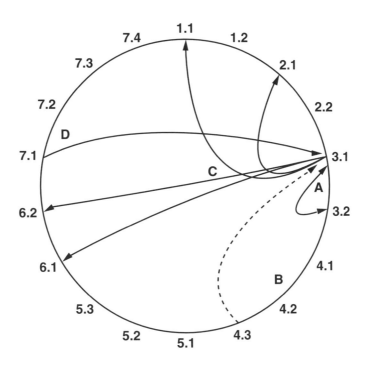

Nature of Relationship

A   Student and stakeholder satisfaction determination [3.2b] helps assess current student expectations and enhance relationships [3.1]. Information about student and stakeholder needs [3.1] is used to build instruments to assess student and stakeholder satisfaction [3.2b].

B   Information from school performance data is analyzed [4.3] and used to help determine ways to assess current and future student requirements [3.1].

C   Information about current and future student requirements [3.1] is used for strategic planning [2.1] to design educational programs and offerings and revise education support processes [6.1 and 6.2], and to help leaders set directions for the school [1.1].

D   Student and stakeholder satisfaction data and comments [7.1] are used to assess student needs and expectations and refine requirements [3.1].

3.1 Knowledge of Student Needs and Expectations
Sample Effective Practices

- Various systematic methods are used to gather data and identify current requirements and expectations of students and stakeholders (for example, surveys and focus groups).
- Key offerings, facilities, and feature services are defined. Product and service features refer to all-important characteristics and performance of offerings that students and stakeholders experience or perceive throughout their use. The focus is primarily on factors that bear on preference such as learning styles and loyalty—for example, those features that enhance or differentiate products and services from competing offerings.
- Student/stakeholder segments are identified or grouped by requirements.
- Various systematic methods are used to identify the future requirements and expectations of students and stakeholders.
- Students of competitors are considered and processes are in place to gather expectation data from potential students.
- Effective listening and learning strategies include the following:
  - Close monitoring of technological, competitive, societal, environmental, economic, and demographic factors that may bear on student and stakeholder requirements, expectations, preferences, or alternatives
  - Focus groups with demanding or leading-edge students and stakeholders
  - Analysis of major factors affecting key students and stakeholders

- Rapid innovation and field trials of products and services are undertaken, to better link research and development (R&D) and design to student and stakeholder requirements. This particularly includes technological innovation.
- Office staff, bus drivers, instructional staff, cafeteria staff, and others are trained in student and stakeholder listening.
- Critical incident data such as complaints are used to understand key service attributes from the point of view of students and stakeholders. These could include cafeteria data, bus incidents, and so on.
- Students that elect to attend out-of-district schools or colleges are interviewed to identify factors that determined their decisions and factors that drive loyalty.
- Post-graduation followup is conducted to determine if requirements were met.
- Methods to listen and learn from students and stakeholders are evaluated and improved through several cycles. Examples of factors that are evaluated include the following:
  - The adequacy and timeliness of student/stakeholder-related information
  - Improvement of survey design
  - Approaches for getting reliable and timely information—surveys, focus groups, student/stakeholder personnel
  - Improved aggregation and analysis of information

3.1 Knowledge of Student Needs and Expectations
Sample Effective Practices for Teachers:
Leaders of the Classroom Learning System

- Various methods are used to identify requirements and expectations of students, parents, and other stakeholders.
- The classroom focuses on the learning style and preferences of the students.
- Meaningful relationships are built, starting with the earliest possible contact date, with parents, students, and other key stakeholders. For example, curriculum and a cover note sent during the summer recess to parents and students is an advance contact and relationship builder.
- Various methods are used to identify student issues and concerns affecting the course such as surveys, focus groups, and suggestion boxes.

3.2 Student and Stakeholder Satisfaction and Relationship Enhancement (40 points)
Approach/Deployment Scoring

Describe how the school determines and enhances the satisfaction of its students and stakeholders to build relationships, to improve current educational services, and to support planning.

In your response, address the following areas:

a. Stakeholder Relationship Enhancement

How the school provides for effective relationships with stakeholders to support and enhance its ability to improve its services. Include

(1) how the school creates clear bases for relationships with key stakeholders. For each stakeholder group, describe (a) key objectives of the relationship; (b) key needs of the stakeholder and how these needs are determined and kept current; and (c) key needs of the school and how these needs are communicated to the stakeholder.

(2) how the school maintains effective stakeholder relationships. Describe (a) how regular and special access needs are addressed; (b) how the school follows up on its interactions with key stakeholders to determine satisfaction and progress in meeting objectives, and to resolve problems; (c) key measures and/or indicators the school uses to monitor the effectiveness and progress of its key relationships; and (d) how the school develops partnerships with key stakeholders to pursue common purposes.

b. Student and Stakeholder Satisfaction Determination

How the school determines student and stakeholder satisfaction and dissatisfaction. Include

(1) how processes, measurement scales, and data are used to determine student satisfaction and dissatisfaction; frequency of determination; and how objectivity and reliability are ensured. Indicate significant differences, if any, in methods and measurement scales for different student groups. Describe also how satisfaction measurements capture key information on factors that bear upon students' motivation and active learning, and how student satisfaction relative to comparable schools is determined.

(2) how the school determines the satisfaction of key stakeholders; a brief description of processes and measurement scales used; frequency of determination; and how objectivity and reliability are ensured. Indicate significant differences, if any, in methods and measurement scales for different stakeholder groups. Describe also how satisfaction measurements relate to education climate and student and stakeholder needs, and how stakeholder satisfaction relative to comparable schools is determined.

Notes:

N1.   Student and stakeholder satisfaction and dissatisfaction determination (3.2b) might include any or all of the following: surveys, formal and informal feedback from students and stakeholders, and complaints. Student and stakeholder dissatisfaction indicators might include dropout rates, complaints, and absenteeism.

N2.   Student and stakeholder satisfaction measurement might include both a numerical rating scale and descriptors assigned to each unit in the scale. An effective (actionable) student and stakeholder satisfaction measurement system is one that provides the school with reliable information about student and stakeholder ratings of specific educational services and/or transactions. The measurement system also provides information on the relationship between these ratings and student learning and student/stakeholder future actions, such as transfer and positive referral.

N3.   Student and stakeholder satisfaction and dissatisfaction results should be reported in Item 7.2. School faculty- and staff-related results should be reported in Item 7.3.

This item addresses how the school determines and enhances the satisfaction of its students and stakeholders to build relationships to improve educational services and to support related planning.

Area 3.2a calls for information on how the school provides for effective relationships with key stakeholders to enhance its ability to improve educational services. Since stakeholders may differ in many ways, the area seeks information segmented by main stakeholder types. For each stakeholder type, this information should cover key objectives of the relationship; key needs of the stakeholder and how these needs are determined and kept current; and the key needs of the school and how these needs are communicated to the stakeholders. Area 3.2a also addresses how the school maintains effective stakeholder relationships. Four key aspects of relationship building are addressed: regular and special access needs; proactive followups with stakeholders; key measures and/or indicators used to monitor the effectiveness of key relationships; and how the school develops partnerships with key stakeholders to pursue common purposes.

Area 3.2b addresses how the school determines student and stakeholder satisfaction and dissatis-

faction for use in improving the school's ability to improve educational and support services.

The first part of the area addresses students and requests information on processes, measurement scales, and data used, and how objectivity and reliability are ensured. A critical part of this process is how the school's measurements capture key information that bears upon students' motivation and active learning. This requires an ongoing search for the key dimensions of satisfaction and dissatisfaction—those factors that best correlate with motivation and learning. Also examined is how the school determines student satisfaction relative to comparable schools. Such comparisons may offer important insights to help the school improve its motivational climate.

The second part of the area addresses key stakeholders and requests information on processes and measurement scales, and how objectivity and reliability are ensured. Also examined are how satisfaction measurements relate to the school's education climate and to student and stakeholder needs and how stakeholder satisfaction compares with comparable schools.

3.2 Student and Stakeholder Satisfaction and Relationship Enhancement

How the school determines and enhances the satisfaction of its students and stakeholders to build relationships, to improve current educational services, and to support planning.

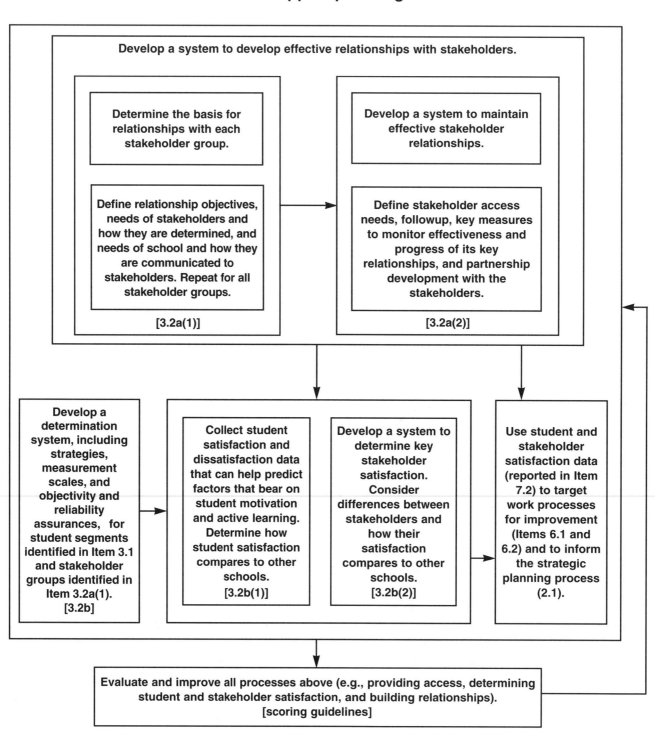

3.2 Student and Stakeholder Satisfaction and Relationship Enhancement Item Linkages

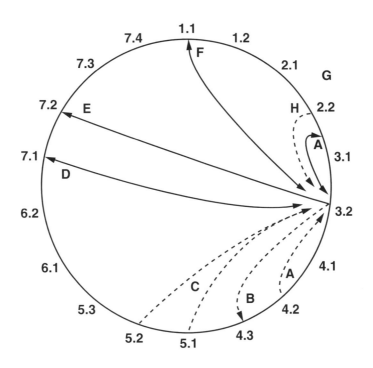

Nature of Relationship

A   Information concerning student needs and expectations [3.1] and benchmark data [4.2] are used to enhance student and stakeholder relationships [3.2a]. Interactions with key stakeholders [3.2a] are used to help assess student needs and expectations [3.1].

B   Student and stakeholder satisfaction information [3.2] is analyzed and used to set priorities for action [4.3].

C   Training [5.2] and improved flexibility and rapid response [5.1] can enhance and maintain a climate conducive to optimal learning [3.2a].

D   Information from stakeholder relations processes [3.2a] can help in the design of satisfaction measures [3.2b] and even pro-

duce data on student performance [7.1]. In addition, student performance results data [7.1] are used to monitor effectiveness and progress of key relationships [3.2a].

E   Efforts of improved accessibility and stakeholder relationship building [3.2a] should result in improved stakeholder satisfaction. These results should be reported in 7.2.

F   Priorities and knowledge of student needs and expectations for faculty and staff [3.2a] are driven by top leadership [1.1]. Leaders at all levels [1.1] personally interact with and build better relationships with students and stakeholders. They receive useful information from those students and stakeholders to improve management decision making.

Continued on next page

G   Goals and strategy [2.2] influence stake-holder relations management [3.2a] and student and stakeholder satisfaction determination processes [3.2b].

3.2 Student and Stakeholder Satisfaction and Relationship Enhancement Sample Effective Practices

A. Stakeholder Relationship Enhancement

- Requirements for building relationships are identified and may include factors such as faculty and staff responsiveness and various stakeholder contact methods.
- Problem resolution priority setting is based on the potential impact of stakeholder decisions to buy, or recommend to others, the offering or service. For example, a business that sponsored and then employed many students would have a direct impact on the school.
- Feedback is sought on the effectiveness of service.
- A systematic approach exists to evaluate and improve stakeholder relationships. For example, schools may want to allow their buildings to be used for community events even at a certain cost to open and strengthen relationships of stakeholders who pay school taxes but do not directly use its services.
- Feedback from stakeholders including faculty and staff is systematically used in the improvement process.
- Several methods are used to ensure ease of student and stakeholder contact, 24 hours a day if necessary (for example, homework hot lines, school calendars with emergency and other numbers listed prominently, websites, toll-free numbers, pagers for contact personnel, surveys, interviews, focus groups, and electronic bulletin boards).
- The process of developing relationships with all key stakeholders is regularly evaluated and improved. Several improvement cycles are evident.
- Procedures are in place and evaluated to ensure that student/stakeholder contact is initiated to follow up on recent transactions to build relationships.
- Training and development plans and replacement procedures exist for first-contact employees (office staff, bus drivers, and cafeteria workers).

B. Student and Stakeholder Satisfaction Determination

- Faculty and staff are empowered to make decisions to address student and stakeholder concerns. For example, parents are asked to talk with instructors before contacting department chairs or principals, and faculty/staff are motivated and have the responsibility to solve problems at that level whenever possible.
- Adequate staff are available for, and their schedules permit, maintaining effective student and stakeholder contact.
- Performance expectations are set for faculty and staff whose jobs bring them in regular contact with customers.

- The process of collecting complete, timely, and accurate stakeholder satisfaction and dissatisfaction data is regularly evaluated and improved. Several improvement cycles are evident.
- The performance of faculty and staff against these expectations is measured and tracked. For example, bus drivers are held responsible for transportation being safe, orderly, and on time.
- A system exists to ensure that student and stakeholder complaints are resolved promptly and effectively.
- Complaints and student/stakeholder concerns are resolved at first contact. This often means training faculty and staff who are first contacts and giving them authority to resolve a broad range of problems.
- Complaint data are tracked and used to initiate prompt corrective action to prevent the problem from recurring.
- An actionable student and stakeholder satisfaction measurement system exists that provides the school with reliable information about ratings of specific offerings and service features and the relationship between these ratings and the student/stakeholder likely future market behavior (loyalty).
- Several satisfaction indicators are used (for example, repeat enrollment within families and schools, praise letters, and direct measures using survey questions and interviews).

- Comprehensive satisfaction and dissatisfaction data are collected and segmented or grouped to enable the organization to predict student and stakeholder behavior (likelihood of remaining a student, positive referrals).
- Several means of collecting satisfaction data are used (for example, surveys, interviews, and focus groups).
- Student/stakeholder dissatisfaction indicators are evaluated, including complaints, refunds, repeat services such as examinations or course content, litigation, performance rating downgrades, and warranty work (if the college guarantees its graduates on-the-job performance or the learning center guarantees a grade level increase), and warranty costs.
- Satisfaction data are collected from former students and stakeholders.
- Competitors' student/stakeholders satisfaction is determined using various means such as external or internal studies.
- Methods are in place to ensure objectivity of these data.
- School-based or independent organization comparative studies take into account one or more indicators of student/stakeholder dissatisfaction as well as satisfaction. The extent and types of such studies depend on industry and organization size.

3.2 Student and Stakeholder Satisfaction and Relationship Enhancement
Sample Effective Practices for Teachers; Leaders of the Classroom Learning System

- Student and stakeholder requirements are included when developing classroom improvement goals.
- Instructional faculty and staff take into account the requirements of the next grade, content level, or course as a basis for curriculum and instructional goals.
- Methods are in place to build, maintain, and track positive relationships with students and stakeholders. (For example, data is kept on return calls or e-mails, number of contacts, tutoring after class, feedback, and so on.)
- The level of student and stakeholder satisfaction/dissatisfaction is routinely assessed, and this information drives improvement in the classroom system.

4 Information and Analysis —80 Points

The Information and Analysis category examines the selection, management, and effectiveness of use of information and data to support key school processes and action plans, and the school's performance management system.

Information and Analysis is the main point within the criteria for examining all key information to manage the school and to drive improvement of educational performance and competitiveness. Category 4 is the brain center or central processing unit (CPU) for the alignment of an educational organization's operations with its strategic directions. However, since information, information technology, and analysis might themselves be primary sources of competitive advantage and productivity growth, the category also includes such strategic considerations.

Educational leaders at all levels use information to plan, set strategic direction and performance goals, monitor performance, set priorities, allocate resources, and take corrective action. Faculty and staff use data and information to manage their work processes and adjust them when they are out of control. Access to data and tools for decision making is a prerequisite to effective faculty and staff involvement, increased initiative, and self-directed responsibility. Without this information and the skill to use it, decisions are left to intuition—and decisions based on intuition are usually retained by more senior leaders and administrators.

Finally, information, information technology, and analysis may also be primary sources of competitive advantage and productivity growth.

4.1 Selection and Use of Information and Data (25 points)
Approach/Deployment Scoring

Describe the school's selection, management, and use of information and data needed to support key school processes and action plans, and to improve school performance.

In your response, address the following area:

a.   Selection and Use of Information and Data

Describe

(1) the main types of information and data and how each type relates to key school processes and action plans;

(2) how the information and data are deployed to all users to support the effective management and evaluation of key school processes;

(3) how key user requirements, including rapid access, ongoing reliability, and confidentiality are met; and

(4) how information and data, their deployment, and effectiveness of use are evaluated, improved, and kept current with changing needs.

Notes:

N1.   *Users* [4.1a(2,3)] refers to school work units and to those outside the school who have access to information and data—students and stakeholders, as appropriate.

N2.   Deployment of information and data might be via electronic or other means. *Reliability* [4.1a(3)] includes reliability of software and delivery systems.

This item examines the selection, use, and management of information and data to support overall school goals, with strong emphasis on the data needed for effective process management, action plans, and performance improvement. Overall, the item represents a key foundation for a performance-oriented organization that effectively utilizes data.

The item examines the main types of data and how each type relates to key organization processes and action plans. In addition, the item examines a central requirement in an effective performance management system—the integration of information and data into measurements that are used for decision making. Also examined is the deployment of information and data to users, with emphasis on alignment of data and information with key school processes and goals. The effective management of the information/data system itself, ensuring rapid access and reliability, is examined in connection with user requirements. Finally, the item examines how overall data and information requirements, including effectiveness of use, deployment, and ability to keep current with changing needs are evaluated.

Although the main focus of this item is on information and data for the effective management of performance, information technology often has major strategic significance as well. For example, information technology could be used to accumulate and disseminate unique knowledge about students and academic achievement, which would enable the organization to customize educational products and services quickly. Also, information technology and the information and data made available through such technology could be of special advantage in educational networks and alliances. Responses to this item should take into account such strategic use of information and data. Accordingly, "users" would include partners as well as school units.

4.1 Selection and Use of Information and Data

How the organization selects, manages, and uses information and data to support decision making for key processes and to improve performance.

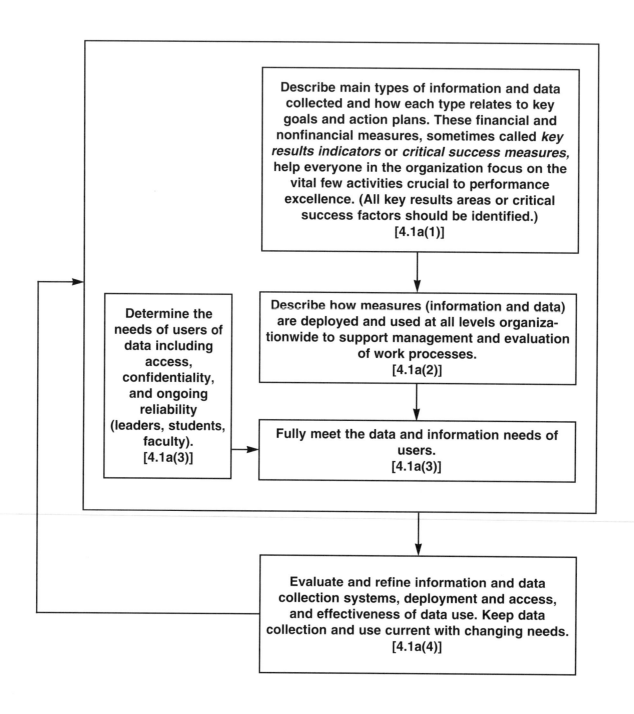

Describe main types of information and data collected and how each type relates to key goals and action plans. These financial and nonfinancial measures, sometimes called *key results indicators* or *critical success measures,* help everyone in the organization focus on the vital few activities crucial to performance excellence. (All key results areas or critical success factors should be identified.)
[4.1a(1)]

Determine the needs of users of data including access, confidentiality, and ongoing reliability (leaders, students, faculty).
[4.1a(3)]

Describe how measures (information and data) are deployed and used at all levels organizationwide to support management and evaluation of work processes.
[4.1a(2)]

Fully meet the data and information needs of users.
[4.1a(3)]

Evaluate and refine information and data collection systems, deployment and access, and effectiveness of data use. Keep data collection and use current with changing needs.
[4.1a(4)]

4.1 Selection and Use of Information and Data Item Linkages

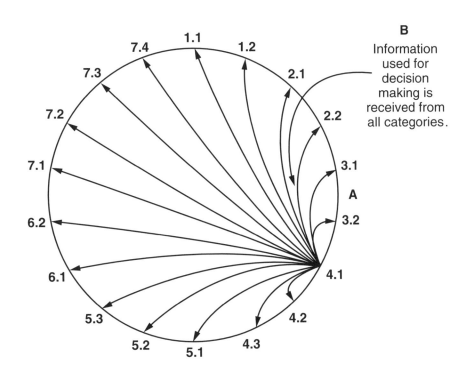

Nature of Relationship

A   Information collected [4.1] is used for planning [2.1], goal setting [2.2], analysis [4.3], benchmarking priority setting [4.2], day-to-day leadership [1.1], setting social responsibility standards (regulatory, legal, and ethical) for community involvement [1.2], monitoring of quality and operational performance results [7.2, 7.3, and 7.4], improving work processes [6.1, 6.2] and faculty and staff systems [5.1, 5.2, 5.3], determining student needs and expectations [3.1], building stakeholder relations [3.2a], and determining student and stakeholder satisfaction [3.2b] and reporting student and stakeholder satisfaction [7.2].

B   Information used for decision making and continuous improvement [4.1] is collected from all categories.

NOTE: Because the information collected and used for decision making links with all other items, the linkage arrows will not all be repeated on the other item maps. The more relevant connections will be identified.

4.1 Selection and Use of Information and Data Sample Effective Practices

- Data collected at the individual faculty and staff level are consistent across the organization to permit consolidation and organizationwide performance monitoring.
- Every person has access to the data they need to make decisions about their work, from top leaders to individuals, work teams, and departments.
- Performance and operational data are collected and routinely used for management decisions.
- Internal and external data are used to describe student and stakeholder satisfaction and product and service performance.
- The cost of poor quality and other financial concerns are measured for internal operations and processes.
- Data are maintained on faculty and staff-related issues of satisfaction, morale, safety, education and training, use of teams, and recognition and reward.
- The data collection and analysis system is systematically evaluated and refined.

- Improvements are made to reduce cycle time for data collection and to increase data access and use.
- Formal processes are in place to ensure data reliability, objectivity, and confidentiality.
- Faculty and staff and stakeholders are involved in validating data.
- A systematic process exists for data review and improvement, standardization, and easy employee access to data. Training on the use of data systems is provided as needed.
- Data used for management decisions' focus on critical success factors are integrated with work processes for the planning, design, and delivery of products and services.
- Users of data help determine what data systems are developed and how data are accessed.

4.1 Selection and Use of Information and Data Sample Effective Practices for Teachers: Leaders of the Classroom Learning System

- Stay knowledgeable about school trends and priorities, and use this knowledge to develop and track goals of the classroom or course.
- Routinely use information systems to track and report results.
- Give students access to their performance data and comparative data to other students and the class (not personally identifiable data).

- Use information systems to support academic and operational improvement for the course or class. (For example, a kindergarten class used a control chart to track and decrease the amount of time they spent on cleanup so they could spend more time on instructional activities like stories).

4.2 Selection and Use of Comparative Information and Data (15 points)
Approach/Deployment Scoring

Describe the school's selection, management, and use of comparative information and data to improve the school's overall performance.

In your response, address the following area:

a. **Selection and Use of Comparative Information and Data**
   Describe
   (1) how needs and priorities for comparative information and data are determined, taking into account key school processes, action plans, and opportunities for improvement;
   (2) the school's criteria and methods for seeking sources of appropriate comparative information and data—from within and outside the academic community;
   (3) how comparative information and data are deployed to all potential users and used to set stretch targets and/or to stimulate innovation; and
   (4) how comparative information and data, their deployment, and effectiveness of use are evaluated and improved. Describe also how priorities and criteria for selecting benchmarks and comparisons are kept current with changing needs and strategies.

Note:

Comparative information and data include benchmarking and competitive comparisons. Benchmarking refers to processes and results that represent best practices and performance for similar activities, inside or outside the academic community. Competitive comparisons refer to performance relative to comparable schools and/or student populations and to competing schools, as appropriate.

The item examines how competitive comparisons and benchmarking information are selected and used to help drive improvement of overall organization performance. The item also examines the key aspects of effective selection and use of competitive comparisons and benchmarking information and data; determination of needs and priorities; criteria for seeking appropriate information—from within and outside the organization's industry and markets; and use of information and data to set stretch targets and to promote major improvements in areas most critical to the organization's competitive strategy.

The item also calls for information on how the organization evaluates and improves its processes for selecting and using competitive and benchmark information to improve planning, to drive improvement of performance and competitive position, and to keep current with changing needs and strategies.

The major premises underlying the requirements of this item are as follows:

• Schools facing tough competition need to know where they stand relative to competitors and to best practices.

- Comparative and benchmarking information often provide impetus for significant (breakthrough) improvement and might alert organizations to competitive threats and new practices.
- Schools need to understand their own processes and the processes of others before they compare performance levels. Benchmarking information may also support analysis and decisions relating to core competencies, alliances, and outsourcing.

It is important to develop and use systematic methods to set priorities for determining targets for collecting competitive comparison and benchmarking information. This will help education organizations avoid wasting resources on frivolous or fruitless searches for information. It is also important to be able to implement the lessons learned from collecting this information. Otherwise, the act of collecting the information will waste resources and not add the value needed to compete effectively. Finally, it is important to learn from and improve the processes of collecting and using comparison and benchmarking information.

4.2 Selection and Use of Comparative Information and Data

How the organization selects, manages, and uses comparative information and data to improve overall performance and competitive position.

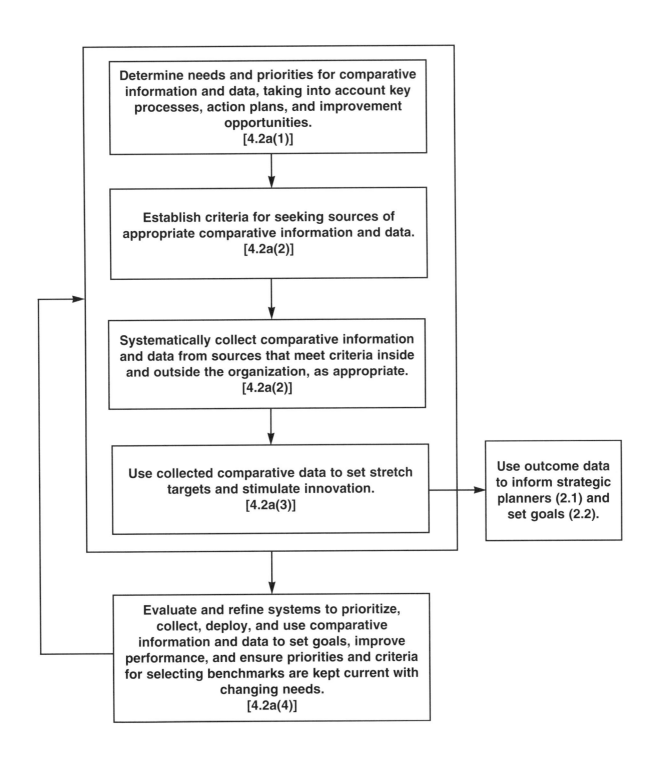

4.2 Selection and Use of Comparative Information and Data Item Linkages

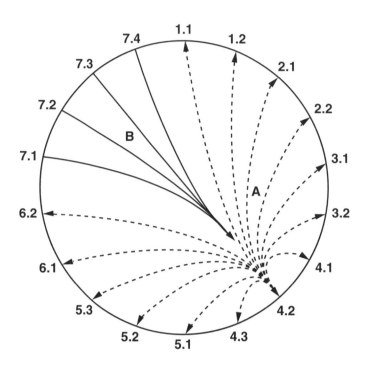

Nature of Relationship

A   Comparison data [4.2] can be used to improve data collection, benchmarking, data analysis [4.1, 4.2, 4.3], leadership effectiveness [1.1], and public responsibility and citizenship [1.2]; to encourage breakthrough improvements in student and stakeholder needs, relationships, and satisfaction [3.1, and 3.2], in design, development, and delivery of educational programs and services [6.1] and education support services [6.2]; for planning [2.1] and to set stretch objectives and goals [2.2]; and to improve faculty and staff well-being and satisfaction [5.3], performance, reward and recognition [5.1], and training [5.2]. Process information is also used to help set improvement priorities [4.3].

B   The need for information to help set priorities for selecting comparison organizations [4.2] is driven by work processes that need improvement as determined by performance [Category 7] results.

NOTE: Because comparison information links with most items, the linkage arrows will not be repeated on all other item maps; however, the most relevant connections will be identified.

4.2 Selection and Use of Comparative Information and Data
Sample Effective Practices

- A systematic process is in place for identifying and prioritizing comparative information and benchmark targets.
- Research has been conducted to identify best-in-class organizations, which may be competitors or noncompetitors.
- Key processes or functions are the subject of benchmarking. Activities such as those that support the organization's goals and objectives, action plans, and opportunities for improvement and innovation are the subject of benchmarking.
- Benchmarking covers key offerings, services, student/stakeholder satisfiers, faculty, and support operations.
- The school reaches beyond its own education facilities to conduct comparative studies.

- Benchmark or comparison data are used to improve the understanding of work processes and to discover the best levels of performance that have been achieved. Based on this knowledge, the organization sets goals or targets to stretch performance as well as drive innovations.
- A systematic approach is used to evaluate and improve processes for selecting, gathering, and using comparative information.
- Benchmarking processes are fully documented.
- Systematic actions have been taken to evaluate and improve the quality and use of comparative information and benchmark data.

4.2 Selection and Use of Comparative Information and Data
Sample Effective Practices for Teachers:
Leaders of the Classroom Learning System

- Use comparative data to track, report, and improve the rate and extent of course and classroom performance improvement.
- When appropriate, students and parents are given data to improve their performance, for example, charts with overall course/class performance, rubrics, flow charts, and timelines.

4.3 Analysis and Review of School Performance *(40 points)*
Approach/Deployment Scoring

Describe how the school analyzes and reviews overall performance to assess progress relative to plans and goals and to identify key opportunities for improvement.

In your response, address the following areas:

a. Analysis of Data

Consider how performance data from all parts of the school are integrated and analyzed to assess overall school performance in key areas. Describe how the principal educational progress and operational performance measures are integrated and analyzed to determine

(1) student and student group performance;

(2) school program performance;

(3) performance of students, student groups, and school programs relative to appropriately selected schools;

(4) school operational performance; and

(5) school operational performance relative to comparable schools.

b. Review of School Performance

Describe

(1) how school performance and capabilities are reviewed to assess progress relative to action plans, goals, and changing needs. Describe the performance measures regularly reviewed by the school's senior leaders.

(2) how review findings are translated into priorities for improvement, decisions on resource allocation, and opportunities for innovation. Describe also how these findings are deployed throughout the school, and, as appropriate, to the school's stakeholders and/or partners.

Notes:

N1.   Analysis includes trends, projections, comparisons, and cause-effect correlations intended to support the setting of priorities for resource use. Accordingly, analysis draws upon all types of data: student, student group, school program, and operational performance.

N2.   Student and school performance results should be reported in Items 7.1, 7.2, 7.3, and 7.4.

Despite the importance of individual facts and data, these alone do not usually provide a sound basis for effectively making decisions, taking actions, or setting priorities. To be effective, these activities depend on developing a solid understanding of the relationships among processes and between processes and business results. Process actions may have many resource implications; results may have many cost and revenue implications as well. Given that resources for improvement are limited and cause-effect connections are often unclear, there is a critical need to provide a sound analytical basis for decisions.

A close connection between analysis and performance review helps to ensure that analysis is kept relevant to decision making. This item is the central analysis point in an integrated information and data system.

Area 4.3a examines how information and data from all parts of the school are aggregated and analyzed to assess overall organization performance. The area covers five key aspects of performance—student and student group; school program; performance of students, student groups, and school programs relative to appropriately selected schools; school operational performance; and school operational performance relative to comparable schools.

Analyses that organizations perform to gain understanding of performance vary widely. Selection depends on many factors, including school type, size, and competitive position. Examples include

- How the educational organization's service improvements correlate with key student/stakeholder indicators such as satisfaction and retention.
- Implications of student- and stakeholder-related problems and problem resolution effectiveness.
- Improvement trends in key operational performance indicators such as productivity, cycle time, waste reduction, new service introduction, and defect levels.
- Relationships between faculty and staff/organization learning and value added per faculty/staff member.
- Financial benefits derived from improved student/faculty/staff safety, absenteeism, and turnover.
- Benefits and costs associated with education and training.
- How the organization's ability to identify and meet faculty/staff requirements correlates with employee retention, motivation, and productivity.

- Cost/revenue implications of employee-related problems and problem resolution effectiveness.
- Trends in individual measures of productivity such as labor productivity.
- Individual or aggregate measures of productivity relative to comparable schools.
- Performance trends relative to comparable schools on key measures and indicators.
- Cost trends relative to comparable schools.
- Relationships between product/service quality and operational performance indicators and overall organization financial performance trends as reflected in indicators such as operating costs, revenues, asset utilization, and value added per faculty/staff member.
- Allocation of resources among alternative improvement projects based on cost/revenue implications and improvement potential.
- Comparisons among school units showing how operational performance improvements affect academic performance.
- Trends in aggregate measures such as total factor productivity.
- Trends in economic and/or market indicators of value.

Area 4.3b examines how the organization reviews performance and capabilities and uses the review findings to improve performance and capabilities relative to action plans, goals, and changing needs. An important part of this review is the translation of review findings into an action plan sufficiently specific so that deployment throughout the organization and to partners is possible.

4.3 Analysis and Review of School Performance

How the organization analyzes and reviews overall performance to assess progress relative to plans and goals and to identify key areas for improvement.

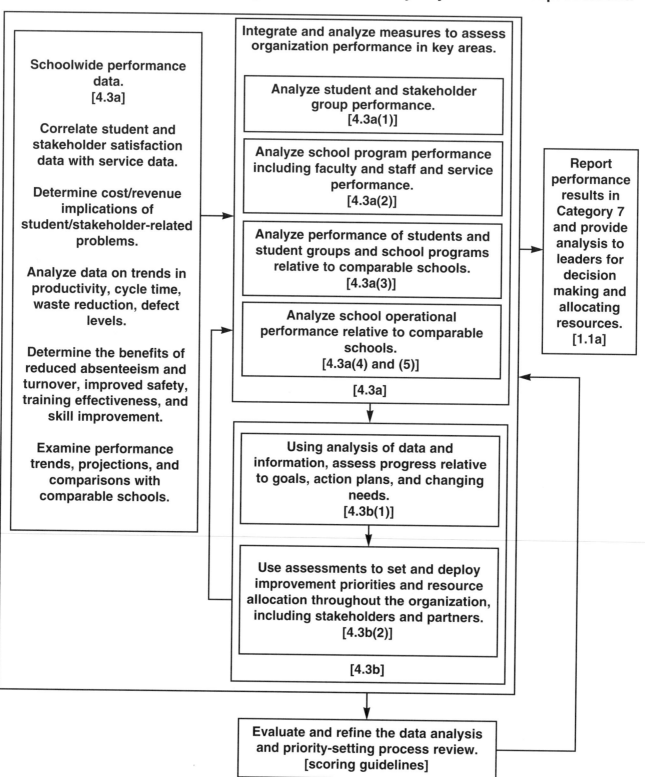

4.3 Analysis and Review of School Performance Item Linkages

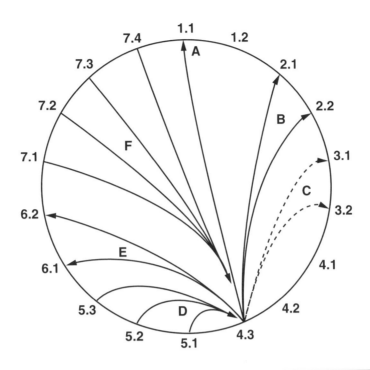

Nature of Relationship

A   Leaders at all levels [1.1] use data and information [4.3b] to review overall performance, assess progress relative to plans, and identify key areas for improvement.

B   Aggregated information is analyzed [4.3a] and used in the strategic planning process [2.1] and to help set goals [2.2b].

C   Information from student performance data are analyzed [4.3a] and used to help determine ways to assess student and stakeholder needs [3.1], to determine standards or required levels of service and relationship development [3.2a], and to design instruments to assess student and stakeholder satisfaction [3.2b].

D   Information regarding faculty and staff capabilities, including work system efficiency, initiative, and self-direction [5.1],

training and development [5.2], and well-being and satisfaction [5.3] is used to set priorities [4.3b] and improve safety, retention, absenteeism, and organizational effectiveness.

E   Data are aggregated and analyzed and used to set priorities [4.3] and improve education design and deliver and education support processes [6.1 and 6.2] that will reduce cycle time and waste, and improve participation and performance.

F   Performance data from all parts of the organization are integrated and analyzed [4.3a] to assess performance in key areas such as student performance [7.1], school-specific performance [7.4], student and stakeholder satisfaction [7.2], and faculty and staff performance [7.3] relative to competitive performance in all areas.

4.3 Analysis and Review of School Performance
Sample Effective Practices

A. Analysis of Data

- Processes are in place for analyzing customer-related data and results (including complaint data) and setting priorities for action.
- Facts, rather than intuition, are used to support decision making at all levels, based on the analyses conducted to make sense out of the data collected.
- The analysis process itself is analyzed to make the results more timely and useful for decision making for quality improvement at all levels.
- Analysis processes and tools, and the value of analyses to decision making, are systematically evaluated and improved.

B. Review of School Performance

- Student and operational performance data, including financial performance data, are used to support performance reviews relative to action plans, planning, and resource allocation.
- Data are used to help leaders improve operations-related decision making, such as determining improvement priorities; evaluating the cost impact of improvement initiatives and trends in key operational indicators (such as cycle time, waste and rework, and product/service quality); and using benchmark data to set improvement priorities and targets.
- Data regarding improvements in performance and financial performance are used in planning, goal setting, and establishing priorities.
- The impacts of improvement activities on stakeholder satisfaction, operational effectiveness, and financial indicators (for example, operating costs, production value per faculty/staff, cost per faculty/staff) are used to set improvement priorities.

5 Faculty and Staff Focus
—100 Points

The Faculty and Staff Focus category examines how the school enables faculty and staff to develop and utilize their full potential, aligned with the school's objectives. Also examined are the school's efforts to build and maintain an environment and climate conducive to performance excellence, full participation, and personal and organizational growth.

Faculty and Staff Focus is the location within the criteria for all key human resource issues and practices, those directed toward creating a school environment with a strong focus on students and learning, and toward developing faculty/staff that enable the school to adapt to change. It addresses these in an integrated way, aligned with the school's mission and strategy. To emphasize this key alignment, the Strategy Development Process (Item 2.1) includes faculty and staff capabilities and needs as key planning considerations.

5.1 Work Systems (40 Points)
Approach/Deployment Scoring

Describe how all faculty and staff contribute to achieving the school's performance and student focus objectives through the school's work design, and compensation and recognition approaches.

In your response, address the following areas:

a. Work Design

How work and jobs are designed and how faculty and staff, including all managers and supervisors, contribute to ensure

(1) design, management, and improvement of school work processes that support school action plans and related faculty and staff resource plans. Include how work processes focus on student achievement and needs. Address faculty and staff work processes separately, as appropriate.

(2) communications, cooperation, and knowledge and skill sharing across work functions, units, and locations; and

(3) flexibility, rapid response, and learning in addressing current and changing student, stakeholder, and operational requirements.

b. Compensation and Recognition

How the school's compensation and recognition approaches for individuals and groups, including all managers and supervisors, reinforce overall school objectives for student learning, performance improvement, and faculty and staff development. Describe significant differences, if any, among different categories or types of faculty and staff.

Notes:

N1.   For purposes of the criteria, staff include the school's permanent, temporary, and part-time personnel, as well as any contract employees or volunteers supervised by the school. Any contract employees supervised by the contractor should be addressed in Item 6.2.

N2.   Work design refers to how faculty and staff are organized and/or organize themselves in formal and informal, temporary, or longer-term units. This includes work teams, problem-solving teams, functional units, cross-functional teams, and departments—self-managed or managed by supervisors. Job design refers to responsibilities, authorities, and tasks of individuals.

N3.   Compensation and recognition refer to all aspects of pay and reward, including promotions and bonuses that might be based upon performance, skills acquired, and other factors. This includes monetary and nonmonetary, formal and informal, and individual and group compensation and recognition.

This item addresses how the school's work and job design, compensation, and recognition approaches enable and encourage all faculty and staff to contribute fully and effectively. Because of differing responsibilities, work organizations, compensation, and recognition systems might differ greatly between faculty and staff units or among faculty units.

Area 5.1a addresses how work processes focus on student achievement and needs and on communications, cooperation, and knowledge and skill sharing. This might involve the use of teams, in some cases involving paraprofessionals and adjunct faculty. Also addressed are flexibility, rapid response, and learning to accommodate to changing needs and operational requirements. Also important is effective communication across schoolwork organizations to ensure a focus on students and learning, and to ensure an environment of encouragement, trust, and mutual commitment.

Area 5.1b addresses the important alignment of incentives with work and job design. The basic thrust of this area is the need for consistency between the school's compensation and recognition system and work structures and processes.

The area calls for information on faculty and staff compensation and recognition—how these reinforce student achievement and school performance improvement. To be effective, compensation and recognition might need to be based, wholly or in part, upon demonstrated skills and/or evaluation by peers in teams.

5.1 Work Systems

How all faculty and staff contribute to achieving the school's performance and student focus objectives through the school's work design, compensation, and recognition approaches.

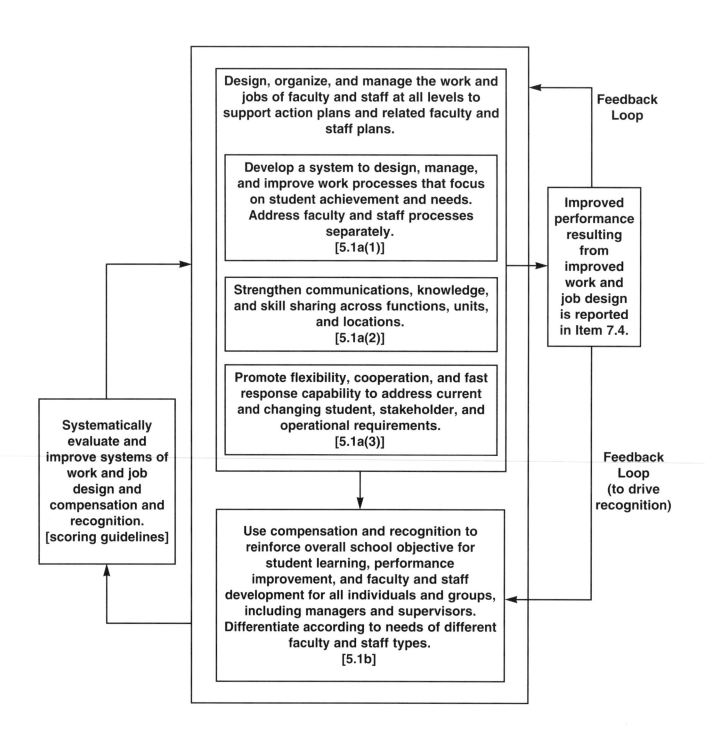

Design, organize, and manage the work and jobs of faculty and staff at all levels to support action plans and related faculty and staff plans.

Develop a system to design, manage, and improve work processes that focus on student achievement and needs. Address faculty and staff processes separately.
[5.1a(1)]

Strengthen communications, knowledge, and skill sharing across functions, units, and locations.
[5.1a(2)]

Promote flexibility, cooperation, and fast response capability to address current and changing student, stakeholder, and operational requirements.
[5.1a(3)]

Use compensation and recognition to reinforce overall school objective for student learning, performance improvement, and faculty and staff development for all individuals and groups, including managers and supervisors. Differentiate according to needs of different faculty and staff types.
[5.1b]

Systematically evaluate and improve systems of work and job design and compensation and recognition.
[scoring guidelines]

Improved performance resulting from improved work and job design is reported in Item 7.4.

Feedback Loop

Feedback Loop (to drive recognition)

5.1 Work Systems Item Linkages

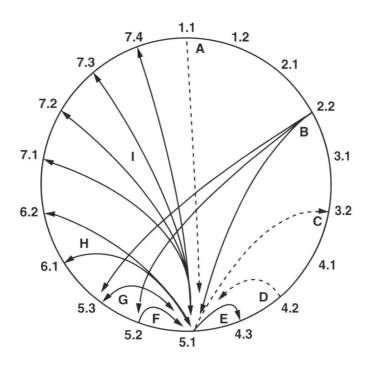

Nature of Relationship

A Leaders at all levels [1.1] set the policies and role model actions essential to improving work system design to enhance faculty and staff performance, initiative, self-direction, and involvement in quality improvement [5.1a].

B Faculty and staff resource plans and performance measures [2.2] address ways to improve faculty and staff performance and involvement [5.1], training [5.2], and satisfaction and well-being [5.3].

C Improved flexibility and self-direction [5.1a] can enhance the effectiveness of student and stakeholder satisfaction [3.2a].

D Key comparison data [4.2] are often used to improve work systems, and reward and recognition [5.1].

E Information regarding work systems effectiveness, design effectiveness, and faculty and staff involvement and recognition [5.1] is used to gain a better understanding of school performance and capabilities and to set priorities for improvement actions [4.3].

F Effective training [5.2] is critical to enable faculty and staff at all levels to improve skills and improve their ability to manage, organize, and design better work processes [5.1a].

G High morale [5.3] enhances faculty and staff participation, self-direction, and initiative [5.1] and vice versa.

H High-performance, streamlined work systems, and effective compensation and recognition [5.1] are essential to improving education and support processes [6.1 and 6.2]. In addition, the analysis of work processes (identifying inefficiencies) is used to inform or drive the improvements in flexibility and job design [5.1a].

I Recognition or rewards [5.1b] are based in part on performance results [Category 7], particularly in areas of operating effec-tiveness [7.4], student performance [7.1], and student and stakeholder satisfaction [7.2]. Improvements in work and job design [5.1] result in improved faculty and staff results and satisfaction [7.3] and improved school-specific results [7.4]. Processes to improve initiative and flexi-bility [5.1a] can enhance all performance results [Category 7].

5.1 Work Systems Sample Effective Practices

A. *Work Design*

- Fully using the talents of all faculty and staff is a basic organizational value.
- School leaders at all levels use cross-functional work teams to break down barriers, improve effectiveness, and meet goals. For example, this could be a team of teachers in the same discipline across several grade levels or cross-disciplinary teams.
- Teams have access to data and are authorized to take responsibility for decisions affecting their work.
- Faculty and staff opinion is sought regarding work design and work processes.
- Prompt and regular feedback is provided to teams regarding their performance. Feedback covers both results and team process.
- Using teams and self-directed faculty and staff to improve performance is the way regular work is done.
- Self-directed or self-managed work teams are used throughout the school to improve performance and address issues and concerns. They have appropriate authority over matters such as curriculum, instruction, and team membership and roles.
- A systematic process is used to evaluate and improve the effectiveness and extent of faculty and staff involvement.
- Many indicators of faculty and staff involvement effectiveness exist, such as the improvements in time or cost reduction produced by teams.
- Initiatives are undertaken to promote labor-management cooperation, such as partnerships with unions and faculty associations.
- Prioritization of faculty/staff problems is based on their potential impact on productivity.

B. *Compensation and Recognition*

- Recognition and rewards are provided for generating successful improvement ideas. Also, a system exists to encourage and provide rapid reinforcement for submitting improvement ideas.
- Recognition and rewards are provided for results, such as for reductions in cycle time and exceeding target schedules with error-free offerings or services at less-than-projected cost.
- Faculty and staff as well as administrators participate in creating the recognition and rewards system and help monitor its implementation and systematic improvement.
- The organization evaluates and improves its approaches to faculty and staff performance and compensation, recognition, and rewards to determine the extent to which faculty and staff are satisfied with them, the extent of their participation, and the impact of the system on improved performance (reported in Item 7.3).
- Evaluations are used to make improvements. Top-scoring organizations have several improvement cycles. (Many improvement cycles can occur in one year.)
- Performance measures exist, and goals are expressed in measurable terms. These measurable goals form the basis for performance recognition.
- Recognition, reward, and compensation are influenced by student and stakeholder satisfaction ratings as well as other performance measures.

5.2 *Faculty and Staff Education, Training, and Development (30 points)*
Approach/Deployment Scoring

Describe how the school's education and training support the accomplishment of key school action plans and address school needs, including building knowledge, skills, and capabilities, and contributing to improved faculty and staff performance and development.

In your response, address the following area:

a. *Faculty and Staff Development*

Describe

(1) how education and training support the school's key action plans and address school needs, including student achievement and faculty and staff personal growth;

(2) how faculty and staff education and training are designed to support the school's work systems. Include how the school seeks input from faculty and staff and their supervisors/managers in education and training design;

(3) how education and training, including orientation of new faculty and staff, are delivered;

(4) how knowledge and skills are reinforced on the job; and

(5) how education and training are evaluated and improved, taking into account school performance, faculty and staff performance, personal development, and other factors, as appropriate.

Notes:

N1.   Education and training delivery [5.2a(3)] might occur inside or outside the school and involve on-the-job, classroom, computer-based, distance education, or other types of delivery.

N2.   Other factors [5.2a(5)] might include effectiveness of incentives in promoting skill building; benefits and costs of education and training; most effective means and timing for training delivery; and effectiveness of cross-training.

This item addresses how the organization develops the workforce via education, training, and on-the-job reinforcement of knowledge and skills. Development is intended to meet the needs of employees and a high-performance workplace, accommodating to change.

Education and training address the knowledge and skills faculty and staff need to meet overall school and personal objectives. Education and training needs might vary greatly depending upon many factors, especially specific faculty and staff responsibilities. Examples include assessment practices, learning styles, problem solving, teamwork, leadership skills, communications, interpreting and using data, use of new technology, process analysis, and other training that affects faculty and staff effectiveness and safety.

The item calls for basic information on the key factors in an effective education and training approach ranging from the linkage between edu-cation and training to school action plans to the evaluation and improvement of the education and training, taking into account school performance, faculty and staff performance, and personal development of faculty and staff. This includes appropriate orientation of new faculty and staff.

Education and training delivery might occur inside or outside the organization and involve on-the-job, classroom, computer-based, distance education, or other types of delivery. This includes the use of developmental assignments within or outside the organization to enhance career opportunities and employability.

The item also emphasizes evaluation of education and training. Such evaluation might take into account faculty and staff self-evaluation. Evaluation might also address factors such as the effectiveness of education and training delivery, impact on organizational unit, and school performance.

5.2 Faculty and Staff Education, Training, and Development

How the school's education and training support the accomplishment of key school action plans and address school needs, including building knowledge, skills, and capabilities, and contributing to improved faculty and staff performance and development.

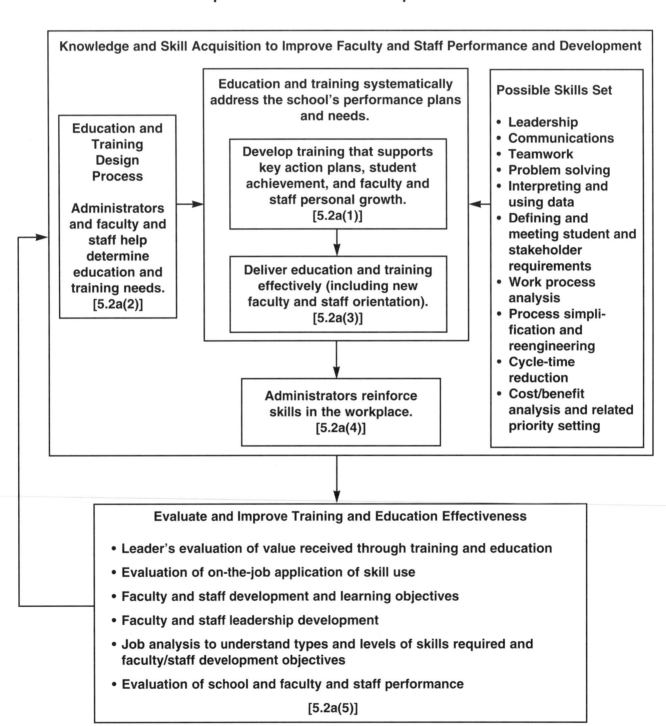

Knowledge and Skill Acquisition to Improve Faculty and Staff Performance and Development

Education and Training Design Process

Administrators and faculty and staff help determine education and training needs.
[5.2a(2)]

Education and training systematically address the school's performance plans and needs.

Develop training that supports key action plans, student achievement, and faculty and staff personal growth.
[5.2a(1)]

Deliver education and training effectively (including new faculty and staff orientation).
[5.2a(3)]

Administrators reinforce skills in the workplace.
[5.2a(4)]

Possible Skills Set

- Leadership
- Communications
- Teamwork
- Problem solving
- Interpreting and using data
- Defining and meeting student and stakeholder requirements
- Work process analysis
- Process simplification and reengineering
- Cycle-time reduction
- Cost/benefit analysis and related priority setting

Evaluate and Improve Training and Education Effectiveness

- Leader's evaluation of value received through training and education
- Evaluation of on-the-job application of skill use
- Faculty and staff development and learning objectives
- Faculty and staff leadership development
- Job analysis to understand types and levels of skills required and faculty/staff development objectives
- Evaluation of school and faculty and staff performance

[5.2a(5)]

5.2 Faculty and Staff Education, Training, and Development Item Linkages

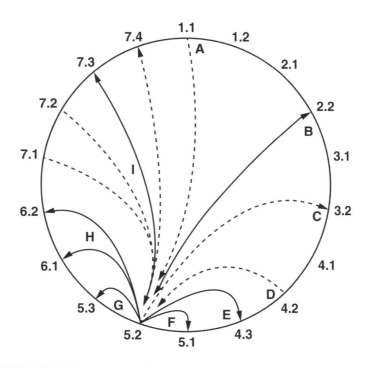

Nature of Relationship

A   Leaders at all levels [1.1] reinforce training on the job to ensure its effectiveness [5.2].

B   Faculty and staff resource plans [2.2a] are used to help align training [5.2] to support the organizational goals [2.2b].

C   Training [5.2] can strengthen customer relationships [3.2a].

D   Key measures and benchmarking data [4.2] are used to improve training [5.2].

E   Information regarding training effectiveness [5.2] is analyzed to set priorities for improvement actions [4.3].

F   Effective training [5.2] enables faculty and staff at all levels to improve skills and their ability to manage, organize, and design better work processes [5.1a].

G   Effective training [5.2] is often critical to maintaining and improving a safe, healthful work environment [5.3a].

H   Training [5.2] is essential to improving work in process effectiveness and innovation [6.1 and 6.2].

I   Results of improved training and development [5.2a] are reported in 7.3. In addition, student performance [7.1], student and stakeholder satisfaction [7.2], and school-specific results [7.4] are monitored, in part, to assess training effectiveness [5.2].

5.2 *Faculty and Staff Education, Training, and Development Sample Effective Practices*

- Hiring criteria and/or standards are developed to produce a workforce with necessary skills.
- Opportunities are created for faculty and staff to learn and use skills that go beyond current job assignments through redesign of processes or organizations.
- Education and training initiatives, including those that involve developmental assignments, are implemented.
- Partnerships with educational institutions are formed to develop faculty and staff or to help ensure the future supply of well-prepared employees.
- Partnerships are established with other organizations and/or networks to share training and/or spread job opportunities.
- Distance learning or other technology-based learning approaches are introduced.
- Systematic needs analyses are conducted to ensure that skills required to perform work are routinely assessed, monitored, and maintained.
- Clear linkages exist between strategic plans and the education and training that are provided. Skills are developed based on work demands and faculty and staff needs. For example, one might expect extensive technology training to be a major budget training item for most schools at all levels.
- Faculty and staff input is considered when developing training plans.

- Faculty and staff career and personal development options, including development for leadership at all levels of the school, are enhanced through formal education and training and through on-the-job training such as rotational assignments or job exchange programs.
- The organization uses various methods to deliver training to ensure that it is suitable for faculty and staff knowledge and skill levels.
- Training is linked to work requirements, which are reinforced on the job. Just-in-time training is preferred (rather than just-in-case training) to help ensure that the skills will be used immediately after training.
- Faculty and staff feedback on the appropriateness of the training is collected and used to improve course delivery and content.
- The organization systematically evaluates training effectiveness on the job. Performance data are collected on individuals and groups at all levels to assess the impact of training.
- Faculty and staff satisfaction with courses is tracked.
- Training is systematically refined and improved based on evaluations.

5.2 Faculty and Staff Education, Training, and Development Sample Effective Practices for Teachers: Leaders of the Classroom Learning System

- Practices that develop and improve the performance of faculty and staff are used to improve student performance. These may include faculty/student cooperation initiatives; creation of assignments for students that go beyond current academic assignments through redesign of processes; developmental assignments such as tutoring or community service; partnerships with other educational providers such as community colleges or distance learning; systematic needs analyses; and tracking student satisfaction.

5.3 Faculty and Staff Well-Being and Satisfaction (30 points)
Approach/Deployment Scoring

Describe how the school maintains a work environment and work climate that support the well-being, satisfaction, and motivation of faculty and staff.

In your response, address the following areas:

a. Work Environment

How the school maintains a safe and healthful work environment. Describe how health, safety, and ergonomics are addressed in improvement activities. Briefly describe key measures and targets for each of these environmental factors and how faculty and staff take part in establishing these measures and targets. Note significant differences, if any, based upon different work environments for faculty and staff groups or work units.

b. Work Climate

How the school builds and enhances its work climate for the well-being, satisfaction, and motivation of all faculty and staff. Describe
(1) school services, benefits, and actions to support faculty and staff; and
(2) how senior leaders, managers, and supervisors encourage and motivate faculty and staff to develop and utilize their full potential.

c. Faculty and Staff Satisfaction

How the school assesses the work environment and work climate. Include
(1) a brief description of formal and/or informal methods and measures used to determine the key factors that affect faculty and staff well-being, satisfaction, and motivation. Note important differences in methods, factors, or measures for different categories or types of faculty and staff, as appropriate; and
(2) how the school relates faculty and staff well-being, satisfaction, and motivation results to key performance results and/or objectives to identify improvement priorities.

Notes:

N1.   Approaches for supporting and enhancing faculty and staff well-being, satisfaction, and motivation [5.3b(1)] might include counseling; career development and employability services; recreational or cultural activities; non-work-related education; day care; special leave for family responsibilities and/or community service; safety off the job; flexible work hours; out-placement; and retiree benefits, including extended health care.

N2.   Specific factors that might affect well-being, satisfaction, and motivation [5.3c(1)] include effective faculty and staff problem or grievance resolution; safety factors; faculty and staff views of administration; faculty and staff training, development, and career opportunities; faculty and staff preparation for changes in technology or work organization; work environment and other work conditions; workload; cooperation and teamwork; recognition; benefits; communications; job security; compensation; equal opportunity; and capability to provide required services to students and stakeholders.

N3. Measures and/or indicators of well-being, satisfaction, and motivation (5.3c) might include safety, absenteeism, turnover, grievances, strikes, other job actions, and worker's compensation claims, as well as results of surveys. Results relative to such measures and/or indicators should be reported in Item 7.3.

This item addresses the work environment and work climate that support and enhances the well-being, satisfaction, and motivation of faculty and staff.

Area 5.3a calls for information on how the school maintains a safe and healthful work environment and how it includes such considerations in its improvement activities. As the safety and health of faculty and staff depend significantly upon specific work environments and responsibilities, it is important to view such factors separately and to segment measures and data accordingly, addressing the principal safety and health issues associated with each work unit.

Area 5.3b calls for information on the school's work climate and how the school seeks to build and enhance the well-being, satisfaction, and motivation of all faculty and staff. Examined are the school's services, benefits, and actions to support faculty and staff, and a summary of how the school's leadership encourages and supports faculty and staff to develop and utilize their full potential.

Most organizations, regardless of size, have many opportunities to contribute to faculty and staff well-being, satisfaction, and motivation. Examples of services, facilities, activities, and other opportunities include the following:
- Personal and career counseling
- Career development and employability services
- Recreational or cultural activities
- Formal and informal recognition
- Non-work-related education
- Day care

- Special leave for family responsibilities or for community services
- Safety off the job
- Flexible work hours
- Outplacement
- Retiree benefits, including extended health care

These services also might include career enhancement activities such as skill assessment, helping employees develop learning objectives and plans, and employability assessment.

Area 5.3c calls for information on how the school assesses its work environment and work climate and determines faculty and staff well-being, satisfaction, and motivation. The area recognizes that many factors affect well-being, satisfaction, and motivation and that these are likely to differ greatly among faculty and staff groups. In addition to formal or informal survey results, other measures of satisfaction, well-being, and motivation might include directly measurable indicators such as safety, absenteeism, turnover, and grievances.

Examples of specific factors that might affect satisfaction, well-being, and motivation include
- Effective faculty and staff problem or grievance resolution
- Safety factors
- Faculty and staff views of leadership and administration
- Faculty and staff training
- Faculty and staff preparation for changes in technology or work organization
- Work environment
- Workload
- Cooperation and teamwork
- Recognition

- Benefits
- Communications
- Job security
- Compensation
- Equal opportunity
- Capability to provide required services to students and stakeholders

Area 5.3c also addresses how the school relates faculty and staff well-being, satisfaction, and motivation results to key school, work unit, and individual performance results to identify improvement priorities. Especially important here is the identification of the principal factors in the work environment that bear upon faculty and staff motivation. Factors inhibiting motivation need to be prioritized and addressed. Further understanding of these factors could be developed through exit interviews with departing faculty and staff.

5.3 *Faculty and Staff Well-Being and Satisfaction*

How the school maintains a work environment and work climate that support the well-being, satisfaction, and motivation of faculty and staff.

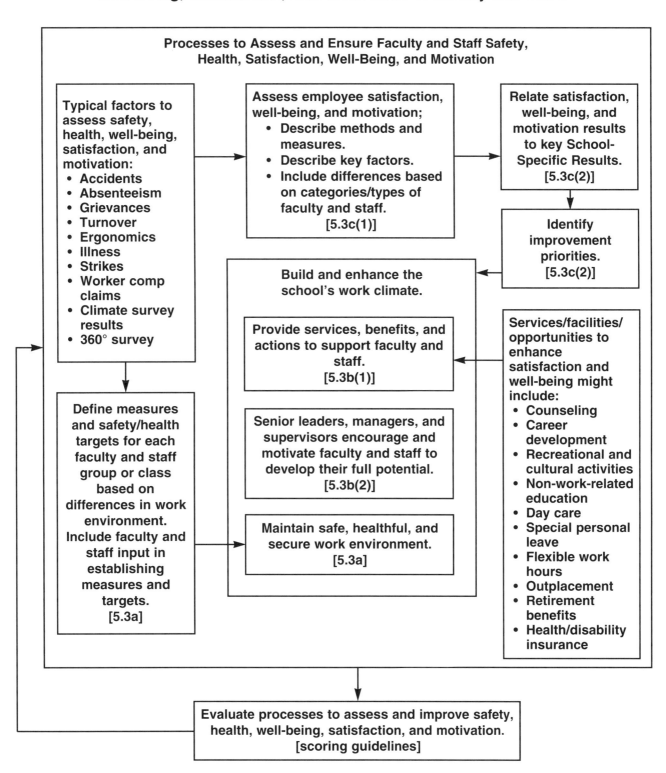

5.3 Faculty and Staff Well-Being and Satisfaction Item Linkages

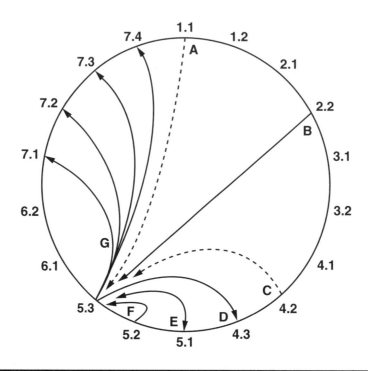

Nature of Relationship

A   Leaders at all levels [1.1] have responsibility for enhancing faculty and staff morale and well-being [5.3].

B   Faculty and staff resource plans [2.2a] address morale and well-being concerns [5.3].

C   Key benchmarking data [4.2] are used to design processes to enhance faculty and staff morale and well-being [5.3].

D   Information regarding faculty and staff well-being and morale [5.3c] is used to gain a better understanding of problems and performance capabilities and to set priorities for improvement actions [4.3].

E   High morale [5.3] enhances faculty and staff participation, self-direction, and initiative [5.1], and vice versa.

F   Training systems [5.2] enhance faculty and staff development, leading to improved morale and well-being [5.3].

G   Systems that enhance faculty and staff satisfaction and well-being [5.3] can boost student and school performance [7.1 and 7.4] and student and stakeholder satisfaction [7.2]. Specific results of faculty and staff well-being and satisfaction systems are reported in 7.3.

5.3 Faculty and Staff Well-Being and Satisfaction Sample Effective Practices

A. Work Environment

- Performance management will consider issues relating to faculty and staff health, safety, and workplace environment. Plans exist to optimize these conditions and eliminate adverse conditions.
- Root causes for health and safety problems are systematically identified and eliminated. Corrective actions are communicated widely to help prevent the problem in other parts of the school.

B. Work Climate

- Special activities and services are available for faculty and staff. These can be quite varied, depending on needs such as the following:
  - Flexible benefits plan including health care, on-site day care, dental, portable retirement, education (both work and non-work-related), maternity, paternity, and family illness leave;
  - Group purchasing power program where the number of participating merchants is increasing steadily; and
  - Special facilities, such as teacher centers, for faculty and staff to discuss their concerns.
- Senior leaders motivate faculty and staff by building a work climate that addresses the well-being of all.

C. Employee Satisfaction

- Key faculty and staff satisfaction opinion indicators are gathered periodically based on the stability of the organization (organizations in the midst of rapid change conduct assessments more frequently).
- Satisfaction data are derived from focus groups, e-mail data, satisfaction survey results, turnover, absenteeism, stress-related disorders, and other data that reflect faculty and staff satisfaction. (A key satisfaction indicator is one that reflects conditions affecting morale and motivation.)
- On-demand electronic surveys are available for quick response and tabulations any time administrators seek faculty and staff satisfaction feedback.
- Administrators use the results of these surveys to focus improvements on work systems and enhance satisfaction.
- Faculty and staff satisfaction indicators are correlated with drivers of performance to help identify where resources should be placed to provide maximum school benefit.
- Creation or redesign of faculty/staff surveys to assess the factors in the work climate that contribute to or inhibit high performance.

5.3 Faculty and Staff Well-Being and Satisfaction
Sample Effective Practices for Teachers:
Leaders of the Classroom Learning System

- Students are viewed as co-producers of knowledge.
- Cooperative approaches and teams of students use learning and decision making.
- Systems are in place that recognize and reward students when they contribute to school and classroom goals.
- Students are motivated and involved in planning and operating the learning system as appropriate for their level. For example, in middle school, students may develop flow charts and rubrics for tasks; in graduate school they may participate on committees that write the exam.

- Focus on the level of student involvement by monitoring, assessment, and improvements.
- Focus on the classroom work climate through assessing and improving well-being and student morale.
- Recognize and focus on specific factors that affect student well-being and satisfaction, such as problem resolution procedures; student view of the faculty; work environment; safety factors; workload; cooperation and teamwork; and equal opportunity.

6 Educational and Support Process Management —100 Points

The Educational and Support Process Management category examines the key aspects of process management, including learning-focused education design, education delivery, school services, and operations. The category examines how key processes are designed, implemented, managed, and improved to achieve better performance.

Educational and Support Process Management is the focal point within the Education Criteria for all key school processes. Built into the category are the central requirements for efficient and effective process management—effective design, evaluation, continuous improvement, and focus on high performance.

6.1 Education Design and Delivery (60 points)
Approach/Deployment Scoring

Describe how educational programs and offerings are designed, implemented, and improved. Describe also how delivery processes are designed, implemented, managed, and improved.

In your response, address the following areas:

a. Education Design

How educational programs and offerings are designed and implemented. Describe how the school ensures that all programs, offerings, and experiences

(1) address student educational and well-being needs, meet high standards, and focus on active learning, anticipating, and preparing for individual differences in student learning rates and styles;

(2) address sequencing and offering linkages;

(3) include a measurement plan that makes effective use of formative and summative assessment; and

(4) have faculty properly prepared.

b. Education Delivery

How the school ensures that ongoing educational programs and offerings meet design requirements. Include

(1) what observations, measures, and/or indicators are used and who uses them;

(2) how the observations, measures, and/or indicators are used to provide timely information to help students and faculty; and

(3) how educational programs and offerings are evaluated and improved. Describe how each of the following is used or considered: (a) information from students, families, feeder schools, and/or receiving schools; (b) benchmarking of best practices in education and other fields; (c) use of assessment results; (d) peer evaluation; (e) research on learning, assessment, and instructional methods; (f) information from employers and governing bodies; and (g) use of new learning technology. Include a description of how improvements are shared among and integrated into school units or departments.

Notes:

N1. Educational programs and offerings may include courses, research, co-op projects, overseas studies, and so on. Education should be interpreted broadly. It includes programs and offerings in trade schools, art and music schools, and other specialized schools.

N2. Education design might take into account distance learning and making offerings available at different locations and times to meet student needs.

N3. Sequencing and offering linkages [6.1a(2)] include not only relationships within a single discipline, but also relationships to related disciplines.

N4. A measurement plan [6.1a(3)] should be holistic and define what is to be assessed and measured, how and when assessments and measurements are to be made, and how the results will be used. For educational programs and offerings, measurements and observations should include key learning and developmental dimensions, for example, enabling early intervention when learning is not progressing adequately.

N5. Proper preparation of faculty [6.1a(4)] should reflect subject matter expertise as well as training/experience in teaching strategies, facilitation skills, learning assessment, understanding how to recognize and use learning research theory information, and reporting information and data on student progress.

N6. Education delivery refers to instructional approaches—modes of teaching and organizing activities and experiences so that learning takes place.

N7. Area 6.1b relates basically to quality assurance. In addition to assessment results, observations, measures, and/or indicators [6.1b(1)] might include enrollment and participation figures, student evaluation of course/instructor, success rates, attendance rates, dropout rates, counselor information, advanced study rates, complaints, feedback from students and families, and observation by school leaders.

N8. Observations, measures, and/or indicators [6.1b(2)] should reveal whether or not the programs or offerings require corrective action. The role of 6.1b(3) is ongoing improvement to achieve better performance. Periodically, programs and offerings might need to be changed or redesigned.

N9. Results of improvements in student performance should be reported in Item 7.1.

This item examines how the school designs, introduces, delivers, and improves its educational programs and offerings. It also examines how these programs and offerings are maintained to meet design requirements and further improved. The item also examines organizational learning, through a focus on how learnings in one school work unit are replicated and added to the knowledge base for other school units.

Area 6.1a calls for information on the design of educational programs and offerings. Four aspects of this design are addressed:
- How student educational and well-being needs are addressed, with a strong focus on active learning and taking into account varying learning rates and styles;
- How sequencing and offering linkages are addressed;
- How design includes a measurement plan that makes use of formative and summative assessments; and
- How the school ensures that faculty are properly prepared.

Design approaches might differ appreciably depending upon many factors, including school mission as well as student age, experience, and capability. Formative and summative assessments need to be tailored to the offering and program goals, and might range from purely individualized to group based.

Area 6.1b calls for information on program and offering delivery. Offering delivery refers to all strategies used to engage students in learning. Examined are the observations, measures, and/or indicators used and how these are used to provide timely information to help students and faculty. Differences among students must be a critical part of the evaluation of key educational processes. Among the key factors to be addressed in assessment are ensuring comparability among students and the relevance of assessment criteria to mission objectives. That is, assessment should be optimally related to the knowledge and skill requirements of offerings, and assessment should provide students and others with key information about what they know and are able to do.

Area 6.1b also calls for information on how processes are improved to achieve better perfor-mance. Better performance means not only bet-ter educational value for the student, but also better operational performance from the point of view of the school. A wide variety of approaches to improvement might be used, depending on the educational program and many student-specific factors. Area 6.1b requests information on how several approaches are used or considered: (a) information from students, families, feeder schools, and/or receiving schools; (b) bench-marking practices of other organizations; (c) use of assessment results; (d) peer evaluation; (e) research on learning, assessment, and instruc-tional methods; (f) information from employers and governing bodies; and (g) use of new learn-ing technology. In some cases, improvement of educational processes might entail complete redesign of programs and offerings, in content, delivery, or both.

6.1 Education Design and Delivery

How educational programs and offerings are designed, implemented, and improved. Also, how delivery processes are designed, implemented, managed, and improved.

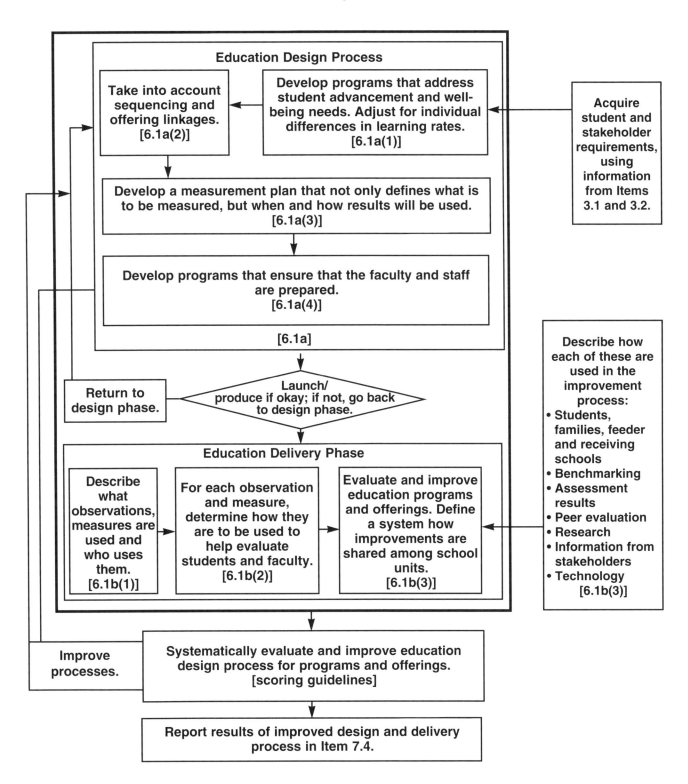

6.1 Education Design and Delivery Item Linkages

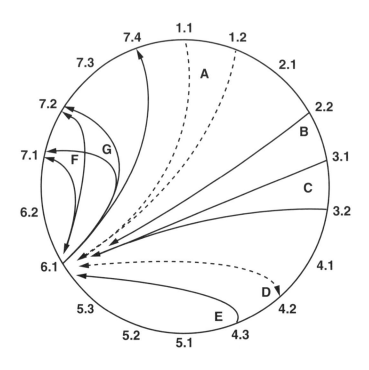

Nature of Relationship

A   Leaders at all levels [1.1] have a responsibility for ensuring that work processes are designed [6.1a] consistent with school objectives, including those relating to public responsibility and corporate citizenship [1.2].

B   Goals, deployed to the workforce [2.2], are used to drive and align actions to achieve improved performance [6.1].

C   Information about student needs and expectations [3.1] and satisfaction information, including that derived from student and stakeholder relationships [3.2a], is used to design or modify educational programs and services to better meet requirements [6.1].

D   Critical education programs and offerings [6.1] are used to help identify and prioritize benchmarking or comparison targets [4.2]. Benchmarking and comparison data [4.2]

are used to develop, share, and integrate improvements [6.1].

E   Priorities for educational programs and offerings improvements [6.1] are set based on performance data analysis [4.3].

F   Information about student performance [7.1] and student and stakeholder satisfaction [7.2] is used to target improvement efforts in educational programs and services design and development processes [6.1].

G   Processes to ensure that educational programs and services are designed to meet student needs and expectations and have a trouble-free introduction [6.1a] affect educational programs and offerings delivery [6.1b], school-specific performance [7.4], student performance [7.1], and student and stakeholder satisfaction [7.2].

6.1 Education Design and Delivery
Sample Effective Practices

A. Design Processes

- A systematic process is used to maintain a focus on students and convert student requirements into the design and delivery of educational programs and offerings.
- The work of various functions is coordinated to bring the program or offering through the design-to-delivery phases. Functional barriers between disciplines, departments, and units have been eliminated schoolwide.
- All design activities are closely coordinated through effective communication and teamwork.
- Internal process capacity and capability are reviewed and considered before educational programs and offerings are finalized.
- Design, production, service, and delivery reviews occur at defined intervals or as needed.
- Steps are taken (such as design testing or prototyping) to ensure that the delivery process will work as designed, and will meet student or stakeholder requirements.
- Design processes are evaluated and improvements made so that future designs are developed faster (shorter cycle time), at lower cost, and with higher quality, relative to key program or offering characteristics that predict student satisfaction.
- The results of improved design process performance are reported in Item 7.4.

B. Production/Delivery Processes

- Performance requirements (from Item 6.1a design processes and requirements) are set using facts and data and are monitored using statistical process control techniques.
- Education delivery processes are measured and tracked. Measures (quantitative and qualitative) should reflect or assess the extent to which requirements are met, as well as consistency.
- For processes that produce defects (out-of-control processes), root causes are systematically identified and corrective action is taken to prevent their recurrence.
- Corrections are monitored and verified. Process used and results obtained should be systematic and integrated throughout the organization.
- Processes are systematically reviewed to improve productivity, reduce cycle time and waste, and increase quality.
- Tools such as flowcharting and work redesign are used throughout the organization to improve work processes.
- Benchmarking, competitive comparison data, or information from users of the process (in or out of the organization) are used to gain insight to improve processes.

6.2 Education Support Processes (20 points)
Approach/Deployment Scoring

Describe how the school's education support processes are designed, implemented, managed, and improved.

In your response, address the following area:

a. Management of Education Support Processes

How key education support processes are designed, implemented, managed, and improved so that current and future requirements are met. Include

(1) how key requirements are determined or set, taking into account the needs of students, faculty, and other stakeholders;

(2) how key support processes are designed and implemented to meet student, faculty and staff, and operational requirements;

(3) a description of the key education support processes and their principal requirements and measures;

(4) how the processes are managed to maintain process performance and to ensure results will meet student, faculty and staff, and operational requirements. Include a description of key in-process measurements and/or student, faculty, and staff information gathering, as appropriate; and

(5) how the processes are evaluated and improved to achieve better performance.

Notes:

N1. Education support processes are those that support the school's overall education activities. This includes student support services such as counseling, advising, placement, tutorial, and libraries and information technology. It also includes recruitment, enrollment, registration, accounting, plant and facilities management, secretarial and other administrative services, security, marketing, information services, public relations, food services, health services, transportation, housing, central receiving, bookstores, and purchasing.

N2. Key education support process performance and improvement results should be reported in Item 7.4.

This item addresses how the school designs, maintains, and improves its support processes. Support processes are those that support the school's overall education activities and operations. This includes learner support services such as counseling, advising, placement, tutorial, and libraries and information technology. It also includes, as appropriate, recruitment, enrollment, registration, accounting, plant and facilities management, secretarial and other administrative services, security, marketing, information services, public relations, food services, health services, transportation, housing, bookstores, and purchasing.

The item calls for information on how the school designs, implements, manages, and improves support processes. Examined are (1) how key support process requirements are determined or set, taking into account the needs of students, faculty, staff, and other key stakeholders; (2) how key support processes are designed and implemented; (3) the key processes themselves and their principal requirements and measures; (4) how the processes are managed on a day-to-day basis to ensure that they are meeting design requirements; and (5) how the processes are evaluated and improved to achieve better performance. Evaluation and improvement might entail the use of activity-level cost information.

6.2 Education Support Processes

How the school's education support processes are designed, implemented, managed, and improved.

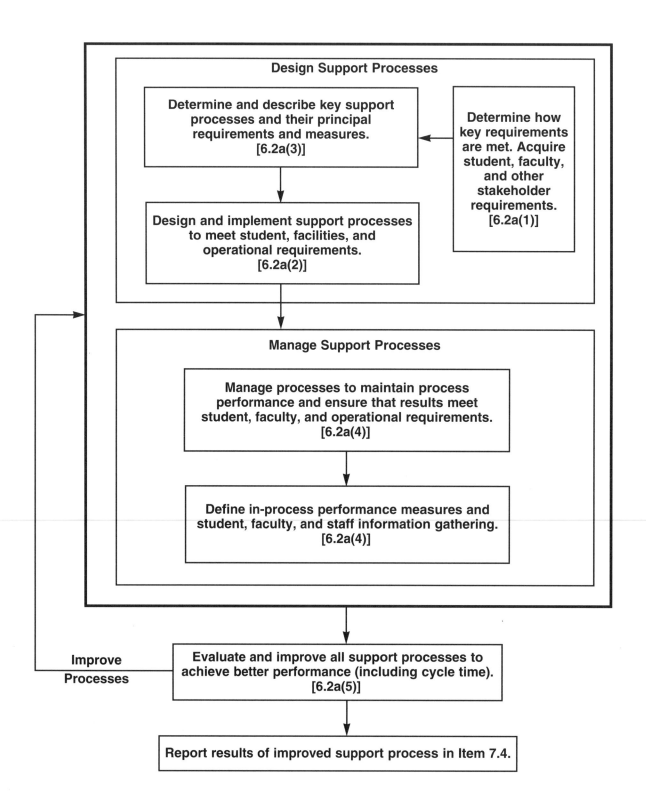

6.2 Education Support Processes Item Linkages

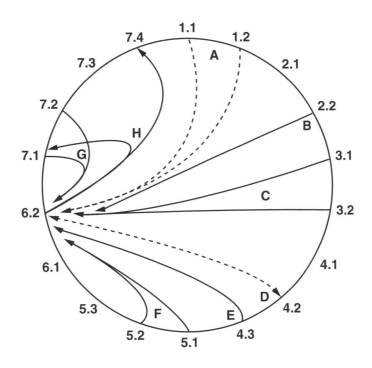

Nature of Relationship

A   Leaders at all levels [1.1] ensure that education support processes [6.2] are aligned with school priorities, including regulatory and public responsibilities [1.2].

B   Goals deployed to the faculty and staff [2.2], are used to drive and align actions to achieve improved education support performance [6.2].

C   Information about student needs and expectations [3.1] and from student and stakeholder satisfaction data [3.2b] is used to identify improvement opportunities in education support processes [6.2].

D   Critical education support processes [6.2] are used to help identify and prioritize benchmarking targets [4.2]. Benchmarking data [4.2] are used to improve support work processes [6.2].

E   Priorities for education support processes improvement [6.2] are set based on performance data and analysis [4.3].

F   High-performance flexible work systems [5.1a] and effective recognition [5.1b] and training [5.2] are essential to improving education support processes [6.2].

G   Information about student performance [7.1] and student and stakeholder satisfaction [7.2] is used to target improvement efforts in education support processes [6.2].

H   Improved education support processes [6.2] produce better educational program and service quality, operational effectiveness [7.4], and student results [7.1].

6.2 Education Support Processes
Sample Effective Practices

- A formal process exists to understand internal user requirements, translate those requirements into efficient support processes, and measure their effectiveness.
- Specific improvements in support services are made with the same rigor and concern for the internal and external stakeholder as improvements in educational design and delivery processes. For example, food service must be operated in a manner that meets student and other stakeholder requirements.
- All support services are subject to continuous review and improvements in performance and user satisfaction.
- Systems to ensure process performance are maintained, and requirements are met.
- Root causes of problems are systematically identified and corrected for processes that produce defects.

- Corrections are monitored and verified. The process used and results obtained are systematic and integrated throughout the organization.
- Support processes are systematically reviewed to improve productivity, reduce cycle time and waste, and increase quality.
- Work process simplification or improvement tools are used with measurable sustained results.
- Stretch goals are used to drive higher levels of performance.
- Benchmarking, competitive comparison data, or information from users of the process (in or out of the organization) are used to gain insight to improve processes.

6.2 Educational and Support Process Management
Sample Effective Practices for Teachers:
Leaders of the Classroom Learning System

- A systematic process is used to design, implement, and deliver teaching and learning products.
- The achievement of learning goals are supported by the physical classroom environment. For example, animals might be part of the science classroom but not if the noise interferes with normal classroom activity.
- Performance improvement tools are taught to students and used daily as part of the classroom. For example, teacher and students use rubrics, flow charts, affinity diagrams, and control charts to plan, monitor, and assess learning and behavior.
- Classroom support processes are monitored and improved. For example, by electronic mail, conferences, and discussion groups.
- Needed requirements for student success, such as materials, timelines, and learning content, are communicated to co-suppliers such as parents or other teachers.

7 *School Performance Results—450 Points*

The School Performance Results category examines student performance, student and stakeholder satisfaction, faculty and staff results, and school-specific performance. Also examined are performance levels relative to comparable schools and/or appropriately selected organizations.

The School Performance Results category provides a results focus for all school improvement activities, using a set of measures that reflect overall mission-related success. Category 7 thus provides "real-time" information—measures and indicators of progress—for evaluating and improving the effectiveness and efficiency of school services, aligned with the school's mission and strategy. The data called for in this category are the major ingredients in Analysis and Review of School Performance (Item 4.3), which is intended to identify causal connections to support improvement activities, planning, and change. Overall, the four items in the category should provide a comprehensive and balanced view of the school's effectiveness in improving its performance, now and in the future.

7.1 Student Performance Results (125 points)
Results Scoring

Summarize student performance results.

In your response, address the following area:

a. Student Performance Results

Summarize current levels and trends in key measures and/or indicators of student performance. Separately address different student groups, as appropriate. Include data showing how student performance and performance trends compare with comparable schools and/or appropriately selected student populations.

Notes:

N1. Results reported might be based upon a variety of assessment methods that reflect the school's primary improvement objectives and together represent holistic appraisals of students. For some measures and/or assessment methods, data might not yet be sufficient to demonstrate meaningful trends. Such data should be reported nevertheless, as they provide useful information regarding the school's current performance levels.

N2. Results may include data indicating performance of recent graduates.

N3. Demonstrations of improvement in student performance should be normalized to comparable student populations. Methods might involve longitudinal studies and cohort studies. Results covering three years or more are preferred.

N4. Comparisons should include a brief description of how the appropriateness of each comparison is ensured. Comparable schools might include those of similar types or sizes, both domestic and international, as well as schools serving similar populations of students.

This item addresses the principal student performance results based upon mission-related factors and assessment methods. Critical to understanding the purposes of this item are the following: (1) student performance should reflect holistic and mission-related results; (2) current levels and trends should be reported, the former to allow comparisons with other schools and/or student populations, and the latter to demonstrate year-to-year improvement; (3) data should be segmented by student group(s) to permit trends and comparisons that demonstrate the school's sensitivity to education improvement for all students. Overall, this item is the most important one as it depends upon demonstrating improvement by the school over time and higher achievement levels relative to comparable schools or student populations.

Proper use of Item 7.1 depends upon appropriate normalization of data to compensate for initial dif-

ferences in student populations. Although better admission criteria might contribute to improved education for all students, improved student performance based entirely upon changing students' entry-level qualifications should not be reported in Item 7.1. However, improvement trends in student admission qualifications are appropriate for inclusion in School-Specific Results (Item 7.4). Improvement in student performance beyond that which could be attributed to entry-level qualifications is appropriate for inclusion in Item 7.1, along with other measures and/or indicators of improvement trends and comparisons.

In order to determine whether results, trends, and levels are good or not, comparative data must be provided.

7.1 Student Performance Results

Summarize current levels and trends in key measures and/or indicators of student performance. Separately address different student groups, as appropriate. Include data showing how student performance and performance trends compare with comparable schools and/or appropriately selected student populations.

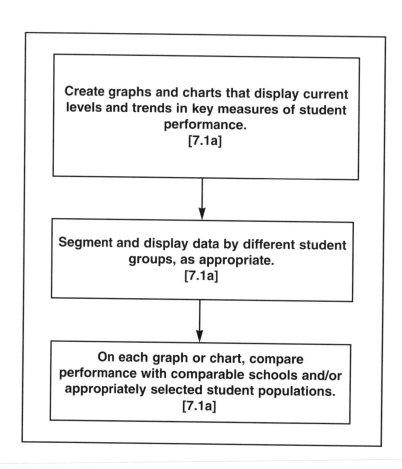

7.1 Student Performance Results Item Linkages

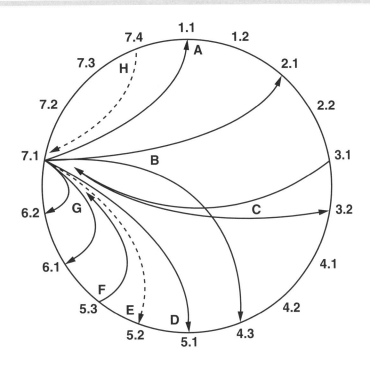

A Data on levels of student performance [7.1] are monitored by leaders at all levels [1.1].

B Data on levels of student performance [7.1] are collected and used to set school performance improvement priorities and to allocate resources [4.3b], and for strategic planning [2.1].

C Processes used to gather information about current student needs and expectations [3.1], strengthen stakeholder relations [3.2a], and determine student and stakeholder satisfaction [3.2b] are used to produce student performance results data [7.1]. In addition, student performance results [7.1] are used to create bases for relationships with key stakeholders [3.2a].

D Recognition and rewards [5.1b] must be based, in part, on student performance results [7.1].

E Student performance results data [7.1] are monitored, in part, to assess training effectiveness [5.2].

F Systems to enhance faculty and staff satisfaction and well-being [5.3] can produce higher levels of student performance results [7.1].

G Data on student performance [7.1] are used to help design educational programs and services and to improve education [6.1] and education support [6.2] processes.

H School-specific results [7.4] provide an adverse indicator of student performance results [7.1].

7.1 Student Performance Results
Sample Effective Results

- Learning trends indicated on examinations, portfolios, and other assessments are positive and sustained over time.
- Key measures and indicators of student performance show steady improvement.

- All-important learning and performance data are presented.
- Comparative data include other schools and comparable organizations, and appropriate comparisons.

7.1 Student Performance Results
Sample Effective Results for Teachers:
Leaders of the Classroom Learning System

- Classroom or course academic performance results are improving.
- Key measures and indicators of student performance show steady improvement.

- All-important learning and performance data are presented.
- Comparative data include other classrooms, courses, and comparable units.

7.2 Student and Stakeholder Satisfaction Results (125 points)
Results Scoring

Summarize the school's student and stakeholder satisfaction and dissatisfaction results.

In your response, address the following area:

a. Student and Stakeholder Satisfaction Results
   Summarize current levels and trends in key measures and/or indicators of satisfaction and dissatisfaction of current and past students and key stakeholders, including satisfaction relative to comparable schools.

Note:

N1.   Results reported in this item derive from methods described in Items 3.1 and 3.2.

N2.   Results data might include student/stakeholder feedback and their overall assessment of education/operations.

N3.   Examples of student/stakeholder dissatisfaction indicators are given in Item 3.2, Note 1.

N4.   Current levels and trends in key measures and/or indicators of student satisfaction relative to comparable schools might address gains and losses of students to other schools or to alternative means of education such as home schooling or corporate educational programs. Results might also include objective information and/or data from independent organizations, including key stakeholders.

N5.   Objective information and/or data from independent organizations, including key stakeholders, might include survey results, competitive awards, recognition, and ratings. The information and/or data should reflect comparative satisfaction (and dissatisfaction), not comparative performance of students. Information on comparative performance of students should be included in Item 7.1.

This item addresses trends and levels in student and stakeholder satisfaction based on relevant measures and/or indicators and these results compared with comparable schools. Effectively used, satisfaction results provide important indicators of school effectiveness and improvement. Effective use entails understanding the key dimensions of satisfaction and dissatisfaction, recognition that satisfaction and dissatisfaction with school services and/or performance might differ among student and stakeholder groups, and that satisfaction/dissatisfaction might change over time, based on longer-term perspective. The underlying purpose of the item is not only to ensure that satisfaction levels provide a useful tool in assessing key climate factors that contribute to or inhibit education. Its purpose is also to encourage inclusion of education and growth dimensions in satisfaction measurement. Satisfaction is thus principally an enabler, not an end in itself. Together, the results reported in item 7.2 should help to guide action leading to improved student performance, recognizing that the action might address climate, curriculum, faculty development, and many other factors. The item should not be interpreted as emphasizing "popularity" or other short-term, non-educational aims.

7.2 Student and Stakeholder Satisfaction Results

Results of improvement efforts using key measures and/or indicators of student and stakeholder satisfaction.

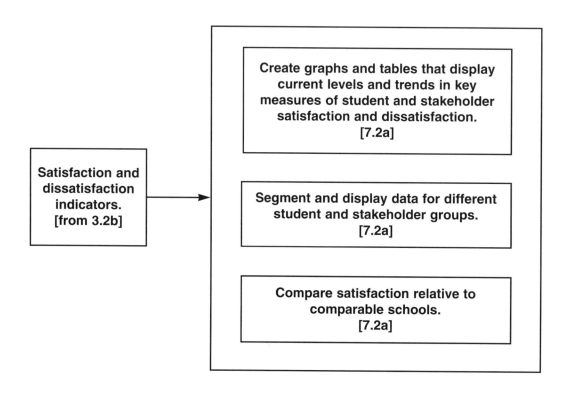

7.2 *Student and Stakeholder Satisfaction Results Item Linkages*

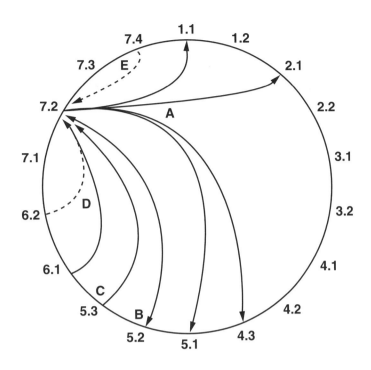

Nature of Relationship

A   Student and stakeholder satisfaction results data [7.2] are used for strategic planning [2.1], leadership monitoring and decision making [1.1], and priority setting [4.3], and may be used as a basis for compensation, recognition, and reward [5.1b].

B   Student and stakeholder satisfaction results data [7.2] are monitored, in part, to assess training effectiveness [5.2].

C   Faculty and staff morale and well-being [5.3] affect student and stakeholder satisfaction results [7.2], and vice versa.

D   Student and stakeholder satisfaction results [7.2] are enhanced by improvements in design and development and by better educational processes [6.1] and education support processes [6.2].

E   School-specific results [7.4] form the basis for student and stakeholder satisfaction results [7.2].

7.2 Student and Stakeholder Satisfaction Results
Sample Effective Results

- Trends and indicators of student and stakeholder satisfaction and dissatisfaction (including complaint data), segmented by student and stakeholder groups, are provided in graph and chart form for all key measures. Multiyear data are provided.
- All indicators show steady improvement. Indicators include data collected in Item 3.2b such as student and stakeholder assessments of education programs and offerings.
- All indicators compare favorably to competitors or similar providers.

- Student and stakeholder satisfaction graphs and information are accurate and easy to understand.
- Data are not missing.
- Results data are supported by student and stakeholder feedback, and overall assessments of education programs and offerings.
- Data are presented concerning student and stakeholder dissatisfaction for the most relevant program or service quality indicators collected through the processes described in Item 3.2b (some of which may be referenced in the School Overview).

7.2 Student and Stakeholder Satisfaction Results
Sample Effective Results for Teachers:
Leaders of the Classroom Learning System

- The level of student involvement and satisfaction results are improving steadily over time.
- Student and stakeholder satisfaction and dissatisfaction results indicate a positive trend.

- Data are not missing.
- Results data are consistent with student and stakeholder feedback.

7.3 Faculty and Staff Results (50 Points)
Results Scoring

Summarize the school's faculty- and staff-related results, including faculty and staff well-being, satisfaction, and development.

In your response, address the following area:

a. Faculty and Staff Results

Summarize current levels and trends in key measures and/or indicators of faculty and staff well-being, satisfaction, and development. Address all categories and types of faculty and staff, as appropriate. Include appropriate comparative data.

Notes:

N1. The results reported in this item should address results from activities described in Category 5. The results should be responsive to key process needs described in Category 6, and the school action plans and related faculty and staff resource plans described in Item 2.2.

N2. Appropriate measures of faculty and staff well-being, satisfaction, and motivation are given in Item 5.3.

N3. Appropriate measures and/or indicators of faculty and staff development and effectiveness might include innovation and suggestion rates, courses or educational programs completed, learning, on-the-job performance improvements, and cross-training.

This item addresses the school's human resource results—those related to well-being, development, satisfaction, and performance of faculty and staff.

Results reported could include generic or school-specific human resource factors. Generic factors include safety, absenteeism, turnover, and satisfaction. School-specific factors might include those created by the school to measure progress against key goals. Results reported might include input data, such as extent of training and development, but should also include measures and/or indicators of effectiveness. Inclusion of demographic and financial data related to diversity/equity are appropriate for inclusion in this item.

The item calls for comparative information so that results can be evaluated relative to comparable institutions.

7.3 Faculty and Staff Results

Results of current levels and trends in key measures and/or indicators of faculty and staff well-being, satisfaction, and development.

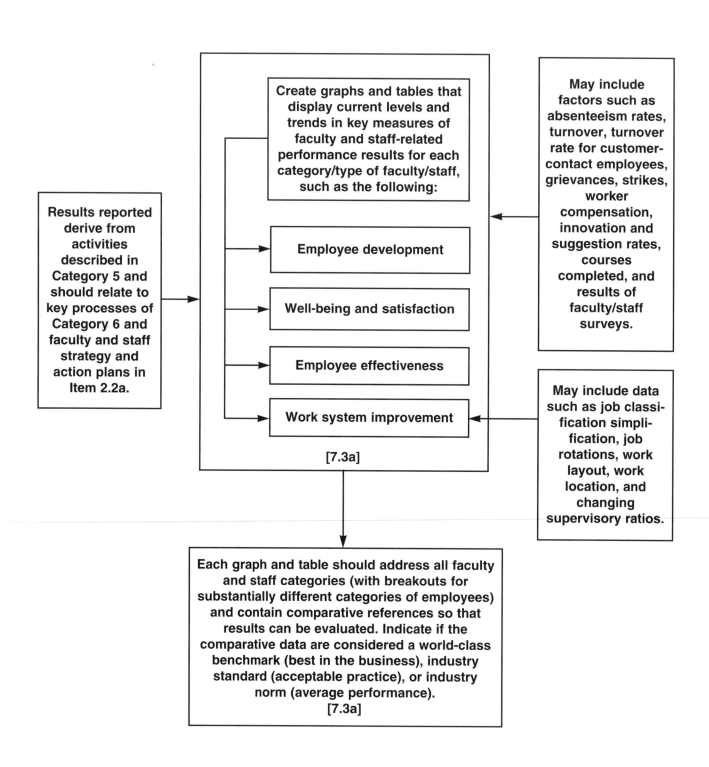

Results reported derive from activities described in Category 5 and should relate to key processes of Category 6 and faculty and staff strategy and action plans in Item 2.2a.

Create graphs and tables that display current levels and trends in key measures of faculty and staff-related performance results for each category/type of faculty/staff, such as the following:

Employee development

Well-being and satisfaction

Employee effectiveness

Work system improvement

[7.3a]

May include factors such as absenteeism rates, turnover, turnover rate for customer-contact employees, grievances, strikes, worker compensation, innovation and suggestion rates, courses completed, and results of faculty/staff surveys.

May include data such as job classification simplification, job rotations, work layout, work location, and changing supervisory ratios.

Each graph and table should address all faculty and staff categories (with breakouts for substantially different categories of employees) and contain comparative references so that results can be evaluated. Indicate if the comparative data are considered a world-class benchmark (best in the business), industry standard (acceptable practice), or industry norm (average performance).
[7.3a]

7.3 Faculty and Staff Results Item Linkages

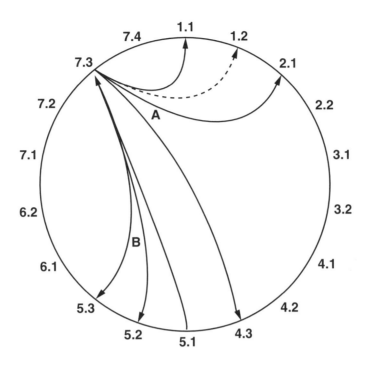

Nature of Relationship

A   Faculty and staff results data [7.3] are collected and used for planning [2.1], for leader decision making [1.1], to provide feedback through the leadership system [1.1], and for priority setting [4.3]. In addition, results in the area of faculty and staff safety [7.3] are used to ensure compliance with regulatory requirements [1.2].

B   Faculty and staff results derive from and are enhanced by improving work systems and enhancing flexibility [5.1a] and by strengthening faculty and staff recognition systems [5.1b], training [5.2], and well-being and satisfaction [5.3]. In addition, faculty and staff results data [7.3] are monitored, in part, to assess training effectiveness [5.2] and improvements in faculty and staff satisfaction [5.3c].

7.3 Faculty and Staff Results
Sample Effective Results

- The results reported in Item 7.3 derive from activities described in Category 5.
- Multiyear data are provided to show sustained performance.
- All results show steady improvement.
- Data are not missing—if faculty and staff results data are declared important, they are reported.
- Comparison data for benchmark or comparable schools are reported.

- Trend data are reported for employee satisfaction with working conditions, safety, retirement package, and other faculty and staff benefits. Satisfaction with administration is also reported.
- Trends for declining absenteeism, grievances, faculty and staff turnover, strikes, and worker compensation claims are reported.
- Data are reported for all faculty and staff categories.

7.4 School-Specific Results (25 Points)
Results Scoring

Summarize key school performance results that contribute to enhanced learning and/or operational effectiveness.

In your response, address the following area:

a. School-Specific Results

Summarize current key school performance results that contribute to enhanced learning and/or operational effectiveness, including school capacity to improve student performance, educational climate, and indicators of operating cost and responsiveness. For all measures and/or indicators of performance, provide current levels and trends. Include appropriate comparative data.

Note:

N1. Results reported in Item 7.4 should address key school requirements and progress toward accomplishment of key school performance goals as presented in the School Overview and Items 1.1, 2.2, 6.1, and 6.2. Include results not reported in Items 7.1, 7.2, and 7.3.

N2. Results reported in Item 7.4 should provide key information for analysis and review of school performance (Item 4.3) and should provide the operational basis for improved student and school performance results (Items 7.1, 7.2, 7.3).

N3. Regulatory/legal compliance results reported in Item 7.4 should address requirements described in Item 1.2.

This item addresses key performance results, not covered in Items 7.1–7.3, that contribute significantly to the school's mission and goals. The item encourages the use of any common or unique measures the school uses to track performance in areas of importance to the school's mission and goals.

Appropriate for inclusion are the following:
- Measures of productivity and operational effectiveness, including timeliness
- Results of compliance and improvement in areas of regulation, athletic programs, and so on
- Improvements in admission standards
- Improvements in school safety and hiring equity
- Effectiveness of research and services
- School innovations
- Utilization of school facilities by community organizations
- Contributions to community betterment
- Improved performance of administrative and other school support functions
- Cost containment
- Redirection of resources to education from other areas

7.4 School-Specific Results

Results of improvement efforts that contribute to school goals to enhance learning or operational effectiveness, including school capacity to improve student performance, educational climate, and indicators of cost effectiveness.

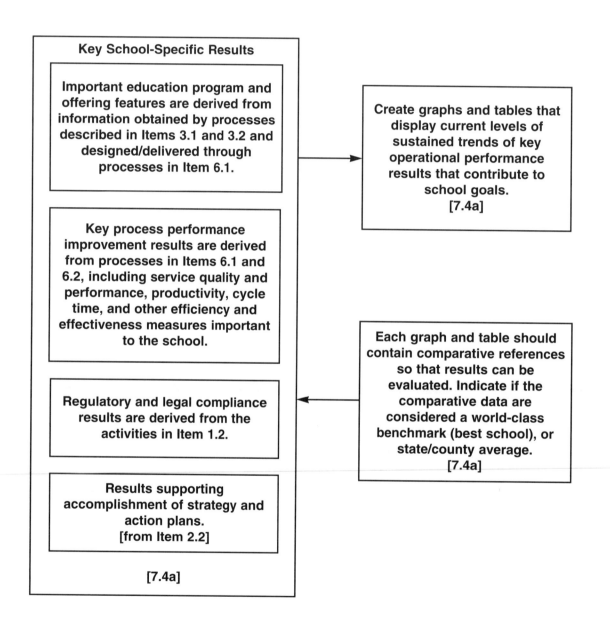

7.4 School-Specific Results Item Linkages

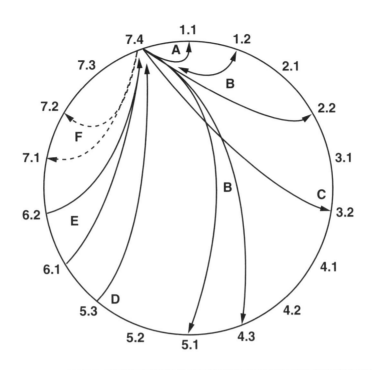

Nature of Relationship

A School quality characteristics and operational performance results data [7.4] are collected and used for planning [2.1], goal setting [2.2], management, monitoring, and decision making [1.1], analysis and priority setting [4.3], and reward and recognition determination [5.1b]. In addition, processes to improve faculty and staff initiative and flexibility [5.1a] can enhance school performance results [7.4].

B Regulatory and legal compliance resulting from the activities in Item 1.2 should be reported in 7.4. In addition, these results are monitored to determine if process changes are needed.

C Student and stakeholder relations systems [3.2a] result in effective and timely problem resolution. These results should be reported in 7.4.

D Faculty and staff morale and well-being [5.3] affect product and service quality results [7.4].

E Designing educational programs and services to meet student needs and expectations, and improve education design and delivery [6.1] and education support performance [6.2], affects overall school performance [7.4].

F School-specific results [7.4] provide the basis for student and stakeholder satisfaction results [7.2] and student performance results [7.1].

7.4 School-Specific Results
Sample Effective Results

- Indices and trend data are provided in graph and chart form for all operational performance measures identified in 6.1, 6.2, 4.1, 1.2, relevant organizational goals (2.2), and the key business factors identified in the School Overview and not reported elsewhere in Category 7.
- Multiyear data are reported.
- All indicators show steady improvement.
- Results data reflect performance relative to specific performance requirements that relate closely to student and stakeholder satisfaction and student retention.
- Product and service measures and indicators address requirements such as accuracy, timeliness, and reliability, and are key to predicting student and stakeholder behavior. Examples include defect levels, repeat services, meeting education program or offering delivery or response times, availability levels, and complaint levels.
- Operational performance measures address productivity, efficiency, and effectiveness such as productivity indices, faculty and staff utilization, waste reduction, energy efficiency, cycle time reduction, and education design improvement measures cycle time reductions.
- Comparative data include comparable best, best competitor, state/county average, and appropriate benchmarks. Data are also derived from independent surveys, studies, laboratory testing, or other sources.
- Data are not missing. (For example, do not show a steady trend from 1991 to 1997, but leave out 1993.)
- Data are not aggregated, since aggregation tends to hide poor performance by blending it with good performance. Break out and report trends separately.

Tips on Preparing a Baldrige Award Application

Preparing the School Overview

The School Overview is an outline. It addresses what is most important to the business of educating students, key influences on how the school operates, and where the school is headed. The overview is intended to help examiners understand what is relevant and important to the school's business of education.

The School Overview is of critical importance to the school because

- It is the starting point for writing and reviewing the application, helping to ensure focus on key education and management issues and consistency in responses, especially in reporting educational performance results.
- It is used by the examiners and judges in the application review, including the site visit.

Guidelines for Preparing the School Overview

The School Overview consists of five sections as follows:

Basic Description of the School

This section should provide basic information on the following:

- The nature of the school's educational products and services.
- School size, location(s), and whether it is publicly or privately owned.

- The school's major markets (local, regional, national, or international) and principal student types (special populations, ages). Note any special relationships, such as partnerships, with businesses or community groups.
- A profile of the school's employee base, including number, types, educational level, bargaining units.
- Major equipment, facilities, and technologies used.
- The regulatory environment affecting the school, such as occupational health and safety, environmental, financial, Education for Handicapped Children, Americans with disabilities, and so on.

If the school is a subunit of a larger school, a brief description of the organizational relationship to the parent and percentage of employees the subunit represents should be given. For example, a college may apply that is a part of a university (the "parent organization"). Briefly describe how the school's products and services relate to those of the parent and/or other units of the parent organization. If the parent organization provides key support services, these should also be described.

Student and Stakeholder Requirements

This section should provide information on key student and stakeholder requirements (for example, safe and orderly environment, fairness in grading, ease of access) for services. Briefly describe all important requirements, and note significant differences, if any, in requirements among student and stakeholder groups.

Relationships to Other Schools or to Other Organizations

This section should provide information on the following:
- Types and numbers of other schools with key linkages
- The most important types of schools, businesses, and other organizations
- Any limitations, special relationships, or special requirements that may exist with some or all schools, businesses, or other organizations

Competitive Factors

This section should provide information on the following:
- The school's position (relative size, growth) in the education industry/sector
- Numbers and types of competitors or similar providers
- Principal factors that determine competitive success, such as productivity, cost reduction, and product and service innovation
- Changes taking place that affect competition

Strategic Context

This section should provide information, as appropriate, on the following:
- Major new thrusts for the school, such as entry into new educational markets or segments
- New partnerships and alliances
- Introduction of new technologies
- The role of and approaches to process and service innovation
- Changes in strategy
- Unique factors such as the impact of restructuring, new leadership, and litigation, to name a few

Page Limit

The School Overview is limited to five pages. These pages are not counted in the overall 50-page application limit.

The School Overview should be prepared first and then used to guide the writing of the document used for assessment.

Guidelines for Responding to Approach/Deployment Items

The criteria focus on key educational performance results. However, results by themselves offer little help in diagnosing why performance is not at required levels. For example, if some results are poor or are improving at rates slower than comparable schools, it is important to understand why this is so and what might be done to accelerate improvement.

Approach/deployment items permit diagnosis of the applicant's most important systems, activities, and processes—the ones that offer the greatest potential for fast-paced performance improvement. Diagnosis and feedback depend heavily on the content and completeness of approach/deployment item responses. For this reason, it is important to respond to these items by providing key education and management process information. Guidelines for organizing and reviewing such information follow. Basic approach/deployment terms are provided in the Scoring System section of the book.

Understand the Meaning of "How"

Items that request information on approach include Areas to Address that begin with the word "how." Responses to such areas should provide a complete picture to enable meaningful evaluation and feedback. Responses should outline key process details such as methods, measures, deployment, and evaluation factors. Information lacking sufficient detail to permit an evaluation and feedback, or merely providing an example, is referred to in the scoring guidelines as anecdotal information.

Show What and How

Describe your system for meeting the requirements of each item. Ensure that methods, processes, and practices are fully described. Use flowcharts to help examiners visualize your key processes.

It is important to give basic information about what the key education and management processes are and how they work. Although it is helpful to include who performs the work, merely stating *who* does not permit effective communication or feedback. For example, stating that "parent satisfaction data are analyzed for improvement by the public relations department" does not set the stage for useful feedback, because potential strengths and weaknesses in the analysis cannot be identified from this very limited information. This makes it impossible to determine if a systematic process is in place.

Show That Activities Are Systematic

Ensure that the response describes a systematic approach, not merely an anecdotal example.

Systematic approaches are repeatable, predictable, and involve the systematic use of data and information for cycles of improvement. In other words, the approaches are consistent over time, build in learning and evaluation, and show maturity. Scores above 50 percent rely on clear evidence that approaches are systematic.

Show Deployment

Ensure that the response gives clear and sufficient information on deployment. For example, one must be able to distinguish from a response whether an approach described is used in one, some, most, or all parts of the organization. Is it used in one school or college or the whole organization?

Deployment can be shown compactly by using summary tables that outline what is done in different parts of the organization. This is particularly effective if the basic approach is described in a narrative.

Show Focus and Consistency

The response demonstrates that the school is focused on key processes and on improvements that offer the greatest potential to improve school performance and accomplish school action plans.

There are four important factors to consider regarding focus and consistency: (1) the School Overview should make clear what is important; (2) the Strategic Planning category, including the strategy and action plans, should highlight areas of greatest focus and describe how deployment is accomplished; (3) descriptions of school-level analysis (Item 4.3) should show how the school analyzes and reviews performance information to set priorities; and (4) the Educational and Support Process Management category should highlight processes that are key to overall school performance. Focus and consistency in the Approach-Deployment Items should yield corresponding results reported in Results Items.

Respond Fully to Item Requirements

Ensure that the response fully addresses all important parts of each item and each Area to Address. Missing information will be interpreted by examiners as a gap in approach and/or deployment. All areas should be addressed and checked in final review. Individual components of an Area to Address may be addressed individually or together.

Cross-Reference When Appropriate

Schools should try to make each item response self-contained. However, some responses to different items might be mutually reinforcing. It is then appropriate to reference responses to other items, rather than to repeat information. In such cases, applicants should use area designators (for example, "see Area 3.2a(1)").

Use a Compact Format

Schools should make the best use of the 50 application pages permitted. Schools are encouraged to use flow charts, tables, and "bulletized" presentation of information.

Refer to the Scoring Guidelines

The evaluation of item responses is accomplished by consideration of the criteria item requirements and the maturity of the school's approaches, breadth of deployment, and strength of the improvement process relative to the scoring guidelines. Therefore, schools need to consider both the criteria and the scoring guidelines in preparing responses.

Guidelines for Responding to Results Items

The Baldrige education criteria place great emphasis on results. All results items remain in Category 7 for 1999. Items 7.1, 7.2, 7.3, and 7.4 call for results related to all key requirements, students, stakeholders, and goals.

Focus on Reporting Critical Results

Results reported should cover the most important requirements for education success, highlighted in the School Overview, and the Strategic Planning categories, and included in responses to other items, such as Faculty and Staff Focus (Category 5) and Educational and Support Process Management (Category 6).

Four key requirements for effective presentation of results data include the following:
- Trends show directions of results and rates of change
- Performance levels show performance on some meaningful measurement scale
- Comparisons show how trends or levels compare with those of other, appropriately selected schools or other organizations
- Breadth of results shows completeness of deployment of improvement activities.

No Minimum Time

No minimum period of time is required for trend data. However, results data might span five years or more for some results. Trends might be much shorter for some of the organization's improvement activities. Because of the importance of showing deployment and focus, new data should be included even if trends and comparisons are not yet well established.

Compact Presentation

Presenting many results can be done compactly by using graphs and tables. Graphs and tables should be labeled for easy interpretation. Results compared with others should be "normalized"— presented in a way (such as use of ratios) that takes into account various size or inflation factors. For example, if the schools faculty and staff has been growing, reporting safety results in terms of accidents per 100 employees would permit more meaningful trend data than in terms of the total number of accidents.

Link Results with Text

Discussion of results and the results themselves should be close together in the report. Use figure numbers that correspond to items. For example, the third figure for Item 7.2 would be 7.2-3. (See the example below.)

The following graph illustrates data that might be presented as part of a response to Item 7.2, Student and Stakeholder Satisfaction Results.

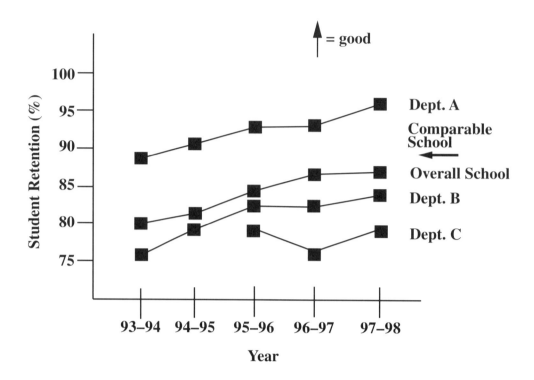

Figure 7.2-3. Student and stakeholder satisfaction results.

Using the graph, the following characteristics of clear and effective data presentation are illustrated:
- Trend lines report data for a key mission objective.
- Both axes and units of measure are clearly labeled.
- Results are presented for several years.
- Meaningful comparisons are clearly shown.
- The school shows, using a single graph, that its departments separately track retention rates.

To help interpret the scoring guidelines, the following comments on the graphed results would be appropriate.
- The overall school performance level is excellent. This conclusion is supported by the comparison with comparable schools.
- The school exhibits an overall excellent improvement record.
- Department A is the current performance leader—showing sustained high perform-

ance well above comparable schools and a positive trend. Department B shows rapid improvement. Its current performance is near that of comparable schools.
- Department C—a new division—is having early problems. The applicant has analyzed and explained the early problems in the application text. Its current performance is not yet at the level of the other departments or comparable schools.

Complete Data

Be sure that results data are displayed for all relevant students and stakeholders, financial concerns, faculty and staff, operational performance, and other performance characteristics. If you identify relevant performance measures and goals in other parts of the analysis, (for example, Items 1.1, 1.2, 2.1, 2.2, 3.1, 3.2, 4.1, 4.2, 4.3, 5.1, 5.2, 5.3, 6.1, and 6.2), be sure to include the results of these performance characteristics in Category 7. As each relevant performance measure is identified in the assessment process, create a blank chart and label the axes. Define all units of measure, especially if they are school-specific or unique to the school. As data are collected, populate the charts. If expected data are not provided in the application, examiners may assume that the trends or levels are not good. Missing data drive the score down in the same way that poor trends do.

Break Out Data

Avoid aggregating the data. Where appropriate, break data into meaningful components. If the school serves several different student and stakeholder groups, display performance and satisfaction data for each group. As the following graph demonstrates, only one of the three trends is positive, although the average is positive. Examiners will seek component data when aggregate data are reported. Only presenting aggregate data instead of meaningful component data could reduce the score.

The Importance of Criteria Notes

Several items are followed by one or more notes that offer some insight and explanation about the item. Often these notes suggest activities or measures that other organizations have used to meet the requirements of the item. There are many ways to manage a high-performance system that are not included in the notes. Notes should be considered suggestions and not requirements.

Data and Measures

Comparison data are required for all items in Category 7. These data are designed to demonstrate how well the organization is performing. To judge performance excellence, one must possess comparison data. In Figure 7.2-4, performance is represented by the line connecting the squares. Clearly the organization is improving, but how "good" is it? Without comparison data, answering that question is difficult.

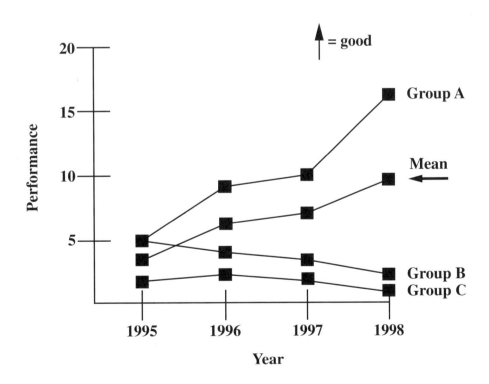

Figure 7.2-4. Chart lacking comparative data.

Now consider the chart with comparison data added.

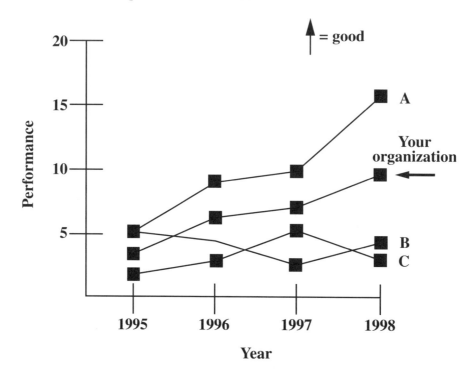

Figure 7.2-5. Chart with comparative data included.

Note the position of three hypothetical comparisons, represented by the letters A, B, and C. Consider the following two scenarios.

- If A represents a state/county average and both B and C represent area competitors, examiners would conclude that the school's performance was substandard, even though it is improving.
- If A represents a best-in-class (benchmark) school and B represents a state/county average, examiners would conclude that organizational performance is very good.

In both scenarios, the organizational performance remained the same but the examiner's perception of it changed.

Measures

Agreeing on relevant measures is a difficult task for schools in the early phases of quality and performance improvement. The task is easier if the following guidelines are considered.

- Clearly define student and stakeholder requirements. Clear requirements are easier to measure. Clearly defined student and stakeholder requirements require probing and suggesting. For example, the student wants better test results reporting. After probing to find what "better" means, we discover that (1) the student wants the grade as well as specific teacher comments (2) better also means quicker results—the next school or class day; and (3) students want an opportunity within two weeks to retake the test and raise their grades.
- For each of the three requirements defined, identify a measure. For example, since the students are concerned with turnaround time for test results, we must assess how long it took the teacher to grade, comment on, and return the test. Measures include time in hours, days, and minutes to produce "better" test results reporting.
- Collect and report data. Several charts might be required to display these factors.

Scoring System

The scoring of school responses to criteria items and feedback are based on three evaluation dimensions: Approach, Deployment, and Results. Schools need to furnish information relating to these dimensions. Specific factors for these dimensions are described as follows:

Approach

Approach refers to how the school addresses the item requirements—the method(s) used. The factors used to evaluate approaches include the following:

- Appropriateness of the methods to the requirements.
- Effectiveness of use of the methods. This includes the degree to which the approach is systematic, integrated, and consistently applied; embodies evaluation, improvement, and learning cycles; and is based on reliable information and data.
- Evidence of innovation and/or significant and effective adaptations of approaches used in other types of schools or businesses.

Deployment

Deployment refers to the extent to which the school's approach is applied to all requirements of the item. The factors used to evaluate deployment include the following:

- Use of the approach in addressing school and item requirements
- Use of the approach by all appropriate work units

Results

Results refers to outcomes in achieving the purposes given in the item. The factors used to evaluate results include the following:

- Current performance
- Performance relative to appropriate comparisons and/or benchmarks
- Rate, breadth, and importance of performance improvements
- Demonstration of sustained improvement and/or sustained high-level performance
- Linkage of results measures to key performance measures identified in the School Overview and in Approach/Deployment Items

Item Classification and Scoring Dimensions

Items are classified according to the kinds of information and/or data those seeking assessment are expected to furnish relative to the three evaluation dimensions.

The two types of items and their designations are
1. Approach/Deployment
2. Results

Approach and Deployment are linked to emphasize that descriptions of Approach should always indicate the Deployment—consistent with the specific requirements of the item. Although Approach and Deployment dimensions are linked, feedback reflects strengths and/or areas for improvement in either or both dimensions.

Results Items call for data showing performance levels and trends on key measures and/or indicators of school performance. However, the evaluation factor, "breadth" of performance improvements, is concerned with how widespread the improvement results are. This is directly related to the Deployment dimension. That is, if improvement processes are widely deployed, there should be corresponding results. A score for a Results Item is thus a composite based upon overall performance, taking into account the breadth of improvements and their importance (see next section).

Importance as a Scoring Factor

The three evaluation dimensions described above are all critical to evaluation and feedback. However, evaluation and feedback must also consider the importance of improvements in Approach, Deployment, and Results to the school. The areas of greatest importance should be identified in the School Overview, and in items such as 2.2, 3.1, 3.2, 6.1, and 7.1. Of particular importance are the key student requirements, key strategies, and action plans.

Assignment of Scores to Responses

The following guidelines should be observed in assignment of scores to responses:

- All relevant areas to Address should be included in the item response. Also, responses should reflect what is important to the school.

- In assigning a score to an item, an examiner first decides which scoring range (e.g., 40% to 60%) best fits the overall item response. Overall "best fit" does not require total agreement with each of the statements for that scoring range. Actual score within the range depends upon an examiner's judgment of the closeness of the item response in relation to the statements in the next higher and next lower scoring ranges.

- An Approach/Deployment Item score of 50% represents an approach that meets the basic objectives of the item and that is deployed to the principal activities covered in the item. Higher scores reflect maturity (cycles of improvement), integration, and broader deployment.

- A Results item score of 50% represents clear indication of improvement trends and/or good levels of performance in the principal results areas covered in the item. Higher scores reflect better improvement rates and/or levels of performance, and better comparative performance as well as broader coverage.

Approach/Deployment

0%	• No systematic approach evident, anecdotal information.
10% to 20%	• Beginning of a systematic approach to the basic purposes of the item. • Major gaps exist in deployment that would inhibit progress in achieving the basic purposes of the item.
30% to 40%	• A sound, systematic approach, responsive to the basic purposes of the item. • Approach is deployed, although some areas or work units are in early stages of deployment. • Beginning of a systematic approach to evaluation and improvement of basic item processes.
50% to 60%	• A sound, systematic approach, responsive to the overall purposes of the item. • Approach is well deployed, although deployment may vary in some areas or work units. • A fact-based, systematic evaluation and improvement process is in place for basic item processes. • Approach is aligned with basic school needs identified in the other criteria categories.
70% to 80%	• A sound, systematic approach, responsive to the multiple requirements of the item. • Approach is well deployed, with no significant gaps. • A fact-based, systematic evaluation and improvement process and organizational learning/sharing are key management tools; clear evidence of refinement and improved integration as a result of organizational-level analysis and sharing exists. • Approach is well integrated with school needs identified in the other criteria categories.
90% to 100%	• A sound, systematic approach, fully responsive to all the requirements of the item. • Approach is fully deployed without significant weaknesses or gaps in any areas or work units. • A very strong, fact-based, systematic evaluation and improvement process and extensive organizational learning/sharing are key management tools; strong refinement and integration, backed by excellent organizational-level analysis and sharing. • Approach is fully integrated with school needs identified in the other criteria categories.

Results

0%	• No results or poor results in areas reported.
10% to 20%	• Some improvements and/or early good performance levels in a few areas. • Results not reported for many to most areas of importance to key school requirements.
30% to 40%	• Improvements and/or good performance levels in many areas of importance to key school requirements. • Early stages of developing trends and obtaining comparative information. • Results reported for many to most areas of importance to key school requirements.
50% to 60%	• Improvement trends and/or good performance levels reported for most areas of importance to key school requirements. • No pattern of adverse trends and no poor performance levels in areas of importance to key school requirements. • Some trends and/or current performance levels—evaluated against relevant comparisons and/or benchmarks—show areas of strength and/or good to very good relative performance levels. • School performance results address most key student, stakeholder, and process requirements.
70% to 80%	• Current performance is good to excellent in areas of importance to key school requirement. • Most improvement trends and/or current performance levels are sustained. • Many to most trends and/or current performance levels—evaluated against relevant comparisons and/or benchmarks—show areas of leadership and very good relative performance levels. • School performance results address most key student, stakeholder, process, and action plan requirements.
90% to 100%	• Current performance is excellent in most areas of importance to key school requirements. • Excellent improvement trends and/or sustained excellent performance levels in most areas. • Evidence of education sector and benchmark leadership demonstrated in many areas. • School performance results fully address key student, stakeholder, process, and action plan requirements.

Supplementary Scoring Guidelines

Authors' note: Many examiners and organizations have found the official scoring guidelines to be somewhat vague, increasing the difficulty of reaching consensus on a score and increasing scoring variation. This year the Baldrige scoring guidelines have been refined, creating 20-point ranges instead of 30-point ranges. However, examiners are still directed to score in 10 percent increments. To make this easier, we developed the following supplemental scoring guidelines. Many state award programs have used these guidelines for several years and found that they make the consensus process easier, reduce scoring variation, and produce comparable scores.

Approach/Deployment

1. For each approach/deployment item, first determine the appropriate level on the approach scale. This sets the upper possible score the applicant may receive on the item.
2. Then read the corresponding level on the deployment scale. For example, if the approach level is 40 percent, read the 40 percent standard on the deployment scale where one would expect "a few minor gaps in deployment exist" and "many work units are in the early stages of deployment." If that is the case, the final score is 40 percent.
3. However, if the deployment score is lower than the approach score, then it establishes the lower range of possible final scores for the item. The actual final score will be between the low and high scores. For example, if only "isolated units are using quality practices; most are not," the lowest possible score would be 10 percent. This final score must be between 40 and 10 percent (e.g., 10, 20, 30, or 40 percent).
4. Never increase a poor approach score based on good deployment.
5. See key terms related to scoring approach/deployment items.

Results

1. For results items, base your assessment only on the standards described on the results scale. Do not consider approach or deployment standards at all.
2. Determine the extent to which performance results are positive, complete, and at high levels relative to competitors or similar providers or an industry standard.
3. To determine the extent to which all important results are reported, examiners should develop a list of the key measures the applicant indicates are important. Start with the measures listed in the overview section. Then add to the key measures list based on data reported in Item 1.2 and the goals in Item 2.2, as well as measures that may be mentioned in Categories 5 and 6. Key measures can be reported anywhere in an application.

Score	Approach	Deployment
0%	No systematic approach evident; anecdotal information.	Anecdotal, undocumented.
10%	Early beginning of a systematic approach consistent with the basic purposes of the item is somewhat evident. Mostly reactive approach to problems. Many key requirements of the item not addressed. In the earliest stages of transitioning from reacting to problems to a general improvement orientation.	Many major gaps exist in deployment. Progress in achieving basic purposes of item is significantly inhibited.
20%	A partially systematic but beginning approach consistent with the basic purposes of the item is evident. Generally reactive to problems. Some key requirements of the item not addressed. In the early stages of transitioning from reacting to problems to a general improvement orientation.	Some major gaps exist in deployment. Progress in achieving basic purposes of item is noticeably inhibited.
30%	A sound systematic approach responsive to the basic purposes of the item is somewhat evident. A few key requirements of the item not addressed. Beginning of a systematic approach to evaluation but little if any improvement of basic item processes is evident. Random improvements may have been made.	The approach is generally deployed although several units are in the earliest stages of deployment. Progress in achieving primary purposes of item is minimally inhibited.
40%	A sound systematic approach responsive to the basic purposes of the item is clearly in place. Several minor requirements of the item are not addressed. Beginning of a systematic approach to evaluation and improvement of basic item processes is evident. Random improvements may have been made.	The approach is deployed although several units are in the early stages of deployment. Progress in achieving primary purposes of item is not inhibited.
50%	A sound systematic approach responsive to the overall purposes of the item is fully developed. Some minor requirements of the item are not addressed. Fact-based improvement system is in place for basic item processes that includes process evaluation in key areas (but no refinements are in place). Random improvements may have been made. The approach is aligned with some basic school needs identified in the other criteria categories.	No major gaps in deployment exist that inhibit progress in achieving primary purposes of item, although deployment may vary in some areas or work units. Some work units are still in the early stages of deployment.
60%	A sound systematic approach responsive to the overall purposes of the item is clearly in place. A few minor requirements of the item not addressed. Fact-based improvement system is in place for the basic requirements of the item including at least one evaluation and improvement cycle completed, including some systematic refinement based on the evaluation in key areas. The approach is aligned with most basic school needs identified in the other criteria categories.	No major gaps in deployment exist that inhibit progress in achieving primary purposes of item although deployment may vary in some areas or work units. A few work units may still be in the early stages of deployment.
70%	A sound systematic approach, responsive to many of the multiple purposes of the item, is clearly in place and fully developed. Organizational learning and sharing are frequently used management tools at many levels. Some systematic evaluation and evidence of refinements and improved integration result from organization-level analysis and learning. The approach is aligned and well integrated with many overall school needs identified in the other criteria categories.	Approach is well deployed with some work units in middle or advanced stages. No significant gaps exist that inhibit progress in achieving the purposes of the item.
80%	A sound systematic approach, responsive to most of the multiple purposes of the item, is clearly in place and fully developed. Organizational learning and sharing are frequently used management tools at most levels. Considerable systematic evaluation and evidence of refinements and integration result from organization-level analysis and learning. The approach is aligned and well integrated with most overall school needs identified in the other criteria categories.	Approach is well deployed with many work units in the advanced stages. No gaps exist that inhibit progress in achieving the purposes of the item.
90%	A sound systematic approach, responsive to all of the multiple purposes of the item, is in place. Considerable systematic evaluation and extensive refinements and improved organizational sharing and learning are key management tools at most levels. Some innovative processes are evident with strong refinement and integration supported by substantial organization-level analysis and sharing.	Approach is fully deployed with most work units in the advanced stages. No significant gaps or weaknesses exist in any areas or work units.
100%	A sound systematic approach, fully responsive to all of the multiple purposes of the item, is clearly in place. Considerable systematic evaluation and clear evidence of extensive refinements and improved organizational sharing and learning are key management tools at all levels. Many innovative processes are evident with strong refinement and integration supported by excellent organization-level analysis and sharing.	Approach is fully deployed with most to all work units in the advanced stages. No significant gaps or weaknesses exist in any areas or work units.

Score	Scoring Results
0%	**No results** or poor results in areas reported.
10%	Results not reported for most areas of importance to the school's key requirements. Limited positive results and/or limited good performance levels are evident for a few areas.
20%	Results not reported for many areas of importance to the school's key requirements. Some positive results and/or early good performance levels are evident for a few of these areas.
30%	Results are reported for many areas of importance to the school's key requirements. Improvements and/or good performance levels are evident for many areas of importance to the school's key requirements. Early stages of developing trends but little or no improvement has been obtained.
40%	Results are reported for most key areas of importance to the school's key requirements. Improvements and/or good performance levels are evident for many areas of importance to the school's key requirements. Early stages of developing trends and obtaining comparative information.
50%	Results are reported for most key student, other stakeholder, process, and action plan requirements. Some positive trends and/or good performance levels—evaluated against relevant comparisons or benchmarks— show a few areas of strength or good relative performance levels. No pattern of adverse trends and no poor performance levels in areas of importance to key school requirements.
60%	Results are reported for most key student, other stakeholder, process, and action plan requirements. Many positive trends and/or good performance levels—evaluated against relevant comparisons and benchmarks—show some areas of strength and good relative performance levels. No pattern of adverse trends and no poor performance levels in areas of importance to key school requirements.
70%	Results are reported for most key student, other stakeholder, process, and action plan requirements. Current performance is good in many areas important to key school requirements. Most improvement trends and/or current performance levels are sustained and many of these—evaluated against relevant comparisons and/or benchmarks—show some areas of leadership and very good relative performance levels.
80%	Results are reported for most key student, other stakeholder, process, and action plan requirements. Current performance is excellent in many areas important to key school requirements. Most improvement trends and/or current performance levels are sustained and most of these—evaluated against relevant comparisons and/or benchmarks—show areas of leadership and very good relative performance levels.
90%	Results fully address key student, other stakeholder, process, and action plan requirements. Current performance is excellent in most areas important to key school requirements. Most improvement trends or current performance levels are sustained and most of these—evaluated against relevant comparisons or benchmarks—show areas of education sector leadership or benchmark leadership in many areas.
100%	Results fully address key student, other stakeholder, process, and action plan requirements. Current performance is excellent in most areas important to key school requirements. Excellent improvement trends and current performance levels are sustained and—evaluated against relevant comparisons and benchmarks— show education sector leadership or benchmark leadership in many areas.

Approach/Deployment Terms

Systematic

Look for evidence of a system that is a repeatable and predictable process that fulfills the requirements of the item. Briefly describe the system. Be sure to explain how the system works. You must communicate the nature of the system to people who are not familiar with it. This is essential to achieve the 30 percent scoring threshold.

Integrated

Determine the extent to which the system is integrated or linked with other elements of the overall management system. Show the linkages across categories for key themes such as those displayed earlier for each item.

Consider the extent to which the work of senior leader is integrated. For example:
1. Senior administrators (Item 1.1) are responsible for shaping and communicating the organization's vision, values, and expectations throughout the leadership system and workforce.
2. They develop relationships with key students and stakeholders (Item 3.2) and monitor their satisfaction (Item 7.2) and educational organization performance (7.4).
3. This information, when properly analyzed (Item 4.3), helps them set priorities and allocate resources to optimize student and stakeholder satisfaction and operational and financial performance.
4. With this in mind, senior administrators participate in strategy development (Item 2.l) and ensure the alignment of the workplace to achieve organizational goals (Item 2.2).
5. Senior administrators may also become involved in supporting new structures to improve faculty and staff work systems [Item 5.1], training effectiveness (Item 5.2), and

faculty and staff well-being and satisfaction (Item 5.3).

Similar relationships (linkages) exist between other items. Highlight these linkages to demonstrate integration.

Prevention-Based

Prevention-based systems are characterized by actions to minimize or eliminate the recurrence of problems. In an ideal world, all systems would produce perfect products and flawless service. Since that rarely happens, high-performing educational organizations are able to act quickly to recover from a problem and then take action to identify the root cause of the problem and prevent it from surfacing again. The nature of the problem, its root cause, and appropriate corrective action are communicated to all relevant faculty and staff so that they can implement the corrective action in their area before the problem arises.

Continuous Improvement

Continuous improvement is a bedrock theme. It is the method that helps organizations keep their competitive edge. Continuous improvement involves evaluation and improvement of processes crucial to organizational success. Evaluation and improvement completes the high-performance management cycle. Continuous improvement evaluations can be complex, data-driven, statistical processes, or as simple as a focus group discussing what went right, what went wrong, and how it can be done better. The key to optimum performance lies in the pervasive evaluation and improvement of all processes. By practicing systematic, pervasive, continuous improvement, time becomes the school's ally. Consistent evaluation and refinement practices can drive the score to 60 percent or 70 percent and higher.

Complete

Each item contains one or more areas to address. Many areas to address contain several parts. Failure to address all areas and parts can push the score lower. If an area to address or part of an area does not apply to your school, it is important to explain why. Otherwise, examiners may conclude that the system is incomplete.

Innovative

The highest-scoring school is able to demonstrate that its processes are innovative, unique, world class, and trendsetters. When the processes are so good that they becomes the benchmark for others (and are deployed throughout the school), the scores move to the 90 percent to 100 percent range.

Anecdotal

If your assessment describes a process that is essentially anecdotal and does not systematically address the criteria, it is worth very little (0 to 10 points).

Deployment

The extent to which processes are widely used by school units affects scoring. For example, a systematic approach that is well integrated, evaluated consistently, and refined routinely may be worth 70 percent to 90 percent. However, if that process is not in place in all key parts of the organization, the 70 percent to 90 percent score will be reduced, perhaps significantly, depending on the nature and extent of the gap.

Major gaps are expected to exist at the 0 to 30 percent level. At the 40 percent to 60 percent level, no major gaps exist, although some units may still be at the early stages of development. At the 70 percent to 90 percent level, no major gaps exist and many to most units are in the advanced stages of development in the area called for in the criteria.

Summary

For each item examined, the process is rated as follows:
- Anecdotal: 0 to 10 percent
- Systematic: 10 percent to 30 percent
- Fully developed: 40 percent
- Prevention-based and evaluated: 50 percent
- Integrated: 50 percent to 100 percent
- Refined: 60 percent to 80 percent
- Widely used, with no gaps in deployment: 70+ percent

Systematic, integrated, prevention-based, and continuously improved systems that are widely used are generally easier to describe than undeveloped systems. Moreover, describing numerous activities or anecdotes does not convince examiners that an integrated, prevention-based system is in place. In fact, simply describing numerous activities and anecdotes suggests that a system does not exist. However, by tracing critical success threads through the relevant items in the criteria, the school demonstrates that its system is integrated and fully deployed.

To demonstrate system integration, pick several critical success factors and show how the school manages them. For example, trace the leadership focus on performance.
- Identify performance-related data that are collected to indicate progress against goals (Item 4.1).
- Show how performance data are used to set work priorities (Item 4.3).
- Show how performance effectiveness is considered in the planning process (Item 2.1) and how work at all levels is aligned to increase performance (Item 2.2).
- Demonstrate the impact of faculty and staff resource management (Item 5.1) and training (Item 5.2) on performance.

- Show how educational design, development, delivery, and support processes (Items 6.1 and 6.2) are enhanced to improve results.
- Report the results of improved performance (7.1, 7.3, and 7.4).
- Determine how improved performance affects student and stakeholder satisfaction levels (Item 7.2).
- Show how student and stakeholder concerns (Item 3.1 and 3.2) are used to drive the selection of key measures (4.1) and impact educational design and delivery processes (6.1).

Note that the application is limited to 50 pages, not including the five-page School Overview. This may not be sufficient to describe in great detail the approach, deployment, results, and systematic integration of all of your critical success factors, goals, or key processes. Thus, you must pick the most important few, indicate them as such, and then thoroughly describe the threads and linkages throughout the application.

Comparisons of the Education Criteria to the Baldrige Award Business Sector Application

In this section, the authors describe linkages overall between the Baldrige Criteria for Business and Education. At the end of the section, the authors note several issues readers may want to consider when implementing the criteria.

Linkages

The 1999 Education Criteria represent the second stage in the development of criteria intended to focus on educational excellence. The Education Criteria incorporate the same core values and concepts used in the 1998 Baldrige Award for Business. This is because the same framework underlies the requirements of all high-performing organizations, including those in education. These requirements however, are not necessarily addressed in the same way. There is a benefit to using the same language and concepts for business and education. The benefit is that it encourages cross-sector cooperation and communication of best practices. The major differences between the two sets of criteria are described below by category.

Leadership

Company Responsibility was changed to Public Responsibility, reflecting the generally public nature of the education enterprise.

Strategic Planning

The six subareas under 2.1(a) were condensed into three areas. The requirements that partner and supplier capabilities be considered in the strategic planning process were eliminated, because of the belief that suppliers were less critical to strategy development in education.

In 2.2, Company Strategy was changed to School Strategy, reflecting the nature of the education enterprise.

Customer Satisfaction and Relationship Enhancement

The name of the category was changed to Student and Stakeholder Satisfaction and Relationship Enhancement. This terminology was changed consistently throughout the criteria. This may reflect a general reluctance on the part of many educators to see education as a business with customers. In the Education Criteria, students are sometimes customers. At other times, stakeholders refer to all other types of customers such as parents, businesses, other schools that may receive the students, and the community (taxpayers).

In Item 3.2, Customer Satisfaction and Relationship Enhancement was changed to Student and Stakeholder Satisfaction and Relationship Enhancement. This again may reflect the preference of the authors of the Education Criteria not to use business terminology but to see students and stakeholders as customers. Item 3.2(c), Relationship Building, was eliminated from the Education Critera. Stakeholder Relationship Building replaced Accessibility and Complaint Management as 3.2(a). Item 3.2(b) includes concepts from Accessibility and Complaint Management.

Information and Analysis

In Item 4.3, Analysis and Review of Company Performance was changed to Analysis and Review of School Performance.

Human Resource Focus

In Category 5, Human Resource Focus becomes Faculty and Staff Focus. "Employee" was changed to "faculty and staff" as well. This language is used throughout the criteria. This reflects a general preference of the authors of the criteria for the terminology of faculty and staff over human resources.

Process Management

In Category 6, Process Management was changed to Education and Support Process Management, reflecting the desire to make clear to educators that they were referring to their education *and* support processes.

In Item 6.1, Management of Product and Service Processes was changed to Education Design and Delivery. In Area 6.1(a), Design Processes are clarified by becoming Education Design, and in Area 6.1(b), Production/Delivery Processes was changed to Education Delivery.

In Area 6.2, Management of Support Processes was changed to Education Support Processes and Area 6.2(a) also added the word "Education" to Support Processes.

The Education Criteria eliminated Item 6.3, Supplier and Partnering Processes. This may reflect the view that schools do not need to pay close attention to suppliers or partners. Authors' note: If your school has suppliers/partners that impact education design and delivery (for example if contracts are used) those should be covered in Item 6.1 or 6.2.

Business Results

Item 7.1, Student Performance Results, is consistent with the Education Criteria's value that student performance results are the most important results. In Business, the first item (7.1) is Customer Satisfaction.

Financial and Market Results was changed to Student and Stakeholder Satisfaction Results. This is similar to Item 7.1 in the Business Criteria.

Item 7.3 remains the focus for Staff and Faculty Satisfaction (it was called Human Resource Results in the Business Criteria)

Item 7.4, School-Specific Results, is the last results area. It is the same as the Business Criteria Company-Specific Results (7.5).

Item 7.2 from the Business Criteria was eliminated. (There are no financial results but these data may be included in Item 7.4 if cost effectiveness is a specific result assessed by the school. Another example would be research results.)

Self-Assessments of Organizations and Management Systems

Baldrige-based self-assessments of education organization performance and management systems take several forms, ranging from rigorous and time intensive, to simple and somewhat superficial. This section discusses the various approaches to organizational self-assessment and the pros and cons of each. Curt Reimann, the first director of the Malcolm Baldrige National Quality Award Office and the closing speaker for the 10th Quest for Excellence Conference, spoke of the need to streamline assessments to get a good sense of strengths, areas for improvement, and the vital few areas to focus leadership and drive organizational change. Three distinct types of self-assessment will be examined: the written narrative, the Likert scale survey, and the behaviorally anchored survey.

Full-Length Written Narrative

The Baldrige application development process is the most time-consuming organizational self-assessment process. To apply for the Baldrige award, applicants must prepare a 50-page written narrative to address the requirements of the performance excellence criteria. In the written self-assessment, the applicant is expected to describe the processes and programs it has in place to drive performance excellence. The Baldrige application process serves as the vehicle for self-assessment in most state-level quality awards. The process has not changed since the national quality award program was created in 1987 (except for reducing the maximum page limit from 85 to 50 pages).

Over the years, three methods have been used to prepare the full-length, comprehensive written narrative self-assessment.

- The most widely used technique involves gathering a team of people to prepare the application. The team members are usually assigned one of the seven categories and asked to develop a narrative to address the criteria requirements of that category. The category writing teams are frequently subdivided to prepare responses item by item. After the initial draft is complete, an oversight team consolidates the narrative and tries to ensure processes are linked and integrated throughout. Finally, top leaders review and scrub the written narrative to put the best spin on the systems, processes, and results reported.

- Another technique is similar to that described above. However, instead of subdividing the writing team according to the Baldrige categories, the team remains together to write the entire application. In this way, the application may be more coherent and the linkages between business processes are easier to understand. This approach also helps to ensure consistency and integrity of the review processes. However, with fewer people involved, the natural "blind spots" of the team may prevent a full and accurate analysis of the management system. Finally, as with the method described above, top leaders review and scrub the written narrative.

- The third method of preparing the written narrative is the least common and involves one person writing for several days to produce the application. Considering the immense amount of knowledge and work involved, it is easy to understand why the third method is used so rarely.

With all three methods, external experts are usually involved. All four 1997 Baldrige Award recipients reported they hired consultants to help them finalize their application by sharpening its focus and clarifying linkages. In fact, the author of this book worked with two of them to do this.

Pros

- All of the Baldrige-winning organizations in 1997 reported, during the 10th Quest for Excellence Conference, that the discipline of producing a full-length written self-assessment (Baldrige application) helped them learn about their organization and identify areas for improvement before the site visit team arrived. The written narrative self-assessment process clearly helped focus leaders on their organization's strengths and areas for improvement—provided that a complete and honest assessment was made.
- All of the winners plan to use the self-assessment processes repeatedly to guide future improvement strategies.
- The written narrative self-assessment also provides rich information to help examiners conduct a site visit (the purpose of which is to verify and clarify the information contained in the written self-assessment).

Cons

- The written narrative self-assessment is extremely time and labor intensive. Organizations that use this approach for Baldrige or state applications, or for internal organizational review, report that it requires between 1,000 and 4,000 person-hours of effort—sometimes more but rarely less. People working on the self-assessment are diverted from other tasks during this period.

- Because the application is usually closely scrutinized and carefully scrubbed, and because of page limits, it may not fully and accurately describe the actual management processes and systems of the organization. Decisions based on misleading or incomplete information may take the organization down the wrong path.
- Although the written self-assessment provides information to help guide a site visit, examiners cannot determine the depth of deployment because only a few points of view are represented in the narrative.
- Finally, and perhaps most importantly, the discipline and knowledge required to write a meaningful narrative self-assessment is usually far greater than that possessed within the vast majority of organizations. Even the four 1997 Baldrige winners hired expert consultants to help them prepare and refine their written narrative.

Short Written Narrative

Two of the most significant obstacles to writing a useful full-length written narrative self-assessment are poor knowledge of the performance excellence criteria and the time required to produce a meaningful assessment. If people do not understand the criteria, it takes significantly longer to prepare a written self-assessment. In fact, the amount of time required to write an application/assessment is inversely related to the knowledge of the criteria possessed by the writers. The difficulty associated with writing a full-length narrative has prevented many organizations from participating in state, local, or school award programs.

To encourage more organizations to begin the performance improvement journey, many state award programs developed progressively higher levels of recognition, ranging from "commitment" at the low end, through "demonstrated progress," to "achieving excellence" of the top of the range. However, even with progressive levels of recognition, the obstacle of preparing a 50-page written narrative prevented many from engaging in the process. To help resolve this problem, several state programs permit applicants who seek recognition at the lower levels to submit a 7-to-20-page short written narrative self-assessment. (Most states still require applicants for the top-level award to complete a full-length written self-assessment.) The short form ranges from requiring a one-page description per category to one page per item (hence the 7-to-20-page range in length).

Pros

- It clearly takes less time to prepare the short form.
- Because of the reduced effort required to complete the self-assessment, states find more organizations are beginning the process of assessing and improving their performance.

Cons

- The short form provides significantly less information to help examiners prepare for the site visit. Although it does take less time to prepare than the full-length version, the short form still requires several hundred hours of team preparation.
- The short form is usually as closely scrutinized and carefully scrubbed as its full-length cousin. This reduces accuracy and value to both the organization and examiners.
- The knowledge required to write even a short narrative prevents organizations in the beginning stages from preparing an accurate and meaningful assessment.
- Finally, there is not enough information presented in the short form to understand the extent of deployment of the systems and processes covered by the criteria.

The Likert Scale Survey

Just about everyone is familiar with a Likert scale survey. These surveys typically ask respondents to rate, on a scale of 1 to 5, the extent to which they disagree or agree with a comment.

The following is an example of a simple Likert scale survey item:

Senior leaders effectively communicate values and customer focus.

1	2	3	4	5
Strongly Disagree				Strongly Agree

A variation on the simple Likert scale survey item has been developed in an attempt to improve consistency among respondents. Brief descriptors have been added at each level as shown below in the descriptive Likert scale survey item:

1	2	3	4	5
None	Few	Some	Many	Most

. . . Senior leaders effectively communicate values and customer focus.

Pros

- The Likert scale survey is quick and easy to administer. People from all functions and levels within the organization can provide input.

Cons

- Both the simple and the descriptive Likert scale survey items are subject to wide ranges of interpretation. One person's rating of 2 and another person's rating of 4 may actually describe the same systems or behaviors. This problem of scoring reliability raises questions about the accuracy and usefulness of both the simple and the descriptive survey techniques for conducting organizational self-assessments.

After all, a quick and easy survey that produces inaccurate data still has low value. That is the main reason why states have not adopted the Likert scale survey as a tool for conducting the self-assessments, even for organizations in the beginning stages of the quality journey.

The Behaviorally Anchored Survey

A behaviorally anchored survey contains elements of a written narrative and a survey approach to conducting a self-assessment. The method is simple. Instead of brief descriptors such as "strongly agree/strongly disagree" or "none-few-some-many-most," a more complete behavioral description is presented for each level of the survey scale. Respondents simply identify the behavioral description that most closely fits the activities in the organization. A sample follows:

	1	2	3	4	5
Reviewing Organization Performance [1.1a(2)]					
1F	The school's leaders evaluate the organization's performance against goals. This review process is not systematic and results in minimal or random adjustments.	Some of the school's leaders review performance against goals but do not systematically use the review process to reinforce directions or drive improvements.	Many of the school's leaders review performance against goals and systematically use the review process to reinforce directions and drive improvements.	Most of the school's leaders review performance against goals and systematically use the review process to reinforce directions and drive improvements.	All of the school's leaders review performance against goals and systematically use the review process to reinforce directions and drive improvements.

How is this done? (Approach) How widely is process used? (Deployment)

How should it be improved?

	1	2	3	4	5	
Leadership System Performance and Accountability [1.1a(2)]						Level
1G	*Performance* evaluations of a few leaders consider high-performance objectives, but they have not been incorporated into the formal review *process.*	*Performance* evaluations of the *leadership system* look at the effectiveness of how some leaders review school performance, but do not consider faculty and staff feedback in the evaluation.	*Performance* evaluations of the *leadership system* look at the effectiveness of how most leaders review school performance and include faculty and staff feedback (such as upward evaluation or 360-degree feedback).	*Performance* evaluations of the *leadership system* look at the effectiveness of how all leaders review school performance and include faculty and staff feedback (such as upward evaluation or 360-degree feedback). A few improvements in leader performance have been made as a result.	*Performance* evaluations of the *leadership system* look at the effectiveness of how all leaders review school performance and include faculty and staff feedback (such as upward evaluation or 360-degree feedback). Continuous improvements in leader performance are being made as a result.	

How is this done? (Approach) How widely is process used? (Deployment)

Suggested action steps to improve, if needed:

Since the behavioral descriptions in the survey combine the requirements of the criteria with the standards from the scoring guidelines, it is possible to produce accurate Baldrige-based scores for items and categories for the entire organization and for any subgroup or division.

The following tables provide sample scores for the entire organization and for two job classifications. The following chart below shows the percent scores for each item. This helps users determine at a glance the relative strengths and weaknesses.

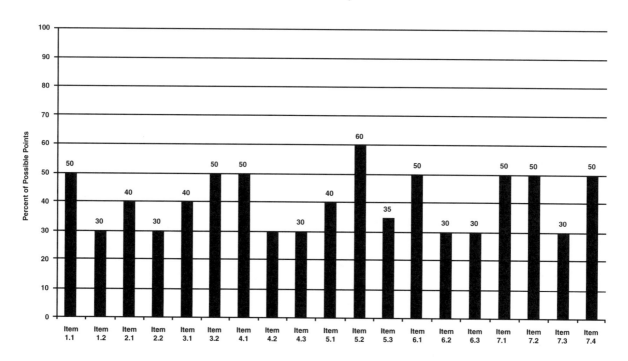

**Enterprise School
Overall Percent Scores by Item**

The following chart shows the ratings by subgroup, in this case, position of administrator or faculty/staff. On the previous graph, Item 1.1, Leadership System reflected a rating of 50 percent. However, according to the breakout below, administrators believe the processes are much stronger (over 60%) than faculty/staff do (less than 35%). This typically indicates incomplete systems development or poor deployment of existing systems and processes required by the item.

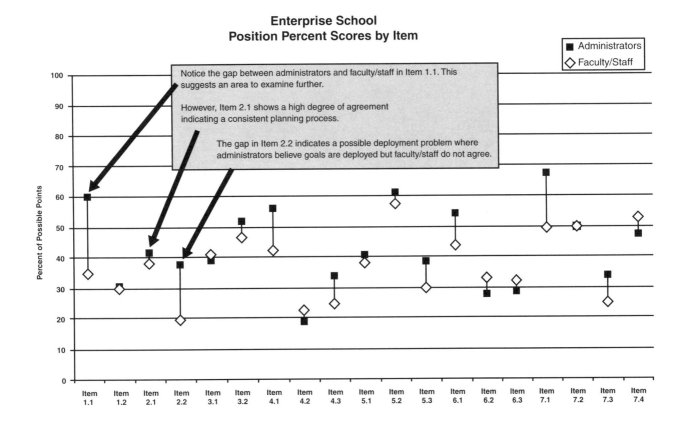

Enterprise School
Position Percent Scores by Item

The following Pareto diagram presents data reflecting the areas respondents believed were most in need of improvement. Continuing with the leadership example, it is clear that respondents believe that leaders need to do a better job of setting clear high performance expectations (Theme D), communicating vision and performance expectations (Theme E), and assessing and improving leadership performance and accountability (Theme G). This helps examiners focus on which areas in leadership may be the most important opportunities for improvement.

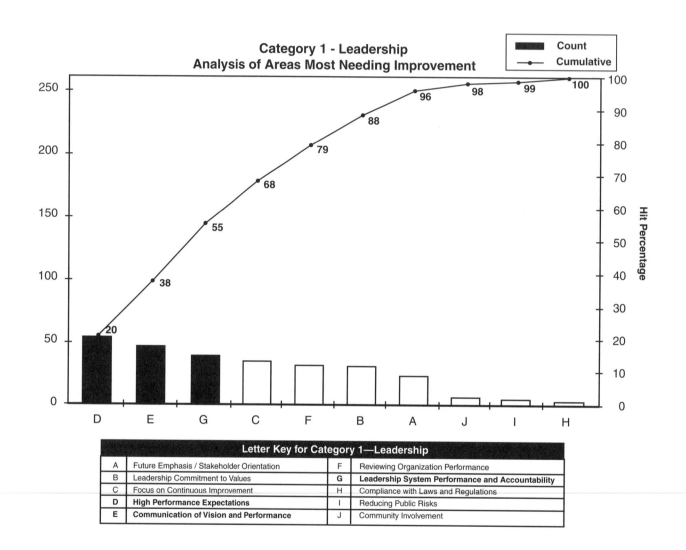

Category 1 - Leadership
Analysis of Areas Most Needing Improvement

Letter Key for Category 1—Leadership			
A	Future Emphasis / Stakeholder Orientation	F	Reviewing Organization Performance
B	Leadership Commitment to Values	G	**Leadership System Performance and Accountability**
C	Focus on Continuous Improvement	H	Compliance with Laws and Regulations
D	**High Performance Expectations**	I	Reducing Public Risks
E	**Communication of Vision and Performance**	J	Community Involvement

The following chart allows examiners to determine what type of employee (in this case administrator or faculty staff) identified the various improvement priorities. Look at "D" and "G" below and you will see that faculty/staff identified the need to improve these areas by a 3 to 1 margin. This tends to indicate a deployment gap and suggests that administrators are not perceived to be as effective as they believe.

Priority Improvement Counts and Percentages — By Position for Leadership Category

1. Leadership

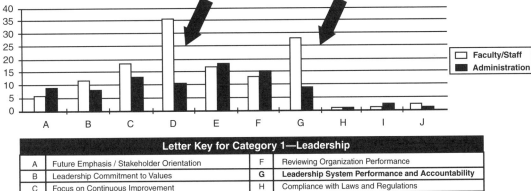

	Count												Percentage (See Chart Below)									
	A	B	C	D	E	F	G	H	I	J		Total		A	B	C	D	E	F	G	H	I	J
Faculty/Staff	6	12	19	36	16	13	28	1	1	2		100		6	12	19	36	16	13	28	1	1	2
Administration	13	12	19	15	29	23	13	1	3	2		150		9	8	13	10	19	15	9	1	2	1

Percentage of "Priority Improvement Hits"

	Letter Key for Category 1—Leadership		
A	Future Emphasis / Stakeholder Orientation	F	Reviewing Organization Performance
B	Leadership Commitment to Values	**G**	**Leadership System Performance and Accountability**
C	Focus on Continuous Improvement	H	Compliance with Laws and Regulations
D	**High Performance Expectations**	I	Reducing Public Risks
E	**Communication of Vision and Performance**	J	Community Involvement

Finally, a complete report of the comments and explanations of the respondents can be prepared and used by examiners and school leaders for improvement planning.

Pros

• Properly written behavioral anchors increase the consistency of rating. That is, one respondent's rating of 2 is likely to be the same as another respondent's rating of 2.

• Although completing a behaviorally anchored survey requires more reading than a Likert scale survey, the amount of time and cost required to complete it is still significantly less than the time and cost required to prepare even a short written narrative.

• Because it is easy and simple to use, the behaviorally anchored survey does not impose a barrier to participation as does the written narrative. States and companies who use surveys with properly written behavioral anchors find the accuracy of the assessment to be as good and in many cases better than that achieved by the narrative self-assessment, and significantly better than Likert scale assessments. By obtaining input from a cross-section of functions and levels throughout the organization, a performance profile can be developed that not only identifies strengths and areas for improvement, but deployment gaps as well—something the written narrative assessments do not effectively provide.

- For organizations doing business throughout the world, the behaviorally anchored survey—translated into the native language of respondents—permits far greater input than the written narrative.
- Finally, accurate survey data, based on behavioral anchors, can be used to compare or benchmark organizations within and among industries, and can also support longitudinal performance studies.

Cons

- Organizations with highly developed performance management systems that seek to apply for top state or national recognition may prefer to practice developing the full-length narrative self-assessment because it is usually required.
- Examiners who are comfortable with the Baldrige application review process, which requires 25 or more hours to conduct an individual review of a full-length narrative self-assessment, may initially find it disconcerting to develop comments and plan a site visit based on data gathered from a survey. Additional training of examiners is required to develop skills at using survey data to prepare feedback and plan site visits.

NOTE: The preceding sample of a behaviorally anchored self-assessment survey is administered by the National Council for Performance Excellence, Winooski, Vermont, and used with their permission. Readers may contact them by calling Wendy Steager at (802) 655-1922 or by writing to NCPE, One Main Street, Winooski, VT 05404. The Vermont Council for Quality, Minnesota Council for Quality, and Florida Sterling Award and their boards of examiners use this survey technique to assess schools, government agencies, and businesses. The behaviorally anchored survey has completely replaced the written narrative self-assessment as the application

for the Vermont Quality Award as well as the Aruba National Quality Award. Examiners successfully use survey data to plan and conduct site visits. At the same time, organization leaders use survey data for improvement planning. The Florida Sterling Award uses the behaviorally anchored survey approach for organizations in the early stages of developing performance excellence systems. Additionally, many private sector organizations are using this type of assessment for internal performance awards.

In Conclusion

- The full-length written narrative self-assessment is costly. It provides useful information both to examiners and the organizations completing it. The process of completing the written self-assessment can help more advanced organizations to focus and work together as a team.
- The usefulness of the short form written self-assessment is marginal especially for beginning organizations; little useful information is provided to examiners and managers/employees of the organization. However, because it takes less time to complete, one of the barriers to participation is lowered.
- Concerns over the accuracy and inter-rater reliability of the simple and descriptive Likert scales make their use in conducting effective organizational assessments of management systems questionable.
- The behaviorally anchored survey combines the benefits of survey speed with the accuracy and completeness of a well developed written narrative self-assessment. In addition, the behaviorally anchored survey can identify gaps in deployment unlike the written narrative self-assessment.

A complete copy of the education self-assessment survey can be obtained from the National Council for Performance Excellence, One Main Street, Winooski, VT 05404.

The Site Visit

Introduction

Many educators and educational organizations have asked about how to prepare for site visits. This section is intended to help answer those questions and prepare the educational organization for an on-site examination. It includes rules of the game for examiners and what they are taught to look for. As we all know, the best preparation for this type of examination is to see things through the eyes of the trained examiner.

Before a school can be recommended to receive the Malcolm Baldrige National Quality Award, it must receive a visit from a team of education assessment experts from the National Board of Examiners. Approximately 25 percent to 30 percent of all organizations applying for the Baldrige Award in recent years have received these site visits. This is the first year of the education award and so no previous percentages are available that isolate educational organizations.

The Baldrige Award site visit team usually includes two senior examiners—one of whom is designated as team leader—and four to seven other examiners. In addition, the team is accompanied by a representative of the National Quality Award Office and a representative of ASQ, which provides administrative services to the Baldrige Award office under contract.

The site visit team usually gathers at a hotel near the organization's central office on the Sunday morning immediately preceding the site visit. During the day, the team makes final preparations and plans for the visit.

Each team member is assigned lead responsibility for one or more categories of the award criteria. Each examiner is usually teamed with one other examiner during the site visit. These examiners usually conduct the visit in pairs to ensure the accurate recording of information.

Site visits usually begin on a Monday morning and last one week. By Wednesday or Thursday most site visit teams will have completed their on-site review. They retire to the nearby hotel to confer and write their reports. By the end of the week, the team must reach consensus on the findings and prepare a final report for the panel of judges.

Purpose of Site Visits

Site visits help clarify uncertain points and verify self-assessment (that is, application) accuracy. During the site visit, examiners investigate areas most difficult to understand from self-assessments, such as the following:
- Deployment—how widely a process is used throughout the organization
- Integration—whether processes fit together to support performance excellence
- Process ownership—whether processes are broadly owned, simply directed, or micro-managed
- Faculty and staff involvement—whether the extent to which employees' participation in managing processes of all types is optimized
- Continuous improvement maturity—the number and extent of improvement cycles and resulting refinements in all areas of the organization and at all levels

Characteristics of Site Visit Issues

Examiners look at issues that are an essential component of scoring and role model determination. They have a responsibility to
- Clarify information that is missing or vague
- Verify significant strengths identified from the self-assessment
- Verify deployment of the practices described in the self-assessment

Examiners will
- Concentrate on crosscutting issues.
- Examine data, reports, and documents.
- Interview individuals and teams.
- Receive presentations from the applicant organization.

Examiners are not permitted to conduct their own focus groups or surveys with students, parents, faculty and staff or to disrupt school processes. Conducting focus groups or surveys would violate the confidentiality agreements as well as be statistically unsound.

Typically Important Site Visit Issues

- Role of senior administration in leading and serving as a role model
- Degree of involvement and self-direction of students, faculty, and staff
- Comprehensiveness and accessibility of the information system
- Utility and validity of available data
- Extent that facts and data are used in decision making
- Degree of emphasis on student and stakeholder satisfaction
- Extent of systematic approaches to school processes
- Deployment and integration of high-performance principles and processes
- Training effectiveness

- Use of compensation, recognition, and rewards to promote key values
- Extent that strategic plans align educational work
- Extent of the use of measurable goals at all levels in the school
- Evidence of evaluation and improvement cycles in all school processes and in system effectiveness
- Improvement levels in cycle times and other operating processes
- Extent of integration of all operational and support processes
- Level of maturity of improvement initiatives
- Extent of ability to make meaningful comparisons to other schools and organizations
- Uncovering improvements since the submission of the application (self-assessment) and receiving up-to-date performance results

Discussions with the Applicant Prior to the Site Visit

Prior to the site visit, all communication between the school and its team must be routed through their respective single points of contact. Only the team leader may contact the school on behalf of the site visit team prior to the site visit. This helps ensure consistency of message and communication for both parties. It prevents confusion and misunderstandings.

The team leader should provide the school organization with basic information about the process. This includes schedules, arrival times, and equipment and meeting room needs.

Schools usually provide the following information prior to the site visit team's final site visit planning meeting at the hotel on the day before the site visit starts:
- List of key contacts
- Organization chart
- Facility layout
- Performance data requested by examiners

The team leader, on behalf of team members, will ask for supplementary documentation to be compiled (such as results data brought up to date) to avoid placing an undue burden on the school at the time of the site visit.

The site visit team will select sites that allow them to examine key issues and check deployment in key areas. This information may or may not be discussed with the school prior to the site visit. Examiners will need access to all areas of the school.

Conduct of Site Visit Team Members (Examiners)

Examiners are not allowed to discuss findings with anyone but team members. Examiners may not disclose the following to the school:

- Personal or team observations and findings
- Conclusions and decision
- Observations about the school's performance systems, either in a complimentary or critical way

Examiners may not discuss observations about other schools, or the names of other award program schools with anyone.

Examiners may not accept trinkets, gifts, or gratuities of any kind (coffee, cookies, rolls, breakfast, and lunch are okay), so schools should not offer them. At the conclusion of the site visit, examiners are not permitted to leave with any of the school's materials, including logo items or catalogs—not even items usually given to visitors. Examiners will dress in appropriate attire for the school.

Opening Meeting

An opening meeting will be scheduled to introduce all parties and set the structure for the site visit. The meeting is usually attended by senior administrators and the self-assessment writing team. The opening meeting usually is scheduled first on the initial day of the site visit (8:30 or 9:00 a.m.). The team leader generally starts the meeting, introduces the team, and opens the site visit. Overhead slides and formal presentations are usually unnecessary.

The school usually has one hour to present any information it believes important for the examiners to know. This includes time for a tour, if necessary.

Immediately after the meeting, examiners are likely to want to meet with senior leaders and those responsible for preparing sections of the self-assessment (application).

Conducting the Site Visit

The team will follow the site visit plan, subject to periodic adjustments according to its findings.

The site visit team will need a private room to conduct frequent caucuses. School representatives are not present at these caucuses. The team will also conduct evening meetings at the hotel to review the findings of the day, reach consensus, write comments, and revise the site visit report.

If, during the course of the site visit, someone from the school believes the team or any of its members are missing the point, the designated point of contact should inform the team leader or the Baldrige Award office monitor. Also, someone who believes an examiner behaved inappropriately should inform the designated point of contact, who will inform the team leader or the award office monitor.

Faculty and staff should be instructed to mark every document given to examiners with the name and work location of the person providing the document. This will ensure that it is returned to the proper person. Records should be made of all material given to team members.

School personnel may not ask examiners for opinions and advice. Examiners are not permitted to provide any information of this type during the site visit.

Team Leader's Site Visit Checklist

This checklist provides a summary of activities required of site visit team leaders.

Preparation

- Size of team and length of visit is determined, with starting and ending date and time selected.
- All team members receive copies of consensus report.
- Team is notified of starting/ending times and locations.
- Background information on new team members (if any) is received.
- Category lead and team pairing assignments are made for each team member.
- New team members complete review of narrative.
- Site visit notebooks are prepared.
- Individual team members prepare assigned site visit issues.
- Subteam members exchange site visit issues for comments.
- Revised site visit issues are received from subteams.
- Site visit issues are reviewed by Team Leader and comments sent to subteams.
- Team is asked to revise site visit themes or issues (as appropriate).

Previsit Meeting

- Examiner introductions are made.
- Site visit issues and themes are reviewed and approaches outlined.
- Sites are selected to visit and logistics reviewed.
- Specific requests for first day are listed (interviews and data).
- Caucus plans are established.

Conduct of Visit

- Conducted opening presentation.
- Followed site visit plan.
- Revised plan as required.
- Caucused frequently.
- Maintained records of findings.
- Maintained records of school documents received.
- Answered all selected site issues; developed information on site visit themes.
- Conducted closing meeting.

Site Visit Report

- Team completed site visit issues.
- Team completed item and category summary forms.
- Completed overall summary form.
- Team initiated report.
- Report copied; original given to award office representative before leaving site.
- Leader kept copy, narrative, and other notes (or a backup person has material).
- Collected and returned all material to school prior to leaving site.
- Collected all narratives, materials, and notes; sent or given to award office.

Feedback Report

- Senior examiner/feedback author collected feedback points during site visit.
- Senior examiner/feedback author reviewed feedback points with team during site visit report writing session.
- Reviewed feedback report completed before leaving site and sent to award office.

Generic Site Visit Questions

Examiners must verify or clarify the information contained in an application, whether or not the examiners have determined a process to be a strength or an area for improvement. Examiners must verify the existence of strengths as well as clarify the nature of each significant area for improvement.

Before and during the site visit review process, examiners formulate a series of questions based on the Baldrige Education Performance Excellence Criteria. Because the site visit must verify or clarify all significant aspects of the school's performance management systems against the criteria, it is possible to identify a series of generic questions that examiners are likely to ask during the site visit process. These questions are presented in the following section to help prepare applicants for the assessment process.

Category 1: Leadership

1. Describe the process your school used in developing your mission, vision, and values. To top leaders: Who was involved with that process? How do you create future opportunities for the school?
   - Please share with us the mission, vision, and values of this school.
   - What are your school's top priorities?
   - How do you ensure that all your faculty and staff know this?
   - How do you know how effective you are at communicating your commitment to the vision and values?
2. How do you, as a leader, see your role in supporting processes to ensure performance excellence?
   - How do you role model the behaviors you want your administrators and other faculty and staff to emulate?
   - What do the leaders do personally to lead this school? What do you do that visibly displays to faculty and staff throughout

the school your personal involvement and commitment to the vision and values? How do you promote improvement?
   - What percentage of your time is spent on performance review and improvement activities?
   - What is your process for evaluating the effectiveness of the leadership system? How do you include or use faculty and staff feedback in the evaluation?
   - Please identify specific examples where the senior leadership improved the leadership system as a result of these evaluations. How do administrators evaluate and improve their own personal leadership effectiveness? How is faculty and staff feedback used here?
3. What are the criteria for promoting administrators within the school?
   - How are you making administrators accountable for performance improvement, faculty and staff involvement, and student and stakeholder satisfaction objectives?
   - What measures do you personally use to track progress toward achieving the school's key educational results drivers? How often do you monitor these measures?
   - Can we see a copy of an administrator's evaluation form?
   - How have you improved the process over the years of evaluating administrators?
4. Share with us what you feel are the most important requirements of your key students and stakeholders.
   - (Pick one of the requirements.) Which department is responsible for delivering this?
   - Please show us evidence of continuous improvement within that department.
5. What is the process used to monitor the performance of your school? How does it relate to the school's strategic business plan?

- Do measurable goals exist?
- How were the goals established?
- How are they monitored? How often?
- How are they key to your students' and stakeholders' primary needs and expectations?
- What are the key success factors (or key results areas, critical success factors) for your school, and how do you use them to drive performance excellence?

6. As a responsible citizen, what is your process for contributing to and improving the environment and society?
   - What do you do to anticipate public concerns over the possible impact of your school? What are some examples? How do you measure progress?
   - What are some ways your school ensures that faculty and staff act in an ethical manner in all school-related matters and activities? How is this monitored to ensure compliance?
   - Tell me about your involvement in the community. How do you promote this involvement to the faculty and staff?
   - Do you have plans or processes in place for systematic evaluation and improvement?

Category 2: Strategic Planning

1. When was the last time the strategic plan was updated? How recent is it? Can we review a copy?
2. How did you develop this plan? What factors did you consider in the development of your strategic plan?
   - How does your strategic plan address faculty and staff capabilities?
   - What role do your students and their expectations play in the development of the strategic plan?
   - How do you identify resources needed to prepare for new opportunities and requirements?
   - What are the objectives for your school that are derived from this plan? If they

are not from the plan, where do they come from?

3. How do you plan for development, education, and training needs of the school? What are the school's faculty and staff development plans (long and short term)?
   - Summarize the school's plans related to work design, flexibility, rapid response, compensation and recognition, faculty and staff development and training, health, safety, ergonomics, special services, and faculty and staff satisfaction.
   - How do these plans optimize the use of faculty and staff?
   - How do these plans align to the strategic plan?
   - What are examples of changes based on inputs from the strategic planning in the following areas: recruitment, training, compensation, rewards, incentives, fringe benefits, and programs?

4. How do you deploy these goals, objectives, and action plans throughout the school to ensure that work is aligned and action is taken to achieve the plan?
   - How do you ensure that school, work unit, and individual goals and plans are aligned?
   - How do you ensure that partner goals are aligned with your strategic plan?

5. Please summarize your process for evaluation and improvement of the strategic planning and plan deployment processes, including the faculty and staff planning process.
   - What are examples of improvements made as a result of this evaluation process? When did they occur?

6. How is performance relative to plan tracked?

7. Who do you consider to be your top competitors, and how does your planned performance compare to theirs?
   - How do you determine who your competitors are?

8. What are your specific goals and objectives? Please provide a copy of your long-range performance projections. How did you go about establishing these projec-

tions? How do these projections compare with your competitors' projections for the same time period?

Category 3: Student and Stakeholder Focus

1. How do you know what your former, current, and future students expect of you? How does your school determine their short- and long-term requirements?
   - How do you engage students in their learning goals and activities?
   - How do you differentiate key requirements from less important requirements and prepare to meet them? How do you anticipate requirements?
   - How do you evaluate and improve processes for determining student requirements?

2. How do you provide easy access for your stakeholders to obtain information and assistance, or make complaints? What do you expect to learn from their complaints?
   - What is your process of handling student and stakeholder complaints? Do you monitor or track complaint data? What do you do with the information?
   - What percent of complaints are resolved at first contact? Describe the training you provide to student and stakeholder contact employees.
   - Describe your process for followup with stakeholders. What do you do with their feedback regarding programs and offerings? What triggers action?
   - What are the key objectives of relationships with your stakeholders? What are their needs? How were they determined? How do you know if they are being met?
   - How do you evaluate and improve the stakeholder relationship process?
   - What are some improvements you have made to the way you determine student and stakeholder requirements? How did

you decide they were important to make, and when were they made?

3. How often do senior administrators talk to students and stakeholders? What do they do with this information?

4. What are your key measures for student and stakeholder satisfaction and dissatisfaction? How do these measures provide information on likely future behavior (loyalty, enrollment, budget votes, and referrals)?
   - How do you measure student and stakeholder satisfaction and dissatisfaction? Do you measure satisfaction/dissatisfaction for all key student and stakeholder groups/segments? What are your groups or segments? How do you determine them? How do you differentiate them in regard to programs, offerings, and services you offer? What process do you use to ensure the objectivity and validity of student and stakeholder satisfaction data?
   - What do you do with the information?
   - How do you disseminate satisfaction/dissatisfaction information to your faculty and staff? What action do they take as a result?
   - How do you know appropriate action is taken?
   - How do you go about improving the way you determine student and staff satisfaction? Please provide some examples of how you have improved it over the past several years. When were the requirements made?

5. What processes do you use to build loyalty, positive referral, and lasting relationships with students and staff?
   - How do you differentiate these process according to student and stakeholder groups?

6. How do you evaluate the effectiveness of processes for building stakeholder relationships? What improvements have resulted from this evaluation? When were they made?

Category 4: Information and Analysis

1. What are the major performance indicators critical to running your school?

2. How do you determine whether the information you collect and use for decision making is complete, timely, reliable, accessible, confidential, and accurate? What is the process you use to determine the relevance of the information to school goals and action plans?
   - How do you ensure that all data collected support the management of school processes?
   - Describe how you obtain feedback from the users of the information. How is this feedback used to make improvements?

3. You have told us what your top priorities are. How do you use comparative information against these? Please describe how needs and priorities for selecting comparisons and benchmarks are determined. Share an example of the process of prioritization.
   - How do you use competitive or comparative performance data generally?
   - How are the results of your comparison efforts used to set stretch targets?
   - How are the results of your comparison efforts used to improve work processes and stimulate innovation?
   - How do you evaluate and improve your comparative and benchmarking processes?
   - Show us samples of comparative studies. Picking some at random, determine the following: Why was the area selected? How were comparison data selected and obtained? How were data in the example used?

4. Please share with us an example of analysis of information important to your students and stakeholders and your own school's success.
   - How are data analyzed to determine relationships between student and stakeholder information and academic performance, or between operational data and student or stakeholder satisfaction?
   - What data and analyses do you use to understand your faculty and staff, your students and stakeholders, and your community?
   - How widely are these analyses used for decision making? What actions are you taking to extend the analysis across all parts of the school?
   - What are you doing to improve the analysis process? What are some improvement examples? When were they made?

5. Please tell us about the process used to review progress relative to your action plans.
   - Can you show us some examples of improvements made as a result of the reviews? When were they made?
   - What measures are reviewed? How often? Who is the principal reviewer(s)?
   - How do you use the findings from the review to prioritize improvements, identify innovation opportunities, and allocate resources? Can you give us some examples? How are they deployed throughout the school?
   - What are you doing to improve the review process? Do you have examples of improvement made? What were they and when did they occur?

Category 5: Faculty and Staff Focus

1. Do faculty and staff know and understand school/department priorities? How do you determine this?
   - What do you do to ensure effective communication among faculty, staff, and departments?
   - What authority do faculty and staff have to direct their own actions and make educational decisions?
   - (To faculty and staff.) What authority do you have to make decisions about resolving problems, changing processes, and communications across departments?

- What is the process you have used to evaluate and enhance opportunities for faculty and staff to take individual initiative and demonstrate self-directed responsibility in designing and managing their work? Show examples of actions taken and improvements made. When were they made?

2. How does the school link recognition, reward, and compensation to reinforce overall school objectives for performance improvement, student learning, and faculty and staff development? Describe your approach to faculty and staff recognition and compensation. How does your compensation and recognition differ for different categories of faculty and staff?
   - (General question for faculty and staff.) Do you feel that your contributions to the school are recognized? How have you been recognized for contributing to achieving the school's action plans?
   - What specific reward and recognition programs are utilized?

3. What ongoing training is provided for your faculty and staff?
   - How is your training curriculum designed and delivered? How do you integrate faculty and staff, chair or team leaders, and administrator feedback into the design of your training program? What methods are used?
   - How does your training program impact operational performance goals? How do you know your training improves your academic results? Show examples.
   - What training and education do you provide to ensure that you meet the needs of all categories of faculty and staff? What training do new faculty and staff receive to obtain the knowledge and skills necessary for success and high performance, including leadership development of faculty and staff at all levels?
   - If applicable, how do faculty and staff in remote locations participate in training programs?
   - What is your system for improving training? Please give us some examples of improvements made and when they were made.

4. What are your targets or measures for employee health and safety? Does your approach to health and safety address the needs of all faculty and staff groups?
   - How do you determine that you have a safe and healthy work environment? How do you measure this?
   - How are you performing against those measures?
   - What are your procedures for systematic evaluation and improvement?

5. How do your senior administrators, chairs, team leaders, and supervisors encourage faculty and staff to develop and put to use their full potential?

6. How is faculty and staff satisfaction measured? What do you do with the information?
   - What are the key areas of concern? What do you do to improve faculty and staff satisfaction systematically? Please give us some examples of improvements. To faculty and staff: What does the school do to enhance your career development?
   - What special services, facilities, activities, and opportunities does your school provide faculty and staff?

Category 6: Educational and Support Process Management

1. What is your process for designing new educational programs and offerings to ensure that student and stakeholder requirements are met?
   - How do partners, students and stakeholders, and support organizations participate in the design process?
   - How are design changes handled and methods used to ensure that all changes are included?
   - How do you ensure that faculty is properly prepared before new programs and offerings are introduced?

- How do you evaluate and improve the process for designing new programs and offerings? Please provide some examples of improvements and when they were made.

2. How do you know that your ongoing programs and offerings are meeting design requirements? What observations, indicators, and performance measures are used and who uses them?
   - What steps have you taken to improve the effectiveness/efficiency of key school delivery processes?
   - What are the processes by which you deliver these programs and offerings to ensure that student and stakeholder expectations will be met or exceeded?
   - Once you determine that a process may not be meeting measurement goals or performing according to expectations, what process do you use to determine root cause and to bring about process improvement?

3. Please give an example of how an observation of a student or stakeholder request or complaint resulted in an improvement of a current process or the establishment of a new process.

4. Please share with us your list of key support processes, requirements, and associated process measures, including in-process measures.
   - How is performance of support services systematically evaluated and refined? Please provide some examples and when they occurred.
   - What are the steps you have taken to design your key support processes? How do you determine the types of services needed? How do your support services interact with and add value to your educational design and delivery processes?
   - How does your school maintain the performance of key support services? Share some examples of processes used to determine root causes of support problems and how you prevent recurrence of problems.

5. Who are your most important (key) suppliers?
   - How do you determine critical characteristics your key suppliers (such as in food service) must meet so that your needs are met? What are the key performance requirements? What type of assistance do you provide your suppliers to help them meet your requirements? Please explain how you measure your supplier's performance and provide feedback.

Category 7: School Performance Results

1. What are the student performance trends and performance levels at this time?
   - Please show a breakout of data by student groups.
   - How do these trends compare with comparable schools or selected student populations?

2. What are the student and stakeholder satisfaction trends and performance levels at this time? [Links to Item 3.2]
   - Please show a breakout of data by student and stakeholder group or segment.
   - How do these student and stakeholder satisfaction trends and levels compare with those of comparable schools or similar educational providers?

3. What are the current levels and trends showing the effectiveness of your faculty and staff practices? [Links to Category 5]
   - Please provide data on key indicators such as safety/accident record, absenteeism, turnover by category and type of faculty/staff and administrator, grievances, and related litigation.
   - How do these trends compare with those of comparable schools or similar providers?

4. How do you measure results that contribute to enhanced learning?
   - Please show us your performance data from your design and delivery processes, regulatory requirements, and any cost-effectiveness measures.

- How do you know which factors are most important to your students and stakeholders? [Links to Item 3.1]
- How does your performance on these key indicators compare to comparable schools or other educational providers?

5. How do you measure support service effectiveness and efficiency? [Links to Item 6.2]
   - Please show us your performance data.
   - How do you know what the key performance indicators should be?
   - How does your performance on these key indicators compare to comparable schools or other educational providers?

General Cross-Cutting Questions Examiners Are Likely To Ask Faculty, Staff, and Administrators

- Who are your key stakeholders?
- What are the school's mission, vision, and values? What are your goals?
- What is the strategic plan for the school? What are the school's goals, and what role do you play in helping to achieve the goals?
- What kind of training do you receive? Is it useful?
- How are you involved in the work and decision making of the school?
- Is this a good place to work? Why or why not?
- What activities are recognized or rewarded?

Summary of Eligibility Categories and Restrictions

This category is open to for-profit and not-for-profit public, private, and government institutions that provide education services in the United States and its territories. Eligible organizations include elementary and secondary schools and school districts; colleges, universities, and university systems; schools or colleges within universities; professional schools; community colleges; and technical schools.

Departments within schools or colleges are ineligible. In addition, subunits providing education support functions are not eligible, including academic resource and development centers, student advising units, counseling units, food services, health services, housing, libraries, safety, information technology resources, human resources, public relations, and purchasing.

Fees

Eligibility: $100
Application
- All not-for-profit institutions: $300
- For-profit institutions with more than 500 employees: $4,500
- For-profit institutions with 500 or fewer employees: $1,500

Multiple-Application Restrictions

A subunit and its parent may not both apply for awards in the same year; only one subunit of an educational institution may apply for an award in the same year in the same eligibility category. A subunit applicant must be self-sufficient in all seven categories and must have a clear definition of the organization to apply. Subunits must be discreet from the parent organization.

Site Visit Review Fees

Site visit review fees will be set when the visits are scheduled. Fees depend upon the number of examiners assigned and the duration of the visit.

Site visit fees cover all expenses and travel costs associated with site visit participation and development of site visit reports. These fees are paid only by those applicants reaching the site visit stage.

Feedback

All applicants receive a feedback report. The feedback report—a tool for continuous improvement—is an assessment written by a team of leading U.S. educational quality and performance experts.

Applicants receive a specific listing of strengths and areas for improvement based on the Baldrige Award criteria. It is used by organizations as part of their strategic planning processes to focus on their customers and to improve productivity.

The report does not provide suggestions or ideas on how to improve.

The feedback report contains the Baldrige Award evaluation team's response to the written application. Length varies according to the detail presented in the written responses to the Baldrige Award criteria. The report includes the following components:

- Background
- Application review process
- Scoring
- Distribution of numerical scores for all applicants
- Overall scoring summary of applicant
- Criteria category scoring summary of applicant
- Details of the applicant's strengths and areas for improvement (Feedback reports often contain more than 150 strengths and areas for improvement.)

Strict confidentiality is observed at all times and in every aspect of application review and feedback.

A survey of recent Baldrige Award applicants conducted by the National Quality Award Office showed that more than 90 percent of respondents used the feedback report in their strategic and business planning processes.

Information about current and past winners and their achievements was drawn from the award office web page. General information on the National Institute of Standards and Technology is available on the World Wide Web at *http://www.nist.gov* and on the Baldrige Award program at *http://www.quality.nist.gov*

State Award Recipients of Educational Excellence Awards

Most states (over 85 percent) have quality or performance awards that recognize performance excellence at different levels. Most recognize education performance as part of the award. The few states that do not are beginning to define criteria for this year. Therefore, we have included all states with Baldrige-based awards and information about any education recipients with which we were provided. Because many states offer progressive or tiered awards that recognize different levels of achievement, we have noted the levels of awards for each state.

Alabama

Contact: Linda Vincent
Telephone: (205) 348-8994
E-mail: Linda@proctr.oba.us.edu
Alabama Quality Award
Award Levels:
Education Recipient

1998 Winner
Mountain Brook City Schools
Dr. Tim Norris, Personnel Director
Mountain City Schools
P. O. Box 130040
Mountain Brook, AL 35213-0040
Telephone: (205) 871-4608
Fax: (205) 877-8303

Arizona

Contact: Dale Parvey
Telephone: (602) 481-3454
E-mail: aqa@tqm.com
Arizona's Pioneer and Governor's Award for
    Quality

Award Levels:
    Pioneer Award
    Governor's Award for Quality

1993 Pioneer Award
Rio Salado Community College

1998 Pioneer Award
Arizona had three Pioneer Award winners for
    1998. They are:

Cyprus Miami Mining Corporation
Richard Dana
P. O. Box 4444
Claypool, AZ 85532
Voice: (520) 473-7214
Fax: (520) 473-7339

Arizona Department of Economic Security
Gloria Diaz
1140 E. Washington
Phoenix, AZ 85034
Voice: (602) 229-2800
Fax: (602) 254-9378

University of Phoenix—Phoenix Campus
Richard Wagner
4605 E. Elwood Street, Ste 445
Phoenix, AZ 85040
Voice: (602) 557-2237
Fax: (602) 929-7414
E-mail: rpwagner@apollogrp.edu

Arkansas

Contact: Barbara Harvel
Telephone: (501) 373-1300
Arkansas Quality Award

Award Levels:
  Quality Interest
  Quality Achievement

1995 Quality Achievement Award
Westark Community College, Business and
  Industrial Institute

California

Contact: Barbara Blalock
Telephone: (510) 210-9766
E-mail: calqed@dnai.com
California Governor's Quality Award
Award Levels:
  Commitment
  Achievement
  Excellence

1995 Eureka Award—Bronze
Marvin Avenue School

California

Contact: Thomas D. Hinton
Telephone: (619) 656-4200
E-mail: ccqs@swmall.com
California Quality Awards
Award Levels:
  Gold
  Silver
  Bronze

Colorado

Contact: Carol Odell
Telephone: (719) 636-5076 x101
E-mail: ppbbb@bbbnet.org
Excellence in Customer Service

1995 Winner—Customer Service
Colorado Technical University

Connecticut

Contact: Brian Will
Telephone: (860) 872-4891

E-mail: brianrwill@aol.com
Connecticut Award for Excellence
Award Levels:
  Nutmeg
  Charter Oak
  Genius (top level)

1996 Nutmeg
Regional School District No. 14—
  Woodbury/Bethlehem
Joseph Sabetella, Superintendent of Schools
Woodbury, CT 06798
Telephone: (203) 263-4339

1996 Nutmeg
Litchfield Center and Elementary Schools,
  Grades K–6
Ann Mirizzi, Principal, Litchfield
  Intermediate School
Andrienne Longobucco, Principal, Litchfield
  Center School
Litchfield, CT 06749
Telephone: (860) 567-7520

Connecticut

Contact: Sheila Carmine
Telephone: (203) 322-9534
E-mail: Cqia@aol.com
Connecticut Quality Improvement Award
Award Levels:
  Entry Level—Connecticut Innovation Prize
  Mid-Level—Connecticut Small Organization
    Component Quality Award
  Connecticut Quality Improvement Award

Delaware

Contact: Zena Tucker
Telephone: (302) 739-4271
Delaware Quality Award
Award Levels:
  The OQA Award
  Award of Merit

1995 Award Of Merit
New Castle County Vocational Technical
   School District
Dr. Donald C. James
Director, Pupil Services/Quality Management
1417 Newport Road
Wilmington, DE 19807
Voice: (302) 995-8030
Fax: (312) 995-8196

Florida

Contact: John Pieno
Telephone: (904) 922-5316
Governor's Sterling Award
Award Levels:
   Governor's Sterling Award
   Sterling Quality Achievement Recognition

1993
Pinellas County Schools
Dr. J. Howard Hinesley, Superintendent
Telephone: (727) 588-6295

1998
Marjorie Kinnan Rawlings Elementary
   School
Shirley Lorenzo, Principal
Telephone: (813) 547-7828

Georgia

Contact: Victoria Taylor
Telephone: (404) 651-8405
Georgia Oglethorpe Award Process

Hawaii

Contact: Norm Baker
Telephone: (808) 545-4394
E-mail: chamber@hula.net
The Hawaii State Award of Excellence
Award Levels:
   Gold
   Red
   Purple
   White

Idaho

Contact: Tom Foster
Telephone: (208) 385-4367
E-mail: risforster@cobfac.idbsu.edu
Idaho Quality Award
Award Levels:
   Idaho Quality Award (Baldrige-based)
   Recognition level

Illinois

Contact: Frederick G. Coggin
Telephone: (312) 258-5185
Lincoln Awards for Excellence
Award Levels:
   Commitment to Excellence
   Progress Toward Excellence
   Achievement of Excellence

1996
Dr. Julio A. Rivera
Charles G. Hammond Elementary School
2819 West 21st Place
Chicago, IL 60623
Telephone: (773) 535-4580
Fax: (773) 535-4579

1996
Dr. Normand R. Wentzel
Community Unit School District #300
300 Cleveland Avenue
Carpentersville, IL 60110
Telephone: (847) 426-1300 ext. 306
Fax: (847) 426-1209

1996
Mr. Bruce E. Andersen
Davea Career Center
301 South Swift Road
Addison, IL 60101-1499
Telephone: (630) 691-7591
Fax: (630) 691-7596

1996

Dr. Linda Helton
Lake Country High Schools, Technology
   Campus
19525 West Washington
Grayslake, IL 60030
Telephone: (847) 223-5989
Fax: (847) 223-7363

1996

Ms. Ann Elizabeth Shorey
Louisa May Alcott Elementary School
2625 North Orchard Street
Chicago, IL 60614
Telephone: (773) 534-5460
Fax: (773) 534-5789

1996

Mr. Raymond Buniak
Thomas Kelly High School
4136 South California
Chicago, IL 60632
Telephone: (773) 535-4900
Fax: (773) 535-4841

1996

Dr. David VanWinkle
Valley View Community Unit School District
   #364-U
755 Luther Drive
Romeoville, IL 60446
Telephone: (815) 886-7246
Fax: (815) 886-7294

1996

Dr. Kenneth B. Allen
Waubonsee Community College
Route 47 at Harter Road
Sugar Grove, IL 60554
Telephone: (630) 466-7900
Fax: (630) 466-9406

1997

Mr. Philip Hunsberger
Community Unity School District #5
410 East LeFevre Road

Sterling, IL 61081
Telephone: (815) 626-5050
Fax: (815) 622-4111

1997

Dr. John Conyers
Community Consolidated School District #15
580 North First Bank Drive
Palatine, IL 60067
Telephone: (847) 934-2809
Fax: (847) 934-2719

1997

Dr. Donald E. Weber
Naperville Community Unit School District
   #203
203 West Hillside Road
Naperville, IL 60540
Telephone: (630) 420- 6311
Fax: (630) 420-1066

1998

Dr. Joseph Dockery-Jackson
Black Hawk College
6600 34th Avenue
Moline, IL 61265
Telephone: (309) 796-1311 Ext. 13587
Fax: (309) 792-5976

1998

Dr. Robert M. Karp
Highland Community College
2998 West Pearl City Road
Freeport, IL 61032
Telephone: (815) 235-6121 Ext. 374
Fax: (815) 235-6130

1998

Dr. Susan Scribner
McKendree College
701 College Road
Lebanon, IL 62254
Telephone: (618) 537-6860
Fax: (618) 537-6417

Indiana

Contact: Chairman
Telephone: (317) 635-3058 ext. 246
E-mail: qualityaward@bmtadvantage.org
State of Indiana Quality Improvement Award

Kansas

Contact: Elaine Hanna
Telephone: (316) 978-3376
Kansas Award for Excellence
Award Levels:
Level 1—Commitment to Excellence Award
Level 2—Performance in Quality Award
Level 3—Kansas Excellence Award

Kentucky

Contact: Joe Walters
Telephone: (606) 255-9458
E-mail: jwalters@tank.rgs.uky.edu
Commonwealth of Kentucky Quality Award
Award Levels:
Level 1—Quality Interest
Level 2—Quality Commitment
Level 3—Quality Achievement
Level 4—Governor's Gold Quality Award

Louisiana

Contact: Corinne Dupui
Telephone: (318) 482-6422
Louisiana Quality Award
Award Levels: two

Maine

Contact: Andrea Jandebeur
Telephone: (207) 621-1988
E-mail: mqc@maine-Quality.org
Award Levels:
Level 1—Commitment
Level 2—Progress
Level 3—Excellence

Gardner Regional Middle School
Contact: Arthur Warren
Telephone: (207) 582-1326

Maryland

Contact: Amit Gupta
Telephone: (301) 405-7099
Maryland Quality Award
Award Levels:
Gold
Silver
Bronze
Certificate of recognition

Maryland

Contact: Tina Romanowski
Telephone: (410) 767-4687
E-mail: cromanow@dbm.state.md.us
Governor's Quality Awards
Award Levels:
Level 1—Quality Excellence (Gold)
Level 2—Quality Achievement (Silver)
Level 3—Quality Commitment (Bronze)
Level 4—Quality Interest

Massachusetts

Contact: Jerold Christen
Telephone: (317) 275-1200
E-mail: jerryc@tiac.net
Massachusetts Quality Award
Award Levels:
Level 1—Self-Assessment
Level 2—Examiner Assessment
Level 3—State Quality Award

Michigan

Contact: William Kalmar
Telephone: (248) 370-4552
Michigan Quality Leadership Award
Award Levels:
Michigan Quality Leadership Award
Honor roll

1995 Silver
Whitehall Shoreline Elementary School

Michigan

Contact: Gayle Miller
Telephone: (616) 728-4642
Muskegon Quality Award
Award Levels:
   Gold
   Silver
   Bronze

1995 Gold
Muskegon Community College

Minnesota

Contact: Patricia Fryer-Billings
Telephone: (612) 851-3181
E-mail: quality@gold.tc.umn.edu
Minnesota Quality Award
Award Levels:
   Bronze (Commitment)
   Silver (Proficiency
   Gold (Mastery)
   Crystal (Excellence)

1996 Education Gold
Alexandria Technical College

Larry Shellito, President
1601 Jefferson Street
Alexandria, MN 56308
Telephone: (320) 762-0221
Fax: (320) 762-4501

David Trites, TQM Coordinator
Alexandria Technical College
1601 Jefferson Street
Alexandria, MN 56308
Telephone: (320) 762-4415
Fax: (320) 762-4421

1997 Education Silver
Eden Prairie Schools, District #272

William Gaslin, Superintendent
8100 School Road
Eden Prairie, MN 55344-2292
Telephone: (612) 975-7010
Fax: (612) 975-7012

Mary Bollinger
Executive Director of Human Resources
8100 School Road
Eden Prairie, MN 55344-2292
Telephone: (612) 975-7101
Fax: (612) 975-7112

1996 Education Silver
Rochester Community and Technical College

Don Supalla, Dean of Student Affairs
851 Southeast 30th Avenue
Rochester, MN 55904-4999
Telephone: (507) 280-3133
Fax: (507) 280-3180

Dave Weber, Director of Communications
851 Southeast 30th Avenue
Rochester, MN 55904-4999
Telephone: (507) 285-7217
Fax: (507) 280-3531

1998 Education Bronze
University of Minnesota, Duluth
Academic Services and Student Life

Mississippi

Contact: Duane Hamill
Telephone: (601) 982-6349
E-mail: dhamill@sbcjc.cc.ms.us
Mississippi Quality Award
Award Levels:
   Quality Interest
   Quality Commitment
   The Excellence Award
   Governor's Quality Award

1995 Quality Interest
Itawamba Community College (Tupelo
   Campus)

Missouri

Contact: John Politi
Telephone: (573) 526-1725
E-mail: jpoliti@mail.state.mo.us
Missouri Quality Award
Award Levels: One level with a best practices
   award built into the process

1995 Winner
University of Missouri-Rolla

1998 Winner
Missouri School for the Blind
Dr. Yvonne Howze, Superintendent
3815 Magnolia
St. Louis, MO 63110
Fax: (314) 772-1561
E-mail: Yhowze@msb.k12.mo.us

Nebraska

Contact: Jack Ruff
Telephone: (402) 471-4167
E-mail: jruff@ded1.ded.state.ne.us
The Edgerton Quality Award
Award Levels:
   Edgerton Award of Commitment
   Edgerton Award of Progress
   Edgerton Award of Excellence

New Hampshire

Contact: Tom Raffio
Telephone: (603) 223-1312
E-mail: tomraffio@nedelta.com
Granite State Quality Award
Award Levels:
   Granite State Quality Award
   Category Awards in each of seven categories

New Jersey

Contact: Richard Serfass
Telephone: (609) 777-0940
Fax: (609) 777-2798
E-mail: rserfass@recom.com
New Jersey Quality Achievement Award

Award Levels:
   Quality Discoverer
   Quality Explorer
   Areas of Excellence Awards
   NJ Quality Achievement

Hunterdon Central Regional High School
Ray Farley, Superintendent
Route 31
Flemington, NJ 08822
Telephone: (908) 284-7135
E-mail:
   farley@star.hcrhs.hunterdon.k12.nj.us

New Mexico

Contact: Julia Gabaldon
Telephone: (505) 262-7955
E-mail: qnm@quality-newmexico.org
New Mexico Quality Awards
Award Levels:
   Pinon (Commitment)
   Roadrunner (Progress)
   Zia (Excellence)

1995 Pinon
Del Norte High School

1995 Pinon
Dona Ann Branch Community College

1995 Pinon
Juan de Onate Elementary School

1995 Pinon
New Mexico State University, Business
   Admin. & Economics

1995 Pinon
Petroglyph Elementary School

1995 Pinon
Western New Mexico University

1994 Pinon
Grants Cibola Co. Schools
Mt. Taylor Elementary School

1994 Pinon
Del North High School

1994 Pinon
Western NM University

1994 Pinon
Luna Vocational Technical Inst.

1994 Roadrunner
San Juan College

New York

Contact: Barbara Harms
Telephone: (518) 482-1747
The Governor's Award for Excellence
Award Levels:
    The Governor's Award for Excellence—New
    York State's highest level of recognition
    for quality
    The ESA Program—Empire State Gold
    Registration/Certification
    Empire State Silver Registration/Certification

1996 Governor's Excelsior Award
Pittsford Central Schools
Dr. John O'Rourke, Superintendent
Pittsford Central Schools
42 West Jefferson Road
Pittsford, New York 14534
Telephone: (716) 218-1000

1995 Governor's Excelsior Award
Sewanhaka Central High School District
Contact: Dr. George Goldstein,
    Superintendent
555 Ridge Road
Elmont, NY 11003
Telephone: (516) 488-9800

1994 Governor's Excelsior Award
Pearl River School District
Contact: Dr. Richard E. Mauer,
    Superintendent
275 East Central Avenue
Pearl River, NY 10965
Telephone: (914) 620-3900

1992 Governor's Excelsior Award
Kenmore Town of Tonawanda Union Free
    School District
Contact: David Paciencia, Superintendent
1500 Colvin Blvd.
Buffalo, NY 14223
Telephone: (716) 874-8400

Winner
St. Elizabeth Hospital

North Carolina

Contact: Mette Leather
Telephone: (800) 207-5485
E-mail: ncqlf@aol.com; drpmbl@aol.com
North Carolina Quality Leadership Award
Award Levels:
    North Carolina Quality Leadership Award
    North Carolina Quality Advancement Award
    North Carolina Quality Commitment Award

1998 Advanced
Wake County Public School System
Toni Patterson
P. O. Box 28041
Raleigh, NC 27611
Telephone: (919) 501-7935
Fax: (919) 850-8953

1998 Commitment
Craven County Schools
Janet Furman, Director of Guidance/
    Communication
3600 Trent Road
New Bern, NC 28562
Telephone: (919) 514-6333
Fax: (919) 514-6351

1997 Honor Roll
New Hanover County Schools
Dianne Avery, Community Relations Director
1802 S. 15th Street
Wilmington, NC 28401
Telephone: (910) 254-4222
Fax: (910) 251-6079 Fax

Ohio

Contact: Charlene Marbury
Telephone: (937) 267-3925
E-mail: marbury,char@dayton.va.gov
Dayton Area Excellence Award
Award Levels:
    Team Excellence Achievement Award
    Serious Commitment
    Exemplary Progress
    Significant Achievement
    Dayton Area Excellence Award

1995 Serious Commitment
Miami-Jackobs College

Oklahoma

Contact: Mike Strong
Telephone: (405) 815-5295
E-mail: mike_strong@odoc.state.ok.us
Oklahoma Quality Award
Award Levels: three

Oregon

Contact: Carolyn Mark
Telephone: (503) 725-2804
E-mail: cmark@oqi.org
Oregon Quality Award
Award Levels:
    Certificate of Quality Commitment
    Certificate of Quality Achievement
    Oregon Quality Award
    Governor's Trophy

1996
Certificate of Achievement
Mountain View High School
Ed Tillinghast, Principal
2755 NE 27th Street
Bend, OR 97001
Telephone: (541) 383-6360
Fax: (541) 383-6469

Pennsylvania

Contact: Tony Tlush
Telephone: (610) 758-4596
E-mail: tony@net.bfp.org
Lehigh Valley Community Quality Award
Award Levels:
    Highest Achievement
    Significant Progress
    Serious Commitment

Pennsylvania

Contact: Betty Rose
Telephone: (717) 397-3531
E-mail: http://www.brose@1cci.com
Lancaster Chamber Business Excellence Award
Award Levels:
    Excellence
    Leadership
    Achievement
    Commitment

Pennsylvania

Contact: Michael Ricci
Telephone: (814) 452-3793
Tri-State Regional Quality Award

Pennsylvania

Contact: Robert Graham
Telephone: (412) 392-4512
Greater Pittsburgh Total Quality Award
Award Levels:
    Highest Achievement
    Significant Progress
    Serious Commitment

1992 Highest Achievement
Millcreek Township School District

1991 Significant Progress
Millcreek Township School District

1990 Significant Progress
Millcreek Township School District

Rhode Island

Contact: Lynne Couture
Telephone: (401) 454-3030
E-mail: race@pcix.com
RI Award for Competitiveness & Excellence
Award Levels:
    Bronze—Competitiveness Commitment
      Award
    Silver—Competitiveness Achievement Award
    Gold—RI Award for Competitiveness and
      Excellence

1995 Winner
*Cranston Area Career & Technical Center,
Cranston*

1994 Winner
Community Prep, Providence

1994 Winner
Narragansett School System, Narragansett

South Carolina

Contact: Jeanette Reeves
Telephone: (864) 503-5990
South Carolina Governor's Quality Award
Award Levels:
    Achiever's Award—Significant Progress
    Governor's Quality Award—Exemplary
      Quality Progress in Quality Management

Tennessee

Contact: Marie Williams
Telephone: (800) 453-6474
E-mail: tqa@bellsouth.net
Award Levels:
    Quality Interest
    Quality Commitment
    Quality Achievement
    Governor's Award

1995 Quality Commitment
King College

1995 Quality Commitment
ETSU—College of Applied Science & Tech.

1995 Quality Commitment
Roane State Community College

1995 Quality Commitment
Walters State Community College

1993 Quality Achievement
Belmont University

Tennessee

Contact: James Lippy
Telephone: (901) 383-4611
E-mail: jlippy@stim.tec.tn.us
Greater Memphis Association for Quality
Award Levels:
    Quality Commitment
    Quality Progress
    Quality Leadership
    Greater Memphis Award for Quality

Texas

Contact: Jim Nelson
Telephone: (512) 322-5603
E-mail: jnelson@austin-chamber.org
Greater Austin Quality Award
Award Level:
    Level 1
    Level 2
    Level 3
    Level 4

1995 Commitment
Pease Elementary School

1995 Commitment
Reading is FUNdamental

1995 Progress
Barrington Elementary School

1994 Progress
University of Texas

1994 Commitment
University of Texas

1994 Commitment
Friends of Reading is FUNdamental

1994 Progress
Ortega Elementary

1994 Progress
Johnson High School

1994 Commitment
Eancs, Independent School District

Texas

Contact: Jay Simons
Telephone: (806) 622-4213
E-mail: simons@arn.net
Northwest Texas Quality Award

Texas

Contact: Jim Carmichael
Telephone: (512) 477-8137
E-mail: qualtex@swbell.net
Texas Quality Award
Award Level:
    Level 1
    Level 2
    Level 3

1998
Texas Quality Award
Brazosport Independent School District
Dr. Gerald E. Anderson, Superintendent
Mr. Mike Abild, Director of Business
    Services, primary contact
P. O. Drawer Z
Freeport, TX 77541
Telephone: (409) 265-6181
Fax: (409) 265-6802

1998
Texas Education Role Model
Amarillo Independent School District
Mr. Bob Morre, Superintendent

Dr. Gary Angell, Exec. Director of Student
    Performance, primary contact
7200 Interstate 40 West
Amarillo, TX 79106-2598
Telephone: (806) 354-4300
Fax: (806) 354-4282

1998
Texas Education Role Model
Cypress Faribanks Independent School
    District
Mr. Richard Berry, Superintendent
Ms. Susan Cory, Coordinator of Continuous
    Improvement, primary contact
P. O. Box 692003
Houston, TX 77269-2003
Telephone: (281) 897-4077
Fax: (281) 897-4149

1998
Rio Vista Independent School District
Dr. Sharron Miles, Superintendent
P. O. Box 369
Rio Vista, TX 76093
Telephone: (817) 373-2241 ext. 222

Utah

Contact: Conroy Whipple
Telephone: (801) 538-3067
E-mail: pedhrm.cwhipple@state.ut.us
Utah Quality Awards
Award Levels:
    Governor's Quality Award
    Quality Progress Award
    Quality Improvement Award

Vermont

Contact: Anne O'Brien
Telephone: (802) 655-1910
E-mail: \vcqual@aol.com
Vermont Performance Excellence Awards
Award Levels:
    Commitment
    Achievement
    Governor's Award for Excellence

Virginia

Contact: Jyl K. Smithson
Telephone: (540) 231-3144
E-mail: JYSLR@vt.edu
U.S. Senate Productivity and Quality Award for
  Virginia
Award Levels:
  Medallion of Excellence
  Plaque for Outstanding Achievement
  Certificate for Significant Achievement
  Award for Continuing Excellence

1995 Winner
Danville Public Schools, Danville

1993 Winner
Danville Public Schools, Danville

1993 Finalist
Portsmouth Public Schools, Portsmouth

Washington

Contact: Michael Tracy
Telephone: (509) 575-1140
E-mail: YCDA@wolfenet.com
New Vision's Quality Recognition Award for
  Yakima County

Washington

Contact: Rocky Blue
Telephone: (206) 575-3840
E-mail: rdacqa@serv.com
Washington State Quality Award
Award Levels:
  Winner
  Achievement

Wyoming

Contact: Jere Hawn
Telephone: (307) 777-7133
E-mail: Wsqa@missc.state.wy.us
Wyoming State Quality Award
Award Levels:
  Certificate
  Amethyst Award
  Sapphire Award
  Ruby Award
  Jade Award
  Diamond Award

Glossary

Action Plans

Principal school-level drivers, derived from short- and long-term strategic planning. In simplest terms, action plans are set to accomplish those things the school must do well for its strategy to succeed. Action plan development represents the critical stage in planning when general strategies and goals are made specific so that effective schoolwide understanding and deployment are possible. Deployment of action plans requires analysis of overall resource needs and creation of aligned measures for all work units. Deployment might also require specialized training for some employees or recruitment of personnel.

An example of an action plan element for a technical school in a highly competitive industry might be to develop and maintain a price leadership position. Deployment should entail design of efficient processes, analysis of resource and asset use, and creation of related measures of resource and asset productivity, aligned for the school as a whole. It might also involve use of a cost-accounting system that provides activity-level cost information to support day-to-day work. Unit and/or team training should include priority setting based on costs and benefits. School-level analysis and review should emphasize overall productivity growth. Ongoing competitive analysis and planning should remain sensitive to technological and other changes that might greatly reduce operating costs for the school or competing educational institutions.

Alignment

Consistency of plans, processes, actions, information, and decisions among school units in support of key school-wide goals.

Effective alignment requires common understanding of purposes and goals and use of complementary measures and information to enable planning, tracking, analysis, and improvement at at least three levels: the school level, key process level (e.g. design, delivery, or support), and the work unit level (e.g. department or classroom).

Benchmarking

The part of an improvement process in which a school compares its performance against that of other schools, determines how those schools achieved higher performance levels, and uses the information to improve its own performance. Although it is difficult to benchmark some processes directly in some education organizations, many of the things one school does are very similar to things that others do. For example, most schools conduct classes, move information, pay people, train them, appraise their performance, and more. A key to successful benchmarking is to identify the process elements of work and find others who are the best at that process.

Continuous Improvement

The ongoing improvement of educational offerings, programs, services, or processes by small increments or major breakthroughs.

Customer

An organization or person who receives or uses a product or service. The customer may be a member or part of another school or the same school, or the community (taxpayers). Examples of customers may include second-grade teachers for first-grade students, students for feedback on assignments or food in the cafeteria, and parents for reports about their children's progress.

Cycle Time

Cycle time refers to time performance—the time required to fulfill commitments or complete tasks.

Data

Numerical information used as a basis for reasoning, discussion, determining status, decision making, and analysis.

Effectiveness

The extent to which a work process produces intended results.

Efficiency

The effort or resources required to produce desired results. More efficient processes require fewer resources than do less efficient processes.

Faculty and Staff Involvement

A practice within a school whereby faculty and staff regularly participate in making decisions on how their work is done, including making suggestions for improvement, planning, goal setting, and monitoring performance.

High-Performance Work

High-performance work, a term used in the item descriptions and comments, refers to work approaches systematically pursuing ever higher levels of overall performance, including quality and productivity.

Approaches to high-performance work vary in form, function, and incentive systems. Effective approaches generally include cooperation between administration, faculty, and staff including workforce bargaining units; cooperation among work units and departments often involving teams; self-directed responsibility (sometimes called empowerment); individual and organizational skill building and learning; flexibility in job design and work assignments; an organizational structure with minimum layering (flattened), decentralized decision making where decisions are made closest to the front line/classroom; and effective use of performance measures, including comparisons. Some high-performance work systems use monetary and nonmonetary incentives based on factors such as school performance, team and/or individual contributions, and skill building. Also, some high-performance work approaches attempt to align the design of schools, work, jobs, and incentives.

Integrated

Refers to the interconnections between the processes of a management system. For example, to satisfy students and stakeholders a school must understand their needs, convert those needs into designs, produce the offering or service required, deliver it, assess ongoing satisfaction, and adjust the processes accordingly. People need to be trained or hired to do the work, and data must be collected to monitor progress. Performing only a part of the required activities is disjointed and not integrated.

Inter-rater reliability

The degree to which multiple raters, observing the same phenomenon, will give it the same rating. If they do, it has high inter-rate reliability; if not, it has low inter-rate reliability.

Leadership System

Leadership system refers to how leadership is exercised throughout the school—the bases for and the way that key decisions are made, communicated, and carried out at all levels. It is based on shared values, expectations, and purposes; communicated and reinforced via interactions among leaders and managers; reflected in the decisions the leaders make; and evident in the actions of the school. It includes the formal and informal mechanisms for leadership development used to select leaders and managers, to develop their leadership skills, and to provide guidance and examples regarding behaviors and practices.

An effective leadership system creates clear values respecting the requirements of the school students and stakeholders and sets high expectations for performance and performance improvement. It builds loyalties and teamwork based on the values and the pursuit of shared purposes. It encourages and supports initiative and risk taking; focuses on simplicity of organizational structure, purpose, and function; and avoids chains of command requiring long decision paths. An effective leadership system includes mechanisms for the leaders' self-examination and improvement.

Measures and Indicators

Measures and indicators refer to numerical information that quantifies input, output, and performance dimensions of processes, products, services, and the overall school (outcomes). Measures and indicators might be simple (derived from one measurement) or composite.

The criteria do not make a distinction between measures and indicators. However, some users of these terms prefer the term *indicator* (1) when the measurement relates to performance, but is not a direct or exclusive measure of such performance. For example, the number of complaints is an indicator of dissatisfaction, but not a direct or exclusive measure of it; and (2) when the measurement is a predictor ("leading indicator") of some more significant performance, for instance, a gain in student satisfaction might be a leading indicator of student retention.

Performance

Performance refers to output results information obtained from processes and services that permits evaluation and comparison relative to goals, standards, past results, and other schools. Performance might be expressed in non-financial and financial terms.

Two types of performance are addressed in the criteria: (1) operational and faculty/staff; and (2) student- and stakeholder-related.

Operational and faculty/staff performance refers to performance relative to effectiveness and efficiency measures and indicators. Examples include cycle time, productivity, and regulatory compliance. Operational performance might be measured at the work unit level, key process level, and school level.

Student- and stakeholder-related performance refers to performance relative to measures and indicators of student and stakeholder perceptions, reactions, and behaviors. Examples include student retention, complaints, and survey results. Student- and stakeholder-related performance generally relates to the school as a whole.

Prevention-Based

Seeking the root cause of a problem and preventing its recurrence rather than merely solving the problem and waiting for it to happen again (a reactive posture).

Process

Process refers to linked activities with the purpose of producing an offering or service for a customer (user) within or outside the school. Generally, processes involve combinations of people, machines, tools, techniques, and materials in a systematic series of steps or actions. In some situations, processes might require adherence to a specific sequence of steps, with documentation (sometimes formal) of procedures and requirements, including well-defined measurement and control steps.

In many schools, particularly when students and/or stakeholders are directly involved in the service, process is used in a more general way—to spell out what must be done, possibly including a preferred or expected sequence. If a sequence is critical, the service needs to include information that helps students and stakeholders understand and follow the sequence. Service processes involving students and stakeholders also require guidance to the providers on handling contingencies related to their likely or possible actions or behaviors.

Some schools do not recognize the importance of the services they provide. Consider the cafeteria again. If the focus is only on making the best coffee and the service is poor—making students and faculty wait too long—the coffee shop will lose customers. Delivery service value must be considered as important to success as delivering product value.

In knowledge work such as strategic planning, research, and analysis, process does not necessarily imply formal sequences of steps. Rather, the process implies general under-standings regarding competent performance such as timing, options to be included, evaluation, and reporting. Sequences might arise as part of these understandings.

Productivity

Productivity refers to measures of efficiency of the use of resources such as buildings, technology, and people. Although the term is often applied to single factors such as staffing (labor productivity), machines, materials, energy, and capital, the productivity concept applies as well to total resources used in producing outputs. Overall productivity is determined by combining the productivities of the different resources used for an output.

Effective approaches to performance management require understanding and measuring single factor and overall productivity, particularly in complex cases when there are a variety of costs and potential benefits.

Refinement

The result of a systematic process to analyze performance or a system and improve it.

Root Cause

The original cause or reason for a condition. The root cause of a condition is that cause which, if eliminated, guarantees that the condition will not recur.

System

A set of well-defined and well-designed processes for meeting the school's quality and performance requirements.

Systematic Approach

A process that is repeatable and predictable, rather than anecdotal and episodic.

Values

The principles and beliefs that guide a school and its people toward the accomplishment of its mission and vision.

Clarifying Confusing Terms

Comparative Information vs. Benchmarking

Comparative information includes benchmarking and competitive comparisons. *Benchmarking* refers to collecting information and data about processes and performance results that represent the best practices and performance for similar activities inside or outside the school's business or industry. Competitive comparisons refer to collecting information and data on performance relative to comparable schools or similar providers.

For example, a college that is community based must recruit and retain students from its local area. Competitive comparisons require that the college know its primary competitors and find out how they are recruiting and retaining its students in an effort to beat them.

Benchmarking would require the school to find any types of organizations who carry out these recruitment and retainment processes better than anyone else and examine both their processes and performance levels. Such organizations may be large companies located elsewhere in the United States. Benchmarking seeks best-practices information. Competitive comparisons look at competitors, whether or not they are the best.

Customer-Contact Employees

Customer-contact employees are any faculty and staff who are in direct contact with students and stakeholders. People who work in school or college offices are examples of contact people. They may be direct service providers or answer complaint calls. Whenever a student or stakeholder makes contact with a school, either in person or by phone or other electronic means, that person forms an opinion about the school and its faculty and staff. Faculty and staff who come in contact with students and stakeholders are in a critical position to influence students and stakeholders for the good of the school, or to its detriment.

Student and Stakeholder Satisfaction vs. Student and Stakeholder Dissatisfaction

One is not the inverse of the other. The lack of complaints does not indicate satisfaction, although the presence of complaints can be a partial indicator of dissatisfaction. Measures of dissatisfaction can include direct measures through surveys as well as complaints.

Student and stakeholder satisfaction and dissatisfaction are complex to assess. They are rarely thoroughly dissatisfied, although they may dislike a feature of a program/offering or an aspect of service. There are usually degrees of satisfaction and dissatisfaction.

Data vs. Information

Information can be qualitative and quantitative. *Data* are information that lend themselves to quantification and statistical analysis. For example, a faculty survey might reflect a percentage of the faculty dissatisfied with recognition programs. This percentage is considered data. These percentages add to the base of information about faculty satisfaction.

Education vs. Training

Training refers to learning about and acquiring job-specific skills and knowledge. *Education* refers to the general development of individuals. A school might provide training in student counseling for its faculty, as well as support the education of faculty through an advanced degree program at a local college.

Empowerment vs. Involvement

Empowerment generally refers to processes and procedures designed to provide individuals and teams the tools, skills, and authority to make decisions that affect their work—decisions traditionally reserved for administrators.

Empowerment as a concept has been misused in many schools. For example, administrators may pretend to extend decision authority under the guise of chartering teams and individuals to make recommendations about their work, while continuing to reserve decision-making authority to themselves.

This practice has given rise to another term—*involvement*—that describes the role of faculty and staff who are asked to become involved in decision making, without necessarily making decisions. Involvement is a practice that many agree is better than not involving them at all, but still does not serve to optimize their contribution to initiative, flexibility, and fast response.

Operational Performance vs. Predictors of Student and Stakeholder Satisfaction

Operational performance processes and predictors of student/stakeholder satisfaction are related but not always the same. Operational performance measures can reflect issues that concern students and stakeholders as well as those that do not. Operational performance measures are used by the school to assess effectiveness and efficiency, as well as predict satisfaction.

In the example of the school cafeteria, freshness of pizza is a key requirement. One predictor of satisfaction might be the length of time, in minutes, between cooking and serving. The standard might be 20 minutes or less to ensure satisfaction. Pizza standing more than 20 minutes old would be discarded.

A measure of operational effectiveness might be how many pizzas were discarded because the

pizza was too old. The student/faculty does not care if the cafeteria throws out stale pizza and, therefore, that measure is not a predictor of satisfaction. However, throwing out pizza does affect profitability and should be measured and minimized.

Ideally, a school should be able to identify enough measures of programs and offerings quality to predict satisfaction accurately and monitor operating effectiveness and efficiency.

Performance Requirements vs. Performance Measures

Performance requirements are an expression of student/stakeholder requirements and expectations. Sometimes performance requirements are expressed as design requirements or engineering requirements. They are viewed as a basis for developing measures to enable the school to determine, generally without asking the student/stakeholder, whether they are likely to be satisfied.

Performance measures can also be used to assess efficiency, effectiveness, and productivity of a work process. Process performance measures might include cycle time or error rate.

Support Services

Support services are those services that support the school's programs and offerings delivery core operating processes. Support services might include finance and accounting, library services, purchasing, management information services, software support, marketing, public relations, personnel administration (job posting, recruitment, payroll), facilities maintenance and management, research and development, secretarial support, and other administration services.

In the faculty/staff resources area (Category 5), the criteria require schools to manage their human resource assets to optimize performance. However, many human resources support services might also exist, such as payroll, travel, position control, recruitment, and employee services. These processes must be designed, delivered, and refined systematically according to the requirements of Item 6.2.

However, the details of developing work specifications, requests for quotations, and other aspects of the procurement process might be assigned to a procurement department. That department would be considered a support service that must design its own products and services to meet the requirements of its internal customer and would be received as a support structure (6.2).

Teams vs. Natural Work Units

Natural work units such as departments reflect the people that normally work together because they are a part of a formal work unit. For example, teachers who teach the same students in a middle school are a natural work unit, or those who all teach mathematics in a college environment.

Teams may be formed of people within a natural work unit or may cross existing (natural) organization boundaries. To design a science curriculum over the summer would be a temporary team.

About The Authors

Mark L. Blazey, Ed.D., is the president of Quantum Performance Group, Inc., founded in 1991 to provide advice and support to governmental, business, and educational organizations on assessment and quality improvement. Dr. Blazey has been a Senior Examiner for the Malcolm Baldrige National Quality Award since 1995 and is the Chief Judge for the New York State, Vermont, and Aruba National Quality Awards. He trains thousands of examiners each year and has written several books on education and performance management, including *Insights to Performance Excellence for Business* and *Baldrige in Brief*. Mark earned a bachelor's degree from Syracuse University and three advanced degrees from the University at Albany: an M.S. in Statistics and Education Psychology; a M.S. in Education; and an Ed.D. in Curriculum, Instruction and Education Policy. He has taught elementary, secondary, postsecondary, and graduate students. From 1989 he was at the Rochester Institute of Technology where he served as dean for Training and Professional Development. From 1980 to 1988 Dr. Blazey served in the Department of Education as director of policy and operations and was a member of the senior executive service.

Karen S. Davison, Ed.D., received her doctoral degree from The University at Albany in 1981. She is the executive officer of Quantum Performance Group, Inc., where she advises private and public sector customers on performance improvement strategies and Baldrige-based assessments. Karen is a senior reviewer for the Empire State Advantage award, and an instructor and mentor for the Aruba Quality award. An educator since 1973, when she taught children with special needs in the Syracuse City School District, she has also directed gifted and talented education and served as chief of curriculum for the Maryland State Department of Education. Dr. Davison serves as vice-chair of the Board of Trustees of Finger Lakes Community College in Canandaigua, New York and is a proud member of the Canandaigua City School Quality Council.

John P. Evans, Ph.D., is a professor and former dean of the Kenan-Flagler Business School at the University of North Carolina at Chapel Hill, where he has been on the faculty for nearly thirty years. While dean, he served as president of the American Assembly of Collegiate Schools of Business, for which he chaired a task force that designed an entirely new accreditation process for business schools, introducing principles of modern quality management and improvement to this accreditation process. Starting in 1989 he served first as an Examiner (1988–89), then as a Senior Examiner (1990–93), and then as a Judge (1996) for the Malcolm Baldrige National Quality Award. He was the principal investigator on a research project sponsored by the National Science Foundation. In this project, with the participation of a number of organizations, he investigated the use of assessment of quality systems in the systematic improvement of organizations. Jack holds baccalaureate, master's, and doctoral degrees from Cornell University.

Index